The Syntax of Nonfinite
Complementation

Linguistic Inquiry Monographs
Samuel Jay Keyser, general editor

The Syntax of
Nonfinite Complementation

An Economy Approach

Željko Bošković

The MIT Press
Cambridge, Massachusetts
London, England

Set in Times New Roman on the Monotype "Prism Plus" PostScript Imagesetter by Asco Trade Typesetting Ltd., Hong Kong.
Printed and bound in the United States of America.

Library of Congress Cataloging-in-Publication Data

Bošković, Željko.
  The syntax of nonfinite complementation : an economy approach / Željko Bošković.
    p.   cm. — (Linguistic inquiry monographs : 32)
  Abstract of thesis (doctoral—University of Connecticut, 1995)
  under the title: Principles of economy in nonfinite complementation.
  Includes bibliographical references and index.
  ISBN 0-262-02429-2 (alk. paper). — ISBN 0-262-52236-5 (pbk. alk. paper)
  1. Grammar, Comparative and general—Syntax. 2. Economy (Linguistics) 3. Minimalist theory (Linguistics) 4. Grammar, Comparative and general—Complement. I. Title. II. Series.
  P295.B67   1997
  415—dc21   97-14912
                                                                   CIP

Mojim roditeljima

Contents

Series Foreword

We are pleased to present the thirty-second in the series *Linguistic Inquiry Monographs*. These monographs present new and original research beyond the scope of the article. We hope they will benefit our field by bringing to it perspectives that will stimulate further research and insight.

Originally published in limited edition, the *Linguistic Inquiry Monographs* are now more widely available. This change is due to the great interest engendered by the series and by the needs of a growing readership. The editors thank the readers for their support and welcome suggestions about future directions for the series.

Samuel Jay Keyser
for the Editorial Board

Preface

This book is a revision of my doctoral dissertation, "Principles of Economy in Nonfinite Complementation," submitted to the University of Connecticut in August 1995. Although the overall structure of the original is retained in this work, numerous substantive revisions and additions have been made within each chapter. The most important changes concern the status of the Minimal Structure Principle in chapter 2 and object shift in chapter 4, where a good deal of completely new material is discussed.

Of all the people who have helped me with this work, my deepest thanks go to Mamoru Saito and especially my thesis advisor Howard Lasnik. I thank them for encouragement, numerous comments, and countless hours of discussion, and for setting an example with their own scholarship and high standards. For discussions, correspondence, and/or comments in connection with different aspects of this work, I also thank Diane Lillo-Martin, Andrew Radford, Javier Ormazabal, Steven Franks, Roger Martin, Daiko Takahashi, Noam Chomsky, Gary Milsark, William Snyder, Michael Hegarty, and an anonymous reviewer.

Parts of this book were presented in seminars at the University of Connecticut and talks at the University of Maryland, Princeton University, City University of New York, Dartmouth College, and the 1994 and 1995 meetings of the Linguistic Society of America in Boston and New Orleans. I thank the audiences at all of these events for helpful comments and thought-provoking questions.

Some of the material in this book has appeared elsewhere in various guises. I thank Kluwer Academic Publishers for kind permission to use portions of the material that appeared in *Natural Language & Linguistic Theory* as Bošković 1996b and Elsevier Science for kindly granting permission to use some parts of the material that appeared in *Lingua* as Bošković 1995b. Thanks are also due to the reviewers and the editors of these articles, particularly Frederick J. Newmeyer, for comments and suggestions on both the content and the presentation of the relevant material.

I am also grateful to Masao Ochi, Sandra Stjepanović, and Arthur Stepanov for their extensive assistance in the final preparation of the manuscript, to Anne Mark for her excellent editorial work, and to all of the members of the University of Connecticut Department of Linguistics for providing a friendly and intellectually stimulating atmosphere to work in.

Finally, my warmest thanks are due to Michèle for her support and patience throughout this project, and especially to my parents for everything they have done for me. Hvala vam na svemu.

Research reported here was supported in part by various grants from the University of Connecticut and by NSF grant SBR-951088 to Howard Lasnik and Željko Bošković.

The Syntax of Nonfinite
Complementation

Chapter 1

Introduction

1.1 Economy and the Minimalist Program

Economy considerations have always played an important role in the generative theory of grammar. In the early theory, they took the form of an evaluation metric for selecting grammars from the format permitted for rule systems. Though the role of economy has changed in the current theoretical framework, an evaluation metric no longer being needed because of the restrictiveness of the theory, economy principles remain important. In fact, they play a central role in the Minimalist Program of Chomsky (1991, 1993, 1994, 1995) and Chomsky and Lasnik (1993).

Starting assumptions of the Minimalist Program fall within the domain of virtual conceptual necessity. Language is assumed to consist of a lexicon and a computational system. The computational system is embedded in two performance systems: articulatory-perceptual and conceptual-intentional. Two linguistic levels, Phonological Form (PF) and Logical Form (LF), are postulated as interfaces with the performance systems. Each linguistic expression, generated by the computational system, is a pair of representations at PF and LF. A computation is said to *converge* at the interface levels if its structural description contains only legitimate PF and LF objects, with all of their morphological features satisfied; otherwise, it *crashes*. However, in current work it has become clear that linguistic expressions cannot be defined simply as pairs (P, L) formed by a convergent derivation and satisfying interface conditions. The operations of the computational system that produce linguistic expressions must be optimal, in the sense that they must satisfy some general considerations of simplicity, referred to as "economy principles." One of these principles, the Last Resort Condition, prohibits superfluous steps in a derivation. It requires that every operation apply for a reason. The workings of the Last Resort Condition will be explored in detail in this book. The possibility will be explored that a similar condition constrains representations, prohibiting superfluous symbols from representations. A second economy principle, proposed by Chomsky and Lasnik (1993) and referred to here as the "Minimize Chain Links Principle," imposes locality restrictions on the operation Move, by requiring that each movement be as short as possible. A third economy principle, also relevant to the operation Move, is Chomsky's (1993) Procrastinate, which favors covert over overt movement, thus delaying the application of Move until LF whenever possible.

In addition to economy conditions on derivations and representations, which require that derivations and representations in some sense be minimal, the very development of the theory has been characterized by natural considerations of simplicity and economy. The general trend in the theory of generative grammar has been to eliminate redundancies that arise when conditions on transformations and representations overlap in their effects. Replacement of distinct transformational rules of the early generative theory by the general operation Affect α has also contributed to developing a simpler and in a way more minimal theory. Elimination of arbitrary mechanisms and unification of superficially different phenomena, driving forces of the theory, are also steps in this direction, which can be illustrated by the reduction achieved with respect to Case theory in the minimalist framework. In the preminimalist framework, Case assignment was assumed to take place in three distinct configurations. Nominative Case was assumed to be assigned by I in a specifier-head (Spec-head) configuration.[1] Accusative Case in simple transitive constructions was assigned in the head-complement relation with a verb.

(1) [$_{IP}$ John [$_{I'}$ I [$_{VP}$ kissed Mary]]]

In exceptional-Case-marking (ECM) constructions such as (2), the verb was assumed to assign accusative Case to the Spec of its complement.

(2) John proved [$_{IP}$ Mary to be innocent]

An arbitrary heterogeneous notion of government was postulated to superficially unify the three configurations in which Case assignment was assumed to take place.

Lasnik and Saito (1991) observe, however, following Postal (1974), that the subject of the embedded clause in ECM constructions behaves as if it were located in an A-position in the higher clause. Thus, as (3) shows, it is capable of binding anaphors contained within higher-clause adverbials.

(3) John proved [Mary and Jane to be innocent] during each other's trials

To account for the grammaticality of (3), Lasnik and Saito propose that the embedded-clause subject moves to the Spec of Kayne's (1989) and Chomsky's (1991) Agr_OP phrase, an A-position, where it is Case-marked in a Spec-head configuration. (The $prove + Agr_O$ complex, created by adjunction of $prove$ to Agr_O, is assumed to undergo movement to a higher head position, which I ignore here.)

(4) John $[_{Agr_OP}$ Mary and Jane$_i$ $Agr_O+prove_j$ $[_{VP}$ t$_j$ $[_{IP}$ t$_i$ to be innocent] during each other's trials]]

Since exceptional and simple accusative seem to be alike in all respects, the next logical step is to assume that direct object NPs in simple transitive constructions, such as *Mary* in (1), are also Case-marked in a Spec-head configuration, after moving to the Spec of Agr_OP (SpecAgr_OP). All structural Case marking is then reduced to a single structural configuration, namely, Spec-head.[2] Furthermore, the need for postulating the arbitrary notion of government, which superficially unified Case assignment configurations in the preminimalist framework, is eliminated, at least with respect to Case theory.

The goal of this book is to explore the role of the economy principles and the possibility of a minimalist reduction in the phenomenon of nonfinite complementation. My discussion of nonfinite complementation will be confined to infinitival and participial complements. Since gerunds have a number of nominal properties that set them apart from infinitives and participles, causing them to behave syntactically very differently from the other two nonfinite forms, I will not investigate them here. I will show that a number of facts concerning infinitival and participial complementation that either have not been previously accounted for or have received unsatisfactory accounts can be explained in a principled way once economy principles and, more generally, the Minimalist Program are adopted. In addition to broadening the empirical coverage of the theory, this book will thus provide empirical confirmation of the economy principles and the Minimalist Program in general. The data examined in the book will also be used to formulate the economy principles more precisely.

1.2 Outline

Chapters 2–4 of this work deal with infinitival complementation, and chapter 5 examines participial complements.

In chapter 2 I examine issues concerning selection and the categorial status of infinitival complements and the distribution of PRO based on traditional ECM, raising, and control infinitivals, which are characterized by the complementary distribution of NP-trace and PRO in their subject position. Under the standard analysis, ECM and raising verbs are assumed to c-select IP infinitival complements, and control verbs CP infinitival complements. I show that selection for different types of infinitival complements should be eliminated and provide evidence that all infinitival complements that are not introduced by an overt complementizer are IPs. I argue that the IP status is forced on these complements by an economy principle, and that the relevant principle forces IP status on *that*-less finite clauses as well. Since the IP analysis of control infinitival complements is incompatible with the standard binding-theoretic account of the distribution of PRO but is consistent with Chomsky and Lasnik's (1993) Case-theoretic account, I argue that the conclusion reached in this chapter concerning the categorial status of control infinitival complements provides evidence for the Case-theoretic approach. I also show that under this account the systematic difference with respect to the licensing of PRO and NP-trace in the subject position of traditional ECM and control infinitival complements can be attributed to the s-selectional requirements of the higher predicates, thus eliminating the need to make recourse to c-selection in accounting for the properties of infinitival complements. Since under the Case-theoretic approach there is also no need to appeal to government to account for the distribution of PRO, the analysis presented in chapter 2 also contributes to the attempt to eliminate government and c-selection from the theory of grammar.

In chapter 3 I examine syntactic properties of Pesetsky's (1992) *wager*-class verbs (Postal's (1974) DOC paradigm), which behave like *believe* in that they disallow PRO in the subject position of their infinitival complement, allow passive raising from their infinitival complement, and are capable of exceptionally Case-marking *wh*-traces. However, in contrast to *believe*, the verbs in question cannot exceptionally Case-mark lexical NPs. Pesetsky (1992) notes that all the verbs belonging to this class are agentive. I provide a principled economy account of the correlation between agentivity and ECM (i.e., Pesetsky's observation that agentive verbs cannot exceptionally Case-mark lexical NPs). I develop a theory of agentivity based on Hale and Keyser's (1993) proposal that agentive constructions involve a null agentive V and my (1994b) claim that movement into θ-positions is allowed in certain well-defined configurations. In this chapter I also examine syntactic properties of the infinitival complement of French *believe*-class verbs, which, in contrast to their English counterparts, allow PRO in their subject position. I provide a principled account of the different behavior of English and French *believe*-class verbs with respect to the licensing of PRO in the subject position of their infinitival complement based on previously unnoticed data concerning temporal properties of French propositional infinitivals and the Case-theoretic approach to the distribution of PRO.

In chapter 4 I investigate the relevance of infinitival complementation for existential constructions and Chomsky's (1986b) expletive replacement hypothesis, the goal being to determine the Case properties of the associate of *there* and identify the driving force behind expletive replacement. I propose a novel analysis of existential constructions based on the expletive replacement hypothesis. I show that the analysis sheds light on the general question of what drives the application of the operation Move and the issue of whether or not lowering operations are allowed. In particular, I argue that Chomsky's (1993) strong version of Greed holds and that lowering operations are allowed at least in LF, where there are no linear ordering requirements, in accordance with Chomsky 1995. I also examine, in some detail, constraints affecting A-positions and A-movement and consequences of adopting Greed for the traditional ECM construction, including the issue of when movement to SpecAgr$_o$P takes place in such constructions.

Finally, in chapter 5 I turn to participial complementation. I discuss the syntax of participles with respect to Serbo-Croatian. To account for the surface position of participles in Serbo-Croatian, a number of theoretically anomalous claims have been made in the literature. Most notably, Serbo-Croatian participles have been argued to undergo long head movement to C^0, across lexically filled X^0 positions (see Rivero 1991 and Roberts 1994, among others). I provide empirical evidence against the long head movement analysis based on previously unnoticed facts and give an analysis of participle movement in Serbo-Croatian that does not involve any theoretically anomalous mechanisms. I extend the analysis to participle movement in Dutch and Polish and show that it has important consequences for several phenomena and theoretical mechanisms, in particular, second position cliticization, excorporation, economy of derivation, and the direction of adjunction operations.

Chapter 2
Selection and the Categorial Status of Infinitival Complements

2.1 Introduction

The development of the Minimalist Program has led to the abandonment of a number of conditions and mechanisms, either because their effects overlap with those of other conditions or because they are arbitrary in nature. The goal of this chapter is to explore the possibility of a minimalist reduction in the phenomena of infinitival complementation and the distribution of PRO.[1]

The standard account of the phenomena is crucially based on two mechanisms that no longer seem to play any role in the grammar: government and c-selection. In the preminimalist framework, government played a central role in the theory. The minimalist framework has witnessed a dramatic decline in the importance of government. A number of phenomena that had previously been defined in terms of government are now characterized independently of it. Thus, as discussed in chapter 1, structural Case assignment, which was previously assumed to take place under government, is now reduced to a single X-bar-theoretic configuration, namely, the Spec-head relation. Locality conditions on movement are also formulated in terms of notions independent of government; more precisely, they seem to follow from general considerations of economy of derivation (see Chomsky and Lasnik 1993 and Takahashi 1994, among others). With the advent of the theory of LF anaphor movement (see Chomsky 1986b), government no longer seems to play a role in binding theory either. In fact, under the standard account of the distribution of PRO and infinitival complementation, which rests on the assumption that PRO cannot be governed, government is still crucially needed only to account for the phenomena in question. Given this and the fact that government is a rather heterogeneous and arbitrary notion, it would be desirable to account for the phenomena in question without making recourse to government. This would open up the possibility that government could be completely eliminated from the grammar.

Another mechanism whose role seems to be limited to infinitival complementation is c-selection. Grimshaw (1979) argues that lexical entries of predicates contain information concerning selection for both syntactic categories (c-selection) and the semantic type of the complement (s-selection). She argues for the autonomy of c-selection and s-selection by noting that there is no one-to-one correspondence between semantic types of complements and their syntactic categories. Crucial examples are provided by the fact that verbs that take the same semantic type may or may not take an NP object. Thus, although both *wonder* and *ask* s-select Question (Q), only the latter allows Q to be realized as an NP.

(1) a.   John wondered [CP what the time was]
    b.   *John wondered [NP the time]
    c.   John asked [CP what the time was]
    d.   John asked [NP the time]

Pesetsky (1982b, 1992), on the other hand, argues that c-selection should be eliminated as an independent syntactic mechanism. Whether or not a predicate can take an NP object is determined by whether or not it can assign Case. Thus, if *ask* but not *wonder* is marked [+accusative], c-selection need not be invoked to rule out (1b). The construction is ruled out independently by the Case Filter.

A potential argument against Pesetsky's claim that c-selection can be eliminated comes from certain facts concerning infinitival complementation. Consider (2a–d).

(2) a.   *John$_i$ is illegal [CP t$_i$ to park here]
    b.   It is illegal [CP PRO to park here]
    c.   John$_i$ appears [IP t$_i$ to like Mary]
    d.   *It appears to Bill [IP PRO to like Mary]

(2a–d) are generally accounted for by invoking c-selection: whereas *illegal* c-selects CP, *appear* c-selects IP. (2a) is then ruled out because it involves NP movement crossing a CP boundary. (2d), on the other hand, is excluded because PRO is governed by *appear*.[2] To the extent that this analysis of (2a–d) is correct, it provides evidence for the existence of c-selection as an autonomous syntactic mechanism. However, if it can be shown that (2a) and (2d) can be excluded by independently needed syntactic mechanisms that do not make reference to c-selection, the data in (2) would not be inconsistent with Pesetsky's position. This would be desirable, given that the facts in (1), which have previously been argued to provide strong evidence for the existence of c-selection, can in fact be accounted for independently of c-selection. Accounting for (2a,d) independently of c-selection would then open up the possibility that c-selection could be altogether eliminated from the theory of grammar.

In this chapter I show that neither c-selection nor the notion of government need be invoked to account for (2a–d). I provide evidence that the standard c-selection/binding-theoretic account, which crucially depends on the notion of government, is empirically inadequate, and I give an account of infinitival complementation based on the Case-theoretic approach to the distribution of PRO and the s-selectional properties of the relevant predicates. I argue that the Case-theoretic account of the distribution of PRO and infinitival complementation is superior to the standard c-selection/ binding-theoretic account on both conceptual and empirical grounds: conceptually, because it enables us to dispense with c-selection for various types of infinitival clauses, as well as a number of stipulations and mechanisms on which the standard account is crucially based, and empirically, because it accounts for certain facts concerning infinitival complementation that remain unaccounted for under the standard c-selection/binding-theoretic account. In sections 2.2 and 2.3 I compare the s-selection/Case-theoretic account and the standard c-selection/binding-theoretic account of infinitival complementation. In section 2.4 I discuss two other accounts of infinitival complementation, by Pesetsky (1992) and Ormazabal (1995).

2.2 Infinitival Complementation and C-Selection

The discussion in this section centers around the well-known paradigm given in (3). I first briefly sum up the standard c-selection/binding-theoretic account of (3) and then develop an account of infinitival complementation based on the Case-theoretic approach to the distribution of PRO that dispenses with c-selection for different types of infinitival clauses. I then provide evidence that the Case-theoretic account of infinitival complementation and the distribution of PRO is superior to the binding-theoretic account.

(3) a.   John believed$_i$ [$_{AgroP}$ him$_j$ t$_i$ [$_{IP}$ t$_j$ to be crazy]]
     b.   *John believed [$_{IP}$ PRO to be crazy]

   c. John tried [$_{CP}$ PRO to win]

   d. *John tried$_i$ [$_{AgroP}$ him$_j$ t$_i$ [$_{CP}$[$_{IP}$ t$_j$ to win]]]

Under the standard analysis (3a–d) are accounted for by recourse to c-selection. Whereas *try* c-selects CP, *believe* c-selects IP.[3] Given that accusative Case is checked in SpecAgr$_o$P, *him* in (3a) and (3d) must undergo LF A-movement to the matrix SpecAgr$_o$P in order to be Case-checked (for relevant evidence, see chapter 1 and section 2.2.3). In (3d) the movement is blocked by the intervening CP. In (3c) the CP protects PRO from being governed by *try*. In (3b), on the other hand, PRO is governed by *believe* and the construction is ruled out by either Condition A or Condition B of the binding theory.

It is well known that the standard account of (3) faces a number of conceptual problems. First, it is based on the assumption that, in contrast to all other NPs, PRO is not Case-marked. This raises an obvious conceptual question, especially if Case marking is a prerequisite for θ-marking, as argued by Chomsky (1981, 1986b).

Second, the account is based on a number of stipulations concerning which elements count as governors. Thus, to maintain the standard account of the distribution of PRO, it is necessary to stipulate that, in contrast to finite I, nonfinite I is not a governor. The same stipulation has to be made for I of Balkan subjunctives, which allow PRO although they exhibit the same verbal morphology as indicatives, including person/number agreement.[4] It is also necessary to stipulate that the null complementizer heading the infinitival complement of *try* in (3c), as well as overt complementizers that head control infinitival complements in the Romance languages (see Rochette 1988 and references therein), does not count as a governor.[5]

Third, the standard binding-theoretic account of (3) is crucially based on the assumption that the infinitival complement of *believe* is an IP, and that of *try* a CP, which is another stipulation. Furthermore, both the mechanism that is responsible for the difference in the categorial status of the infinitival complements in (3) (namely, c-selection) and the notion of government (which plays the central role in the standard account) are theoretically very problematic. In fact, as noted above, in the current theoretical framework they seem to be needed merely to account for the facts in (3a–d).

Chomsky and Lasnik's (1993) proposal that PRO is always Case-marked opens up a new way of analyzing (3a–d) that makes no reference to either c-selection or government. Chomsky and Lasnik note that, as illustrated by (4), PRO must undergo NP-movement from non-Case positions and is not allowed to undergo NP-movement from Case positions even to escape government.

(4) a.   John tried PRO$_i$ to be arrested t$_i$
　　b.   *John tried PRO$_i$ to seem to t$_i$ that the problem is unsolvable

To account for (4a–b), Chomsky and Lasnik reject the binding-theoretic account of the distribution of PRO and argue that, like all other argument NPs, PRO is always Case-marked. They propose that PRO is marked for null Case, which is restricted to PRO and checked via Spec-head agreement with nonfinite I. They show that, given this proposal, (4b) is ruled out by the Last Resort Condition, which forbids NP-movement from Case-checking to Case-checking positions.[6] NP-movement in (4a), on the other hand, is in accordance with the Last Resort Condition; PRO moves from a non-Case position to a position in which Case can be checked. Given the data in (4a–b), I will adopt Chomsky and Lasnik's Case-theoretic account of the distribution of PRO, with a modification proposed by Martin (1992b).[7]

Martin modifies Chomsky and Lasnik's (1993) account by arguing that not every nonfinite I has the ability to check null Case. Restricting attention to infinitival complements, only [+tense] nonfinite I can check null Case. Martin adopts Stowell's (1982) proposal that, in contrast to ECM infinitives, control infinitives are specified for Tense. More precisely, they denote a possible future; this is, they specify a time frame that is unrealized with respect to the Tense of the matrix clause (note, for example, the interpretation of *John remembered to bring the wine*). To account for this, Stowell proposes that infinitival complements of control verbs have an independent Tense value; that is, they are specified as [+tense]. In contrast to control infinitives, ECM infinitives have no independent Tense value; that is, they are specified as [−tense]. Their time frame is determined by the time frame of the higher clause. They have no internally organized Tense.[8]

Martin notes that certain facts concerning the occurrence of eventive predicates in infinitival complements confirm the correctness of Stowell's proposal. Enç (1991) argues that eventive predicates contain a temporal argument that needs to be bound. Tense, the aspectual *have* and *be*, and adverbs of quantification serve as binders for the temporal argument. It is well known that under the nonhabitual reading eventive predicates can be embedded under control predicates, but not under ECM predicates.

(5) a. John tried to bring the beer
    b. *John believed Peter to bring the beer

Martin (1992b) observes that, given Stowell's proposal concerning the presence versus absence of Tense in infinitival complements and Enç's claim that eventive predicates contain a temporal argument that must be bound, the contrast in (5) can readily be accounted for. The Tense of the control infinitival can serve as a binder for the temporal argument of *bring* in (5a). On the other hand, (5b) is ruled out because, ECM infinitivals being Tenseless, the temporal argument of *bring* remains unbound.[9] Stowell's proposal concerning temporal properties of control and ECM infinitivals thus seems to be well motivated. Building on Stowell's proposal, Martin (1992b) modifies Chomsky and Lasnik's Case-theoretic approach to the distribution of PRO by proposing that the [+tense] feature of nonfinite I ([+tense,−finite] I) rather than nonfinite I in general checks null Case via Spec-head agreement.

Independent evidence for Martin's proposal is provided by certain facts concerning VP-ellipsis. Lobeck (1990) and Saito and Murasugi (1990) note that functional heads can license ellipsis of their complement only when they undergo Spec-head agreement. Thus, (6a–f) show that tensed I, *'s*, and [+wh]-C, which according to Fukui and Speas (1986) undergo Spec-head agreement, license ellipsis, whereas the nonagreeing functional categories *to*, *the*, and *that* do not.[10]

(6) a. John liked Mary and Peter [$_{I'}$ did e] too
    b. *John believed Mary to know French but Peter believed Jane [$_{I'}$ to e]
    c. John's talk about the economy was interesting but Bill [$_{D'}$'s e] was boring
    d. *A single student came to the class because [$_{D'}$ the e] thought that it was important
    e. John met someone but I don't know who [$_{C'}$ [+wh]-C e]
    f. *John thinks that Peter met someone but I don't believe [$_{C'}$ that e]

Note now that, in contrast to what happens in ECM infinitives, VP-ellipsis is not blocked in control infinitives.

(7) John was not sure he could leave, but he tried PRO [$_{I'}$ to e]

Martin notes that this contrast between ECM and control infinitives is exactly what is expected if, in contrast to what happens in ECM infinitives, Tense in control infinitives checks null Case via Spec-head agreement with

PRO in SpecIP. Since *to* in (7) undergoes Spec-head agreement, its complement can be deleted. The contrast between (6b) and (7) thus provides evidence for the Case-theoretic approach to the distribution of PRO.[11] Given the ellipsis data discussed above, I will adopt Martin's proposal that PRO is Case-checked under Spec-head agreement with [+tense, −finite] I.

I believe that the difference between *believe* and *try* with respect to the Tense specification of their complement, which is responsible for the contrast between (6b) and (7), can best be stated in terms of s-selection. Suppose that, in contrast to *believe*, which s-selects Proposition (here I am ignoring constructions in which *believe* and *try* take NP complements), *try* s-selects a nonpropositional complement, which I will refer to as "Irrealis." This seems plausible given that there are several semantic differences between the infinitival complements of *believe* and *try*. For example, it is well known that truth and falsity can be predicated of the infinitival complement of *believe* but not *try* (e.g., *John believed Peter to have played football, which was false* vs. **John tried to play football, which was false*). Let us assume that the defining property of irrealis complements is that the truth of the complement is left unspecified at the time of the utterance, which straightforwardly explains the impossibility of predicating truth or falsity of the complement of *try*. Given this defining property, the presence of Stowell's unrealized Tense in the complement of *try* may well be a consequence of the s-selectional properties of *try*. If *try* takes a finite or [−tense] infinitival complement, its complement will not be interpreted as irrealis and its s-selectional properties will not be satisfied. As for *believe*, the possibility of its taking an infinitival complement specified for unrealized Tense can also be excluded via s-selection; if *believe* takes such a complement, which I assume can have only irrealis interpretation, its s-selectional requirements will not be satisfied.

Note that verbs taking factive infinitival complements (8a), which presuppose the truth of their complement, and verbs taking implicative infinitival complements (8b), which assert the truth or falsity of their complement, can be treated in the same way as verbs taking irrealis infinitival complements.

(8) a. John hated to win the championship last year
    b. John managed to bring the beer yesterday

Pesetsky (1992) argues that factive and implicative *to* are modalized Tense morphemes whose presence is necessary to yield factive and implicative interpretations; that is, their presence is forced by the s-selectional properties of the higher predicates. Given that, in the absence of adverbs of quantification and the aspectual *have* and *be*, eventive predicates are allowed only in clauses that are specified as [+tense], the grammaticality of (8a–b) on the nonhabitual reading indicates that, like irrealis infinitivals and unlike propositional infinitivals, factive and implicative infinitivals are specified as [+tense]. As noted above with respect to irrealis infinitivals and as discussed at length below, given that factive and implicative infinitivals are specified as [+tense, −finite], the possibility of PRO in these infinitivals is predicted under the Case-theoretic account of the distribution of PRO. Note also that, as expected under this account, VP-ellipsis is allowed with implicative and factive infinitivals, just as it is with irrealis infinitivals.

(9) a. Peter liked to play football and John hated to
    b. I didn't think Sam could finish the job but he managed to

Since implicative and factive infinitivals pattern with *try* in all relevant respects, from here on I will use the term "*try*-class verbs" to refer not only to irrealis but also to implicative and factive infinitivals.

In summary, under the Case-theoretic approach to the distribution of PRO, like other NP arguments, PRO is always Case-marked. Its Case is checked via Spec-head agreement with [+tense,−finite] I. As a result of the s-selectional properties of the relevant predicates, this element is present in the infinitival complement of *try*-class verbs but not *believe*-class verbs.[12]

2.2.1 Case Checking with ECM Verbs

Now that the Case-theoretic account of the distribution of PRO has been introduced, we are ready to return to the paradigm in (3). Let us first reconsider the infinitival complement of *believe* in (3a–b), repeated here as (10a–b).

(10) a. John believed$_i$ [$_{AgroP}$ him$_j$ t$_i$ [$_{IP}$ t$_j$ to be crazy]]
     b. *John believed [$_{IP}$ PRO to be crazy]

Under the Case-theoretic approach to the distribution of PRO, (10b) is excluded by Case theory: since the embedded Tense does not check null Case, PRO in (10b) cannot be Case-checked. Notice that (10b) is now ruled out regardless of whether the embedded clause is a CP or an IP. Even if the embedded clause is a CP, (10b) is still excluded via Case theory. Given this, we do not need to stipulate that *believe* c-selects IP. We can let *believe* take either a CP or an IP complement and rule out ungrammatical constructions by independently needed mechanisms. Thus, if *believe* takes a CP complement in (10a), the construction is ruled out because it involves A-movement—namely, movement of *him* to the matrix SpecAgr$_O$P—across a CP boundary. More specifically, under the standard analysis it is ruled out either by the Empty Category Principle (ECP) (if *him* moves directly to the matrix SpecAgr$_O$P, crossing the CP/IP pair) or by the Improper Movement Constraint (if *him* moves via the embedded SpecCP).[13] The derivation in which the complement of *believe* is an IP, however, proceeds without problems. Given this, I conclude that under the Case-theoretic approach to the distribution of PRO there is no need to appeal to c-selection to account for (10a–b). *Believe* can be allowed to take either a CP or an IP infinitival complement. As for raising predicates such as *appear*, the reader can verify that (2c–d), repeated here as (11a–b), can also be accounted for without invoking c-selection.

(11) a.   John$_i$ appears [t$_i$ to like Mary]
    b.   *It appears to Bill [PRO to like Mary]

2.2.2   *Try*-Class Verbs and Case Checking

Let us now turn to control verbs, which under the binding-theoretic account of the distribution of PRO c-select CP. I will show that under the Case-theoretic account control verbs can be allowed to take either a CP or an IP complement. This will enable us to account for the possibility of PRO and the impossibility of NP-trace in control infinitivals without recourse to c-selection. Notice first that since the Case-theoretic account permits PRO to be governed, there is nothing wrong with the complement of *try* being an IP. What is important is that the [+tense] feature of the complement can check null Case, which PRO is marked for. The question remains, however, whether (12a–c) can be ruled out if *try* is allowed to take an IP complement.

(12) a.   *John$_i$ was tried [t$_i$ to leave]
    b.   *John tried [him to leave]
    c.   *Who$_i$ did John try [t$_i$ to leave]

If the embedded clauses in (12a–c) are IPs, we cannot appeal to the impossibility of A-movement out of CPs to rule them out. (12b–c), as well as (12a) under the standard assumption that only [+accusative] verbs can be passivized (see, however, section 4.3.2), could be ruled out via Case theory if *try* is not a Case assigner. However, the grammaticality of *John tried something* provides evidence that *try* is a Case assigner. Some other control verbs (e.g. *demand*, which behaves like *try* in all relevant respects) also uncontroversially assign Case, as *John demanded Mary's resignation* illustrates.

Given that, as argued by Hornstein and Lightfoot (1987), Larson (1991), Koster (1984), and Sportiche (1983), among others, (13) is ruled out because PRO lacks an appropriate controller, the ungrammaticality of (12a) cannot be related to the ungrammaticality of (13).[14]

(13) *It was tried [PRO to leave]

This is so because, unlike (13), (12a) does not contain PRO. Recall, however, that under the Case-theoretic approach to the distribution of PRO the possibility of having PRO in a particular position provides evidence that null Case can be checked in that position. As discussed above and as illustrated by (3c), PRO can appear in the subject position of the infinitival complement of *try*. Given this, *John* in (12a) is located in a Case-checking position prior to movement to the matrix SpecIP. What we have in (12a), then, is NP-raising originating from a Case-checking position, a possibility that is ruled out by the Last Resort Condition.[15] Assuming that *him* in (12b) and *who* in (12c) must move to the matrix SpecAgr$_O$P for Case checking, (12b–c) also involve NP-movement from a Case-checking position and therefore are ruled out by the Last Resort Condition. (12a–c) can then be ruled out in the same way as (4b), discussed above. Given that (12a–c) are ruled out by the Last Resort Condition, I conclude that it need not be specified in the lexicon that control verbs such as *try* take a CP infinitival complement in order to account for the impossibility of ECM and passive raising with such verbs. Under the Case-theoretic approach to the distribution of PRO, control verbs can take either a CP or an IP complement. ECM and passive raising with control verbs are ruled out by the Last Resort Condition.

Control adjectives such as *illegal* are amenable to the same analysis as control verbs. Under the Case-theoretic approach, the infinitival clause in (2b) can be either a CP or an IP. Like (3d), (2a) is ruled out by the Last Resort Condition regardless of the categorial status of the embedded clause.

In summary, in the preceding two sections I have considered the behavior of *try*-class and *believe*-class verbs with respect to ECM, passive raising, and the licensing of PRO. I have shown that under the Case-theoretic approach to the distribution of PRO the relevant facts can be accounted for without appealing to c-selection. Stowell's (1982) difference in the temporal properties of *try*-class and *believe*-class infinitivals, which determine the status of infinitival SpecIP with respect to Case checking, plays a crucial role in the phenomena under consideration. Since the difference in the temporal properties is a result of the s-selectional requirements of *try*-class and *believe*-class verbs, the systematic difference with respect to the licensing of PRO and NP-trace in the subject position of the infinitival complement of the verbs ultimately follows from their s-selectional requirements.

2.2.3   Case Checking with *Want*-Class Verbs

So far I have considered infinitival complements in which PRO and lexical subjects are in complementary distribution. The complementary distribution breaks down with *want*-class verbs.

(14) a. I want him to leave
      b. I want PRO to leave

The grammaticality of (14a) is potentially problematic for the analysis developed here. Under this analysis *him* cannot be Case-checked in the matrix SpecAgr$_O$P. Given that the infinitival clause receives irrealis interpretation and that its subject position can be filled by PRO and is therefore a Case-checking position, NP-raising into the matrix clause is ruled out by the Last Resort Condition. The ungrammaticality of (15), where passivization has occurred, confirms this.

(15) *John was wanted to leave

Following Bach (1977), Lasnik and Saito (1991) provide evidence that, in contrast to *him* in (3a), *him* in (14a) does not move into the matrix clause. Consider (16), taken from Lasnik and Saito 1991.

(16) a. ?Joan wants him$_i$ to be successful even more fervently than
          Bob's$_i$ mother does
      b. ?*Joan believes him$_i$ to be a genius even more fervently than
          Bob's$_i$ mother does

Given that the embedded subject in (16b) raises to SpecAgr$_O$P in LF for Case checking, it c-commands the matrix adverbial at LF, thus causing a Condition C violation. The grammaticality of (16a) indicates that Condition C is not violated in this construction, which in turn provides evidence that the embedded subject does not undergo A-movement into the matrix clause. It follows that it must be Case-checked within the infinitival complement. The constructions in (14a) and (16a) thus do not raise a problem for the Last Resort account given above.

The following constructions from Lasnik and Saito 1991 involving anaphor binding (17) and negative polarity item (NPI) licensing (18) provide further evidence that the subject of the infinitival complement of *believe*, but not *want*, undergoes A-movement into the matrix clause. In (17a) and (18a) the embedded-clause subject can license an anaphor and an NPI located within a matrix adverbial; such licensing is not possible in (17b) and (18b).

(17) a.   ?I believed [those men$_i$ to be unreliable] because of each other's$_i$
          statements
     b.   ??*I wanted [those men$_i$ to be fired] because of each other's$_i$
          statements

(18) a.   ??I believed [none of the applicants to be qualified] after reading
          any of the reports
     b.   ??*I wanted [none of the applicants to be hired] after reading any
          of the reports

A question now arises about how the embedded subject is Case-checked in constructions such as (14a). In Bresnan 1972, Chomsky 1981, Snyder and Rothstein 1992, and Bošković 1994a, among others, it is argued that the infinitival complement in (14a) is headed by a null complementizer, a phonologically null counterpart of the complementizer *for*, which heads the infinitival complement of *want* in (19). The embedded-clause subject in (14a) can then be Case-checked in essentially the same way as in (19).[16]

(19) I want (very much) for him to leave

An important clue to how exactly the embedded-clause subject is Case-checked in (14a) and (19) is provided by the possibility of VP-ellipsis in (20a–b).

(20) a.   ?You wanted for Mary to cook but Peter wanted for John [$_{I'}$ to e]
     b.   Mary didn't ask Peter to leave but she really wanted C him
          [$_{I'}$ to e]

Recall Lobeck's (1990) and Saito and Murasugi's (1990) generalization that only complements of agreeing functional heads can undergo ellipsis. As discussed above, Martin (1992b) argues that, given this generalization, the possibility of VP-ellipsis with control infinitivals (as in (7)) and its impossibility with ECM infinitivals (as in (6b)) indicate that the subject of control infinitivals but not the subject of ECM infinitivals is Case-checked under Spec-head agreement with the infinitival I. Returning now to (20a–b), note that the grammaticality of these constructions indicates that, like PRO in (7) and unlike *Jane* in (6b), the embedded subject in (20a–b) is Case-checked under Spec-head agreement with the embedded-clause I. What we need to do now is capture the standard assumption that C and *for* are responsible for Case-checking the infinitival subject in (20a–b) and still have the embedded subject undergo Case checking under Spec-head agreement in the embedded SpecIP. Watanabe's (1993) analysis of *for-to* constructions achieves this result. Following a suggestion by Noam Chomsky, Watanabe proposes that the *for-to* complex is generated under I, with *for* undergoing movement to C^0. (Roger Martin (personal communication) has suggested a similar analysis.) Under this proposal, *John* in (20a) is Case-checked in SpecIP under Spec-head agreement with the *for-to* complex, prior to the raising of *for*.[17] I assume that the null counterpart of *for* in (20b) behaves like *for* in all relevant respects. Note incidentally that the contrast between (20b) and (6b) provides more evidence that, in contrast to the subject of the infinitival clause embedded under *believe*, the embedded subject in constructions such as (20b) and (14a) is Case-checked within the embedded clause, and not by undergoing object shift to the matrix SpecAgr$_o$P. If the latter were the case, we would expect VP-ellipsis to be disallowed in (20b), just as it is in (6b).

One question concerning the infinitival complement of *want* that still has to be addressed is why *for* and its null counterpart are allowed with *want*. The answer may lie in Pesetsky's (1992) l-selection. Pesetsky argues that regardless of whether or not c-selection is eliminated, in addition to s-selection, which may simply be a coherence condition on semantic interpretation, we need selection for terminal elements, which he refers to as "l-selection." L-selection is limited in scope and involves arbitrary selection for lexical items and features associated with them that cannot be reduced to either s-selection or c-selection. L-selection does not refer to syntactic categories, but instead refers to individual lexical items and specific features such as [+/−finite]. For example, it involves selection for individual prepositions. The fact that the noun *love* allows either *for* or *of*, whereas *desire* requires *for*, is a matter of l-selection. According to Pesetsky, l-selection can see a particular lexical item such as *for*, but it cannot see the node P^0 that dominates it. L-selection thus has nothing to do with syntactic selection. Note that c-selection itself cannot make the necessary distinction between *love* and *desire*, since c-selection could only provide information that both the noun *love* and the noun *desire* take a PP complement.

Concerning *want*, it seems plausible that the presence of *for* and its null counterpart with *want* is a result of the l-selectional properties of *want*, given that we are dealing here with selection for particular terminal elements and not merely selection for CP. (In fact, even under the standard c-selection account of infinitival complementation we still need a way of saying that some verbs taking a CP infinitival allow *for* and some do not.) Given the facts concerning the mobility of infinitival complements to be discussed in section 2.2.4.1, I assume that l-selection for a prepositional complementizer with *want*-class verbs is optional (see also section 2.4 for relevant discussion). However, I should note here that Kiparsky and Kiparsky (1970) observe that the complementizer *for* (and I assume that the same holds for its null counterpart) occurs only with a particular class of predicates, namely, emotive predicates. Building on their observation, Bresnan (1972) argues that the complementizer *for* is semantically active. It expresses subjective reason or cause, purpose, use, or goal. Given Bresnan's proposal, we could perhaps let *for* freely appear in any infinitival complement as long as its meaning is compatible with the semantics of the higher predicate. (Pesetsky (1992) also argues that whether or not an infinitival complement can be introduced by *for* is determined by the semantics of the higher predicate, in fact, the whole higher clause.)[18]

To sum up, I have shown in this section that the lack of complementary distribution of lexical subjects and PRO in the infinitival complement of *want*-class verbs does not pose a problem for the Case-theoretic account of the distribution of PRO and the Last Resort account of the impossibility of ECM and passive raising out of control infinitival complements. The relevant facts are accounted for without invoking c-selection.

2.2.4 The Categorial Status of Control Infinitives

We have seen that we no longer need to specify that control verbs c-select CP infinitival complements. In this section I show in fact that were we to specify this, certain grammatical constructions would be ruled out. In other words, I show that under certain circumstances complements of control verbs must be IPs, a possibility that is not available under the c-selection/binding-theoretic account of infinitival complementation, but is consistent with the s-selection/Case-theoretic account.

2.2.4.1   Empty Complementizers and the ECP   Stowell (1981) argues that the distribution of empty complementizers can be accounted for if they are subject to the ECP. In (21a) the empty complementizer is properly governed by the verb; in (21b–c) it is not.[19]

(21) a.   It is believed [$_{CP}$ C [$_{IP}$ he is crazy]]
    b.   *[$_{CP}$ C [$_{IP}$ He would buy a car]] was believed at that time
    c.   *It was believed at that time [$_{CP}$ C [$_{IP}$ you would fail her]]

Infinitival clauses behave quite differently from finite clauses in the relevant respect.

(22) a.   I tried at that time [$_{CP}$ C [$_{IP}$ PRO to fail her]]
    b.   [$_{CP}$ C [$_{IP}$ PRO to buy a car]] was desirable at that time

The grammaticality of (22a–b) is unexpected. Since the empty C in (22) is not properly governed, we would expect (22a–b) to be ruled out by the ECP on a par with (21b–c). The grammaticality of the constructions suggests that the infinitives in (22a–b) are not CPs and therefore do not contain a null complementizer. Under the analysis developed here (22a–b) can be accounted for. Given that under the Case-theoretic approach to the distribution of PRO control infinitivals can be IPs, the CP projection does not have to be present in (22a–b). Since the null complementizer is not present, no problems with respect to the ECP arise in (22a–b) under this analysis. The contrast between (22a–b) and (21b–c) is thus straightforwardly accounted for.[20]

(23) also shows that control infinitivals can be IPs.

(23) a.   What the terrorists tried was [$_\alpha$ PRO to hijack an airplane]
    b.   They demanded and we tried [$_\alpha$ PRO to visit the hospital]
    c.   *What the terrorists believe is [$_\alpha$ they will hijack an airplane]
    d.   *They suspected and we believed [$_\alpha$ Peter would visit the hospital]

Assuming that (23c–d) are ruled out by the ECP because the null head of α is not properly governed, the question arises why (23a–b) are grammatical. It seems plausible that α in (23a–b) must match the selectional restrictions of the relevant predicates. Since under the c-selection account of infinitival complementation both *demand* and *try* are assumed to take a CP complement, (23a–b) are ruled out by the ECP on a par with (23c–d). On the other hand, given my assumption that *demand* and *try* can freely take an IP complement, the grammaticality of (23a–b) can readily be accounted for.

Consider also (24a–b), which provide more evidence that control infinitivals can be IPs.

(24) a. *Mary believed Peter finished school and Bill [α Peter got a job]
     b. Mary tried to finish school and Peter [α PRO to get a job]

Aoun et al. (1987) argue that governing heads cannot be gapped. Given this, (24a) is ruled out by the ECP because the null C heading α cannot be properly governed. The grammaticality of (24b), then, provides evidence that control infinitivals can be IPs; if they had to be CPs, (24b) would be ruled out by the ECP on a par with (24a).

Factive infinitivals (25a–c) and implicative infinitivals (25d–f) pattern with irrealis infinitivals in all relevant respects; this behavior suggests that they can also be IPs.

(25) a. John hated at that time to play football early in the morning
     b. What John hated was to play football early in the morning
     c. John loved and Sam hated to play football early in the morning
     d. John managed at that time to leave
     e. What John managed was to leave as soon as they arrived
     f. John disdained and Sam declined to work for a living

The line of reasoning employed here leads me to conclude that adjunct infinitivals, such as the one in (26), are also IPs.

(26) John went there [PRO to meet Mary]

If the infinitival in (26) were a CP, the construction would be ruled out by the ECP because the null complementizer is not properly governed, the adjunct CP being a barrier to government.

Note that the CP-deletion approach to infinitival complementation fares no better than the c-selection approach with respect to (22)–(25). Given the assumption that *try, demand, desirable*, and the verbs taking factive and implicative infinitivals in (25) do not trigger CP-deletion, the infinitival clauses in (22)–(25) would have to be CPs, and, as a consequence, the relevant constructions would be ruled out by the ECP. To maintain the CP-deletion hypothesis in light of these data, we would have to assume that, in contrast to ECM predicates, which always trigger CP-deletion, control predicates trigger CP-deletion only in the contexts given in (22)–(25). Since triggering CP deletion is a lexical property, this cannot be done in a principled way.

To sum up, I have argued in this section that in certain contexts control infinitives must be IPs. Given that the infinitives in (22)–(25) are IPs, I see no principled way of ruling out the IP option for the infinitives in (12a–c) and (3c–d). Since the standard binding-theoretic account of the distribution of PRO is crucially based on the CP status of control infinitival complements, this leads me to reject this account in favor of the Case-theoretic account.[21]

2.2.4.2 Scrambling out of Control Infinitives Certain facts concerning scrambling out of control infinitives provide more evidence for the IP status of such infinitives and for the Last Resort Condition analysis of A-movement out of infinitival complements. As noted by Mahajan (1990) and Nemoto (1991), in contrast to scrambling out of finite CPs, scrambling out of control infinitives exemplifies A-movement. The following examples from Serbo-Croatian, involving the scrambled quantifier *nekoga* 'someone', illustrate this.

(27) a. Nekoga$_i$ njegov$_{j/?*i}$ otac veruje da oni mrze t$_i$
         someone his   father believes that they hate
         'Someone, his father believes that they hate'
     b. Nekoga$_i$ njegov$_i$ otac planira   PRO kazniti   t$_i$
         someone his   father is-planning   to-punish
         'Someone, his father is planning to punish'

It is well known that, as illustrated by (28), Ā-movement, but not A-movement, induces weak crossover effects. In other words, quantifiers moved to A-positions, but not Ā-positions, can locally bind pronouns.

(28) a. Everyone$_i$ seems to his$_i$ father t$_i$ to be crazy
     b. Everyone$_i$, his$_{j/?*i}$ father kissed t$_i$

The fact that the preposed quantifier in (27a) cannot be coindexed with the pronoun it c-commands indicates that, like *everyone* in (28b), it is located in an Ā-position. It is generally assumed in the literature on scrambling that the lack of weak crossover effects in constructions such as (27b) indicates that, like *everyone* in (28a), the scrambled quantifier in (27b) is located in an A-position. Bearing this in mind, consider (29a), where passive raising out of an infinitival complement has occurred.

(29) a. *Jovan$_i$ je planiran [t$_i$ poljubiti Mariju]
          Jovan is planned   to-kiss Maria
          'Jovan was planned to kiss Maria'
     b. cf. Jovan je planirao [PRO poljubiti Mariju]
          'Jovan planned to kiss Maria'

Given that A-movement out of the control infinitival in (27b) is possible, the question is why (29a) is bad. Under the standard approach to the distribution of PRO, it is not clear how the contrast between (27b) and (29a) can be accounted for. Assuming that control complements are CPs, we would expect *both* (29a) and (27b) to be ruled out because they involve A-movement crossing a CP boundary, which, as is well known, is not allowed (see note 13). If, as suggested above, infinitival passives such as (13) are ruled out because they lack an appropriate controller for PRO, (29a) cannot be ruled out in the same way, because PRO is not present in (29a). However, the contrast between (29a) and (27b) receives a straight-forward account under the Case-theoretic approach. Given that a position in which PRO can appear is a Case-checking position, (29a) is ruled out by the Last Resort Condition because it involves movement from a Case-checking position into a Case-checking position. The grammatical (27b), on the other hand, does not involve movement into a Case-checking position.[22]

As for the contrast between (27b) and (27a), the fact that long-distance scrambling in (27a) does not exhibit properties of A-movement is not surprising, since it is well known that A-movement cannot take place across a CP boundary. As noted above, A-movement out of CPs is ruled out either by the ECP or by the Improper Movement Constraint, both of which are reducible to economy principles (see note 13). Since, as shown by the lack of weak crossover effects in (27b), scrambling out of control infinitivals has properties of A-movement, it must be the case that the movement in question does not cross a CP boundary. It follows that the control infinitival in (27b) cannot be a CP, a conclusion that is consistent with the proposals made here, but not with the traditional accounts of infinitival complementation.[23]

To summarize the discussion in this section, I have argued that the traditional c-selection and CP-deletion accounts of infinitival comple-mentation and the binding-theoretic account of the distribution of PRO should be rejected in favor of the Case-theoretic account of the distribu-tion of PRO and infinitival complementation. I have provided evidence that in certain contexts control infinitival complements must be of category IP, contrary to what is predicted by the c-selection/binding-theoretic account, but in accordance with the Case-theoretic account. (For more evidence for the Case-theoretic account based on French propositional infinitivals and English *wager*-class verbs, see chapter 3.) In addition to accounting for the phenomena discussed in this section, the Case-theoretic account of the distribution of PRO enables us to dispense with c-selection for different types of infinitival clauses and a number of stipulations concerning which elements count as governors. I have shown that infinitival complements can be allowed to vary freely between IP and CP within the limits set by the l-/s-selectional properties of the higher predicate, the Case requirements of the infinitival subject, and economy conditions responsible for the impossibility of A-movement out of CPs.

2.3   Economy and the Categorial Status of Clauses

In this section I will introduce a principle of economy of representation proposed by Law (1991). I will illustrate the workings of the principle, and establish its theoretical and empirical validity, by examining the categorial status of null-operator relatives and finite declarative complements. Having established the validity of the principle, I will show that it has important consequences for infinitival complementation. In particular, I will show that it imposes IP status on control infinitival complements and eliminates the possibility that control infinitivals may be CPs.

2.3.1   Null-Operator Relatives and Economy of Representation

Consider the following null-operator relatives:

(30) a. the man [Op_i that John likes t_i]
      b. the man [Op_i John likes t_i]

It is a standard assumption that, just like null-operator relatives introduced by *that*, zero null-operator relatives are CPs. However, Law (1991) proposes a version of the principle of economy of representation, which, as he notes, effectively forces IP status on zero null-operator relatives. In (31) I give a modified version of that principle, which I will refer to as the "Minimal Structure Principle" (MSP).[24]

(31) *The Minimal Structure Principle*
      Provided that lexical requirements of relevant elements are satisfied,
      if two representations have the same lexical structure and serve the
      same function, then the representation that has fewer projections is
      to be chosen as the syntactic representation serving that function.

The MSP requires that every functional projection be motivated by the satisfaction of lexical requirements; that is, structures can contain only as many functional projections as are needed to satisfy lexical requirements.

Given the MSP, the relative clause in (30b), which is potentially ambiguous in that it can be either a CP (32b) or an IP (32a), is disambiguated in favor of the more economical IP option.[25]

(32) a. the man [$_{IP}$ Op$_i$ [$_{IP}$ John likes t$_i$]]
  b. the man [$_{CP}$ Op$_i$ [$_{C'}$ C [$_{IP}$ John likes t$_i$]]]

There is also empirical evidence for the IP status of the relatives in question. The IP analysis straightforwardly accounts for the long-standing problem of the ungrammaticality of short zero-subject relatives involving Op.[26]

(33) *the man [$_{IP}$ Op$_i$ [$_{IP}$ t$_i$ likes Mary]]

Given that the relative clause in (33) is simply an IP, the only possible landing site for Op is the IP-adjoined position. The ungrammaticality of short zero-subject relativization then reduces to the ungrammaticality of short subject topicalization, since the two have the same structure in all relevant respects. (For arguments that topicalization involves IP-adjunction, see Baltin 1982, Iwakura 1978, Lasnik and Saito 1992, Rochemont 1989, and Saito 1985, among others.)

(34) *I think that [$_{IP}$ John$_i$, [$_{IP}$ t$_i$ likes Mary]]

Lasnik and Saito (1992) provide convincing evidence that short subject topicalization is disallowed. Thus, they observe that if vacuous subject topicalization were allowed, *wh*-movement in (35a) and (35b) would incorrectly be predicted to have the same status, since the two sentences would have the same structure in all relevant respects.

(35) a. ?*Who do you think that [friends of t] kissed Mary
  b. ?Who do you think that [friends of t] Mary kissed

Lasnik and Saito also note that if short subject topicalization were allowed, we would expect that, as in (36a), *John* and *himself* can be co-indexed in (36b). However, this is not possible.

(36) a. John$_i$ thinks that himself$_i$ Peter likes
  b. *John$_i$ thinks that himself$_i$ likes Peter

Under the IP analysis, the ungrammaticality of short zero-subject relatives such as (33) thus reduces to the ungrammaticality of (34). Apparently, movement from SpecIP to the IP-adjoined position must be disallowed. The ungrammaticality of (37) confirms this.

(37) *Who$_i$ do you think [$_{CP}$ t''$_i$ [$_{C'}$ that [$_{IP}$ t'$_i$ [$_{IP}$ t$_i$ likes Mary]]]]

As noted by Saito and Murasugi (1993), if *who* could move from SpecIP to the IP-adjoined position, the Comp-trace (C-trace) effect would be voided in (37), since the original trace t would be licensed by t'. (t' itself would still be a problem. However, being an intermediate trace, it could be deleted.) To rule out (37), Saito and Murasugi (1993) propose a condition on the length of chain links.[27] The condition, which Saito and Murasugi argue is derivable from the economy principles—in particular, the ban on superfluous steps—is given in (38).

(38) a. A chain link must be at least of length 1.
    b. A chain link from A to B is of length n iff there are n "nodes" (X, X', or XP, but not segments of these) that dominate A and exclude B.

(38a) requires that each chain link have some length. Since, given (38b), the chain link from SpecIP to the IP-adjoined position is of length 0, all the derivations in (33), (34), and (37) are ruled out by (38a).[28] The reader can verify that, unlike what happens in (33), no problems with respect to (38) arise in (39). (I ignore irrelevant details of the structure, as well as intermediate traces.)[29]

(39) a. the man [$_{IP}$ Op$_i$ [$_{IP}$ Mary [$_{VP}$ likes t$_i$]]]
    b. the man [$_{IP}$ Op$_i$ [$_{IP}$ you [$_{VP}$ claim [$_{IP}$ t$_i$ likes Mary]]]]

Constructions corresponding to (33) are, however, grammatical in some languages. Pesetsky (1982a) conjectures that such constructions can be grammatical only in languages that allow null subjects and do not require complementizers. Rizzi (1990a) gives 15th-century Italian as an example.

(40) Ch'è faccenda [$_{IP}$ Op$_i$ [$_{IP}$ ex [$_{VP}$ tocca   a noi t$_i$]]]
    for is matter   concerns to us
    'For this is a matter that concerns us'

This is predicted under the IP analysis, since in null-subject languages such as 15th-century Italian the operator can be extracted from SpecVP, with SpecIP being filled by a null expletive. As a result, (38) is not violated.[30]

An interesting confirmation of the IP analysis is provided by relatives containing resumptive pronouns. Saito (1985) shows that such pronouns are not allowed in adjunction structures. He gives scrambling, embedded topicalization, and heavy NP shift, all of which he claims involve adjunction, as examples. Note that to avoid the possibility of analyzing the clause involving embedded topicalization as a superficial matrix clause involving left dislocation, which I assume is a root process involving a base-generated phrase in the Spec of a functional category associated with a resumptive pronoun, following Lasnik and Saito (1992) I give an example of embedded topicalization within a subject clause.

(41) a. *Scrambling*

John$_i$-o, Mary-ga   (*kare$_i$-o) mita (koto) (Japanese)

John-ACC Mary-NOM   he-ACC   saw (fact)

'John, Mary saw him'

  b. *Embedded topicalization*

That this solution, I proposed (*it) last year is widely known

  c. *Heavy NP shift*

John met [$_{NP}$ a man that bought (*it$_i$) for his mother [$_{NP}$ that painting by Rembrandt]$_i$]

Given Saito's observation, the IP analysis predicts that, unlike null-operator relatives introduced by *that*, zero relatives should disallow resumptive pronouns. As (42a–b) (taken from Kayne 1984) show, the prediction is borne out.[31]

(42) a. *the book [$_{IP}$ Op [$_{IP}$ I was wondering whether I would get it in the mail]]

  b. the book [$_{CP}$ Op [$_{C'}$ that I was wondering whether I would get it in the mail]]

Under the IP analysis Op in (42a) is located in an adjoined position. As a result, the gap associated with Op cannot be filled by a resumptive pronoun. Since in the relative clause introduced by *that* Op is located in SpecCP rather than in an adjoined position, the gap can be filled by a resumptive pronoun.[32] The contrast in (42) thus provides more evidence for the IP status of zero null-operator relatives, forced by the MSP.

The following constructions, however, raise a potential problem for the IP analysis of null-operator relatives:

(43) a. *The person stood up [$_{IP}$ Op [$_{IP}$ John criticized t]]

  b. *The person stood up [$_{IP}$ Op [$_{IP}$ t criticized John]]

  c. The person stood up [$_{CP}$ who/that t criticized John]

  d. The person stood up [$_{CP}$ who/that John criticized t]

The question is why, in contrast to (43c–d), (43a–b) are ungrammatical. It is generally assumed that constructions such as (43a–b) are ruled out by the ECP because the null complementizer, which under standard assumptions heads the extraposed relative clause, is not properly governed. However, suppose that, following Travis (1991), we extend Stowell's (1981) proposal that null complementizers must be properly governed to the requirement that all phonologically null heads must be properly governed. Notice now that under checking theory verbs are taken from the lexicon with agreement/tense inflection. I is simply a set of features without lexical content and therefore is subject to the ECP.[33] I assume that in constructions such as (32a) the head of the relative clause is properly governed either by the determiner (under the DP hypothesis) or by the noun head of the relative, possibly through the agreement relation holding between the noun head of the relative and the head of the relative clause (see Rizzi 1990a). (43a–b), on the other hand, are ruled out because the head of the relative clause is not properly governed. As for (43c–d), it seems plausible that whatever is responsible for licensing C in (44) with respect to the ECP is also responsible for satisfying the ECP in (43c–d) when the complementizer is not phonologically overt. (I assume that C properly governs I of its complement.)

(44) [CP What C [IP he likes]] is apples

As noted above, for some reason, null heads that are in a Spec-head relation with an operator are exempt from the ECP. Returning now to (43a–b), notice that their ungrammaticality in fact provides evidence that zero null-operator relatives are not headed by a null complementizer that is in a Spec-head relation with an operator. If this were the case, we would expect (43a–b) to be grammatical. The data under consideration are thus consistent with the IP analysis of the relatives under consideration. However, they are not consistent with the CP analysis.[34]

2.3.2 Finite Declarative Complements and Economy of Representation

In the preceding section I have argued that null-operator relatives that are not introduced by *that* are IPs, the IP status being forced on them by the MSP. Another construction where we would expect the effects of the MSP to be detectable involves finite declarative complements, such as the embedded clause in *I believe John likes Mary*. In this section I will provide evidence that zero finite declarative complements are indeed IPs, and I will attribute their IP status to the MSP.[35] Notice first that the very possibility of finite relative clauses being IPs provides evidence that the presence of Tense does not require a CP projection, contra Stowell (1982) and Pesetsky (1982b), which clears the way for the IP analysis of finite declarative complements that are not introduced by *that*. Furthermore, under the IP analysis it need not be stipulated that finite and nonfinite complements of verbs such as *believe* differ in their categorial status. Under the IP analysis both the finite and the nonfinite complements of *believe* can be IPs. As shown in Bowers 1987 and Bošković 1992, the IP analysis also provides a straightforward account of the lack of C-trace effects in constructions such as (45a), which contrasts with (45b).

(45) a.   Who do you believe likes Mary
     b.   *Who do you believe that likes Mary

The reason why (45a) does not exhibit a C-trace effect under the IP analysis is trivial: no C is present in the embedded clause. On the other hand, providing a principled account of the grammaticality of (45a) and the contrast between (45a) and (45b) has proved to be a recurring problem for the CP analysis of zero finite declarative complements (see Bowers 1987 and Bošković 1992 for much relevant discussion). Another argument for the IP analysis involves obligatoriness of *that* with embedded topicalization, a phenomenon that has not received a satisfactory account, although it has recently come under intensive scrutiny. I discuss this phenomenon in detail in the next section.[36]

2.3.2.1 Topicalization It is well known that, in contrast to main-clause topicalizations, embedded topicalizations must include *that* (see Authier 1992, Kayne 1994, Rochemont 1989, Watanabe 1993, among others).[37]

(46) a.   [$_{IP}$ Mary, [$_{IP}$ John likes]]
     b.   Peter doesn't believe that [$_{IP}$ Mary, [$_{IP}$ John likes]]
     c.   *Peter doesn't believe [$_{IP}$ Mary, [$_{IP}$ John likes]]

The long-standing problem of the obligatoriness of *that* with embedded topicalization is readily accounted for under the IP analysis. Given that the embedded clause in (46c) is an IP and that topicalization involves adjunction to IP, (46c) is ruled out because it involves adjunction to an argument, which, as is well known (see Chomsky 1986a), is not allowed. Given that (as proposed by Chomsky (1986a), who follows Kyle Johnson on this point) the ban on adjunction to arguments follows from θ-theory, the ungrammaticality of (46c) can ultimately be traced to θ-theory. (According to Chomsky (1986a, 16), adjoined elements interfere with θ-role assignment to the phrase they adjoin to, which leads to a θ-Criterion violation.) Since the relevant IP is not an argument, the problem noted above with respect to (46c) does not arise in (46a–b). The facts in (46) thus receive a straightforward account under the IP analysis. On the other hand, under the CP analysis they remain a mystery.

The only CP accounts of the facts under consideration that I am aware of are offered by Authier (1992) and Watanabe (1993). However, their accounts are rather problematic. Both Authier and Watanabe adopt the CP-recursion analysis of topicalization, according to which the topicalized phrase is located in the lower SpecCP of a CP-recursive structure. To account for the obligatoriness of *that* with embedded topicalization, Authier stipulates that topicalized CPs cannot be selected. However, this does not rule out the possibility of the higher C being null.

(47) *Peter doesn't believe [$_{CP}$ C [$_{CP}$ Mary, [$_{C'}$ C [$_{IP}$ John likes]]]]

Watanabe accounts for (47) by stipulating that when the higher C is null, the CP-recursive structure is unrecoverable. However, as Watanabe himself notes, this incorrectly rules out matrix topicalization (46a), which under Watanabe's analysis also involves CP-recursion.

Returning now to the CP/IP account of the obligatoriness of *that* with embedded topicalization, notice that if, following Rochemont (1989), instead of restricting topicalization to IP-adjunction, we simply assume that topicalization involves clausal adjunction (i.e., adjunction to either CP or IP), a rather natural move, the analysis of the facts in (46) given above can be straightforwardly extended to account for (48). (I assume that the marginality of (48a,c) is due to a Subjacency violation; see Lasnik and Saito 1992.)

(48) a. ??[$_{CP}$ To John, [$_{CP}$ which book should Peter give]]
      b. *I wonder [$_{CP}$ to John, [$_{CP}$ which book Peter should give]]
      c. ??I wonder [$_{CP}$ to whom [$_{IP}$ this book, [$_{IP}$ Peter should give]]]
      d. *John believes [$_{CP}$ this book, [$_{CP}$ that Peter should give to Mary]]

Like (46c), (48b) is ruled out because it involves adjunction to an argument, this time a CP. The same holds for (48d). On the other hand, since the relevant CP in (48a) and IP in (48c) are not arguments, no adjunction to arguments takes place in these constructions.[38] The fact that under the analysis presented here the data in (46) and (48) receive a uniform account —and that the account exhibits such simplicity—provides evidence for the analysis.

The analysis can also be extended to account for some otherwise puzzling facts concerning long *wh*-movement and topicalization in American Sign Language (ASL), which have not been accounted for in the literature. The ASL facts in question also confirm that the presence or absence of the CP projection and not the distinction between lexical and null complementizers is responsible for the contrast between (46b) and (46c).

Petronio (1992) shows that in ASL some verbs do, and some do not, allow *wh*-extraction from their clausal complement. Thus, as (49) shows, THINK but not FEEL allows long *wh*-extraction. (Following standard practice, capital letters are used for ASL signs and "___wh-q" and "___t" are used for signs accompanied by nonmanual *wh*-question and topicalization gestures.)

<pre>
                            wh-q
(49) a. ?*WHO BILL FEEL [JOHN LIKE t]
                            wh-q
     b.   WHO YOU THINK [RAY LIKE t]
</pre>

Lillo-Martin (1990) argues that the unacceptability of (49a) results from a Subjacency violation. Building on a proposal made by Tiedeman (1987), she argues that because of a feature conflict with the null declarative complementizer in ASL, which is specified as [−wh], WHO cannot pass through the embedded SpecCP in (49a).[39] As a result, *wh*-movement in (49a) violates Subjacency. The question now is why (49b) is fully acceptable. I propose that the embedded clause in (49b) is an IP, the IP status being imposed on the clause by the MSP. Given this, we can straightforwardly account for the fact that, in contrast to (49a), (49b) does not violate Subjacency. Furthermore, the IP analysis predicts that there should be a correlation between long *wh*-extraction and embedded topicalization. If the clausal complement of FEEL is a CP and that of THINK an IP, the analysis predicts that embedded topicalization will be allowed with FEEL, but not with THINK. The prediction is borne out.

<pre>
                        t
(50) a. BILL FEEL [cp[ip JOHN [ip MARY LIKE t]]]
                        t
     b. *BILL THINK [ip JOHN [ip MARY LIKE t]]
</pre>

Under the proposals made here, the contrast between (50a) and (50b) is accounted for in the same way as the data in (46) and (48). Like (46c) and (48b,d), (50b) is ruled out by the ban on adjunction to arguments, which, as noted above, is derivable from θ-theoretic considerations. Since, as in (46a–b) and (48a,c), the clause hosting topicalization is not an argument in (50a), no problems with respect to the ban on adjunction to arguments arise in (50a).

It is worth mentioning here that there is some variation with respect to the possibility of long *wh*-extraction in ASL. Boster (1991) observes that for some signers, but not for others, long *wh*-extraction is allowed from the clausal complement of HOPE. It is interesting, however, that the correlation between long *wh*-extraction and embedded topicalization, predicted by the proposals made above, still holds. As noted by Boster, the signers who accept (51a) disallow embedded topicalization with HOPE. On the other hand, the signers who disallow (51a) accept (51b).

(51) a. $\overline{}$ wh-q
          WHAT JOHN HOPE [MARY BUY t]

      b. JOHN HOPE [$\overline{\text{BOOK}}$ MARY BUY t]

Notice also that, as expected, all signers allow topicalization in root clauses, which are not arguments.

(52) $\overline{}$ t
      MARY JOHN LIKE

The ASL data under consideration thus provide more evidence that finite clauses can be IPs. The fact that the proposed analysis of the English data in (46), which is crucially based on the IP hypothesis, can be generalized so as to account for the otherwise puzzling ASL data provides more evidence for this analysis.

Before concluding this section, I will briefly demonstrate that, as shown in Bošković 1994a, the IP analysis can be straightforwardly extended to account for certain facts concerning topicalization in Romanian subjunctives. As (53a) shows, subjunctive IPs in Romanian are headed by the subjunctive particle *să*, which must be present in all subjunctive clauses. (See Terzi 1992 and references therein for arguments that *să* is an I element. The Romanian data considered in this section are taken from Terzi 1992.) The constructions in (53) demonstrate that, in contrast to the I element *să*, the complementizer *ca* is only optionally present in Romanian subjunctive complements.[40]

(53) a. Vreau [$_{IP}$ *(să) vină   Ion mîine]
          I-want   PRT comes Ion tomorrow
          'I want Ion to come tomorrow'

      b. Vreau [$_{CP}$ ca să vină   Ion mîine]
          I-want   that PRT comes Ion tomorrow

Given the above discussion, we would expect (53a) and (53b) to differ in the categorial status of the complement. The complement in (53b), headed by an overt complementizer, is clearly a CP. On the other hand, under the proposals made here we would expect the complement in (53a) to be an IP, on a par with the embedded clause in *John believes Peter left*. The facts concerning topicalization in subjunctive complements confirm that this is indeed the case.[41] Topicalization is allowed in subjunctive complements when the complement is headed by the complementizer *ca* (54b). However, it is not allowed when the subjunctive complement is headed by the I element *să* (54a).

(54) a. *Vreau [$_{IP}$ mîine   [$_{IP}$ să   vină   Ion]]
         I-want   tomorrow   PRT comes Ion
     b. Vreau [$_{CP}$ ca [$_{IP}$ mîine   [$_{IP}$ să   vină   Ion]]]
         I-want   that   tomorrow   PRT comes Ion

Assuming that topicalization involves adjunction to IP, this is exactly what the IP analysis predicts. Given that the embedded clause in (54a) is an IP, the construction is ruled out because it involves adjunction to an argument. Since the relevant IP in (54b) is not an argument, the ban on adjunction to arguments is not violated in (54b) and the construction is correctly predicted to be grammatical.[42] The contrast between (54a) and (54b) is thus accounted for in the same way as the contrast between (46b) and (46c). The fact that the IP analysis of (46b–c) can readily be extended to account for the Romanian and ASL data examined in this section, as well as the English data in (48), provides strong evidence that the IP analysis of the contrast between (46b) and (46c) is on the right track.

2.3.2.2 *Wanna-Contraction* In Bošković 1994a I gave an argument for the IP status of zero declaratives based on PF contraction.[43] Consider (55).

(55) a. *Who$_i$ do you wanna t$_i$ buy a car
     b. cf. I wanna PRO buy a car

Under standard assumptions, contraction in (55a) is blocked by the *wh*-trace. However, the following constructions, taken from Schachter 1984, provide evidence that *wh*-traces do not block PF contraction. (For discussion of contraction across PRO, see Bošković 1994a, where it is argued that PRO remains in SpecVP at S-Structure (SS) and moves to SpecIP in LF.)[44]

(56) a. What$_i$ do you think's t$_i$ happening there tomorrow
   b. cf. What$_i$ do you think t$_i$ is happening there tomorrow
   c. What$_i$ do you think's t$_i$ been happening there today
   d. cf. What$_i$ do you think t$_i$ has been happening there today

Since a *wh*-trace clearly intervenes between the contracted auxiliary and its host, Schachter's data can be interpreted as indicating that *wh*-traces are invisible at PF.[45] Returning now to (55a), note that there are actually two elements intervening between *want* and *to* that could potentially block contraction. (Recall that a null C must be present in (57) to Case-check the embedded-clause subject.)

(57) Who$_i$ do you want [$_{CP}$ C [$_{IP}$ t$_i$ to buy a car]]

If, as suggested by the grammaticality of (56a,c), *wh*-traces do not block PF contraction, C is left as the only obstacle to PF contraction in (57).[46] Since under the IP analysis C is not present in the embedded clause in (56a,c), the possibility of contraction in these constructions can then be straightforwardly accounted for. Given this analysis, I argue in Bošković 1994a that the contrast between (55a) and (56a,c) provides more evidence for the IP analysis of zero finite declarative complements.

The analysis given in Bošković 1994a can also be readily extended to account for (58a–b), if we make the natural assumption that not only *wh*-traces but traces in general are invisible at PF.

(58) a. John$_i$ is sposta t$_i$ leave on Monday
   b. John$_i$ is supposed t$_i$ to leave on Monday

Under standard assumptions the raising infinitival in (58a–b) is an IP. The only element intervening between the infinitival particle and the higher verb is then a trace, which is invisible at PF (see below for an account of the PF invisibility of traces).

Under the analysis given in Bošković 1994a, summed up here, the contrast between (55a) and (58a–b) is thus accounted for without stipulating that some traces do, and some traces do not, block PF contraction, as the standard analysis proposed by Jaeggli (1980) does. Under this analysis the contrast between (55a) and (58a–b) is accounted for by stipulating that Case-marked traces are visible at PF and therefore block contraction, whereas non-Case-marked traces are invisible at PF and do not block contraction. Since *wh*-trace is Case-marked, it is assumed that it blocks contraction in constructions such as (55a). On the other hand, not being Case-marked, NP-traces do not block contraction; hence the grammaticality of (58a–b). Even if we disregard the problem raised for the standard analysis by the grammaticality of (56a,c), where an intervening *wh*-trace clearly does not block contraction, the standard analysis is conceptually rather problematic in the current system, since it appeals to Case theory at PF. However, under current theoretical assumptions Case theory has no PF relevance. Under the checking theory all NPs are taken from the lexicon with a Case feature, which must be checked under Spec-head agreement before the level of LF is reached. NPs whose Case features remain unchecked are illegitimate LF objects and cause the derivation to crash. On the other hand, the presence of an unchecked Case feature does not make an NP an illegitimate PF object. Thus, under the standard minimalist analysis the Case feature of the object NP in (59) is assumed to be checked only after the NP undergoes LF movement to SpecAgr$_O$P. Yet the presence of an NP with an unchecked Case feature does not cause the derivation to crash at PF.

(59) a. SS John [$_{VP}$ likes Mary]
     b. LF John likes$_i$ [$_{Agr_OP}$ Mary$_j$ t$_i$ [$_{VP}$ t$_i$ t$_j$]]

Under current theoretical assumptions the Case Filter is thus interpreted as an LF requirement—a conceptually desirable result. If Case is a condition on θ-marking, as argued by Chomsky (1981, 1986b), we would not expect an ultimately thematic requirement to have consequences for levels other than LF, an expectation that is inconsistent with Jaeggli's analysis of *wanna*-contraction.[47] On the other hand, it is easy to verify that under the analysis presented here, based on the IP analysis of zero finite declarative complements, the facts concerning PF contraction (in particular, the ungrammaticality of (55a) and the grammaticality of (56a,c) and (58a–b)), can be accounted for without appealing to Case theory at PF—another conceptually desirable result.

One remaining question that needs to be addressed under the current analysis is why traces do not block contraction. Chomsky (1993) argues that traditional traces are in fact copies of moved elements, which are identical to the moved elements. In PF, copies are deleted under identity with the element that is pronounced. It is easy to verify that if PF copy deletion is freely ordered with respect to other PF processes, such as contraction and merger, the desired result that copies do not affect PF contraction is achieved. In fact, an additional stipulation concerning ordering of PF processes would be needed to ensure that copies such as *wh*-trace block PF contraction. Since no additional stipulations have to be made under the account of PF contraction presented here, which is based on the

IP analysis of zero finite declarative complements, this account provides another conceptual argument for this analysis.

To summarize the discussion in the preceding two sections, I have argued that English zero finite declarative complements and null-operator relatives, as well as finite complements of ASL verbs such as THINK and *ca*-less subjunctives in Romanian, must be IPs. The MSP provides a uniform theoretical explanation for the IP status of the clauses in question.[48]

2.3.3 Infinitival Complementation and Economy of Representation

Returning now to infinitival complements, note that the MSP forces IP status on the infinitival complement in (60), just as it does on English zero finite declarative complements, null-operator relatives, finite complements of ASL verbs such as THINK, and *ca*-less subjunctives in Romanian.

(60) John tried [$_{IP}$ PRO to kiss Mary]

Given the MSP, the infinitive in (60), which is potentially ambiguous between CP and IP, is disambiguated in favor of the IP option. Having fewer projections, the IP option is more economical than the CP option. We thus have a theory-internal argument that the infinitival complement of *try*-class verbs is always an IP. This argument is based on the requirement that structures contain only as many functional projections as are needed to satisfy relevant lexical requirements. The requirement fits in well with the general considerations of economy outlined in Chomsky 1991 and, as shown above, is empirically well motivated.

Interestingly, a number of authors have recently independently proposed principles that are quite similar to the MSP.

(61) a. *Minimal Projection* (Grimshaw 1994, 1)
          A functional projection must be functionally interpreted.
      b. *Structural Economy Principle* (Safir 1993, 64)
          At any point in a derivation, a structural description for a natural language string employs as few nodes as grammatical principles and lexical selection require.
      c. (Speas 1994, 186–187)
          Project XP only if XP has content. A node X has content if and only if X dominates a distinct phonological matrix or a distinct semantic matrix.
      d. *Minimal Projection Principle* (Radford 1994, 11)
          S-structures are the minimal well-formed projections of the lexical items they contain.

e. (Chomsky 1995, 294)

  α enters the numeration only if it has an effect on output.

The basic idea behind all the principles in (61) is that superfluous projections are not allowed in representations. Though what counts as superfluous differs slightly in the definitions in (61), like the MSP, all the principles in (61) impose IP status on control infinitival complements. In other words, they strengthen the conclusion reached in section 2.2 from "Control infinitival complements can be IPs" to "Control infinitival complements *must* be IPs."

A question now arises concerning how principles such as (61a–e) and the MSP (31) interact with Chomsky's (1994) *numeration*, which can be defined roughly as an array of lexical items that is mapped by the computational system into a linguistic expression (a PF-LF pair). Chomsky views the numeration as fixing the reference set for determining whether a particular derivation is optimal. In Chomsky 1995 he proposes that (61e) enters into determining the numeration itself. Conceptually, this is rather problematic because of its globality. To determine the effects of (61e), one needs to know PF and LF outputs. But the numeration, which is determined by (61e), must be present in the initial stage of the derivation. There are two ways of solving the problem. One is to drop the notion of numeration and/or find another way of determining the reference set, which is a nontrivial task. Another is to redefine the notion of numeration so that elements affected by principles such as (61a–e) and the MSP are not present in the numeration. This can be done rather straightforwardly if we adopt the MSP as the formulation of the relevant principle of economy of representation.[49] All we need to do, then, is define the numeration, and with it the reference set, on lexical elements only. Under this view only lexical elements would be present in numerations. (This seems natural if the contents of numerations are determined by what we want or choose to say.) Repeated access to the lexicon would then be allowed to ensure that we have all the purely functional elements that are necessary to build legitimate structures. Instead of positing the MSP, we could then simply require that the lexicon be accessed only when needed (i.e., when a certain functional category becomes necessary in structure building). This amounts to assigning cost to merger or, to be more precise, merger of elements that are not taken from the numeration. Under this view merger of such elements is subject to the ban on superfluous operations (i.e., it is a last resort operation). Note that lexical insertion from the numeration need not be exempted from the ban on superfluous operations since taking an element out of a numeration and inserting it into the structure can be considered a step toward a well-formed derivation. This is essentially the position taken by Collins (1994). The position could be made more precise by assuming that derivations that do not exhaust numerations do not converge. Inserting an element from the numeration into the structure is then a step toward convergence and therefore is in accordance with the ban on superfluous steps in a derivation. A tacit assumption here is that forming a numeration (i.e., selecting lexical elements into a numeration) is not subject to economy principles and therefore is costless. Assigning cost to numeration formation, or trying to determine why one numeration is formed rather than another, would mean bringing the question of what we want to say into the domain of inquiry covered by linguistics or, to be more precise, the study of the working of the computational mechanism of human language, which is what this book is concerned with. As Chomsky (1995) observes, requiring the computational mechanism of human language to deal with the issue of what people choose to say and why they choose it would be no different from requiring a theory of the mechanism of vision or motor coordination to explain what people choose to look at or reach for and why they choose it.

Under the approach to numerations and lexical insertion taken above, the MSP can be dispensed with. Its effects are derivable from the ban on superfluous steps in a derivation (i.e., the Last Resort Condition). This is desirable, since the ban applies locally (i.e., an operation is evaluated with respect to the ban at the point of its application). The MSP, on the other hand, has an element of globality, especially when compared to the derivational approach developed in this section. The representations that the MSP rules out in favor of other, more economical representations cannot even be built under the derivational approach since they inevitably violate the ban on superfluous operations. Dispensing with the MSP—or, to be more precise, replacing it with the approach to lexical insertion and numerations adopted above—is thus a step toward eliminating globality from the system, which is a desirable move conceptually. It is also in accordance with the recent trend of maximizing derivational constraints at the expense of representational constraints (see Epstein 1995).

In summary, I have argued in this section that economy principles impose IP status on control infinitivals and eliminate the possibility of control infinitivals being CPs. Control infinitivals not only can be, but also must be, IPs.[50]

2.4   Other Recent Accounts of Infinitival Complementation

In the previous sections I have argued that, contrary to standard assumptions, c-selection plays no role in infinitival complementation and that control as well as ECM infinitival complements are IPs. Two other recent works also attempt to eliminate c-selection from infinitival complementation, differ from standard assumptions concerning the categorial status of infinitival complements, and emphasize the role of s-selection in infinitival complementation. Pesetsky (1992) argues that all clausal complements, including control and ECM infinitivals, and possibly all clauses are CPs.[51] Ormazabal (1995) presents a mixed account on which, as in Pesetsky 1992, ECM infinitivals are CPs and, as in Bošković 1992 and 1996b (and here), control infinitivals are IPs. Both Pesetsky and Ormazabal dispense with c-selection for different types of infinitival clauses. For Pesetsky, the CP status of infinitival complements is a result of a more general requirement that all clauses be CPs, the question of what the requirement could follow from being left open. For Ormazabal, the categorial status of infinitival complements is a result of the s-selectional properties of higher predicates, much as in the current analysis.[52] I will first discuss Pesetsky's account, concentrating on his claim that, contrary to what is argued here, control infinitivals are CPs. I will then examine Pesetsky's and Ormazabal's claim that ECM infinitivals are CPs.

Pesetsky's analysis is based on a number of stipulations, as well as several theoretical assumptions that are inconsistent with the theoretical framework adopted here. First, his analysis of the different behavior of *believe*-class and *try*-class infinitivals with respect to the possibility of PRO and passive raising is crucially based on the stipulation that the null complementizer heading the infinitival complement of *believe* is specified as [+affix] whereas the complementizer heading the infinitival complement of *try* is specified as [−affix]. This stipulation is reminiscent of Chomsky's (1986b) CP/IP distinction between different types of infinitival complements. (In Pesetsky's system, C-affixation, which takes place through syntactic incorporation, results in the infinitival subject position being governed by the higher verb.) The stipulation also has an unfortunate consequence in that it forces Pesetsky to abandon his position that null morphemes are universally affixes, thus losing a firm criterion for determining the morphological status of null morphemes, which play a crucial role in his system. Another stipulation that plays a crucial role in Pesetsky's analysis is that, in contrast to null heads, traces of null heads count as governors. As a result of this stipulation, incorporation of the [+affix] C into the higher verb (the operation takes place only with *believe*-class verbs) results in the higher verb governing the infinitival subject position, given Baker's (1988) Government Transparency Corollary, which in Pesetsky's interpretation states that a category into which an item is incorporated governs everything that the trace of the incorporated item governs. However, given that, in contrast to traces of null heads, null heads themselves are not governors, [−affix] Cs, which occur with *try*-class verbs, fail to govern the subject position of *try*-class infinitivals. The position then has the usual characteristics of ungoverned positions.

Pesetsky's analysis is crucially based on government, which is involved in Case licensing and in determining the distribution of PRO. This is inconsistent with the minimalist framework, which does not have a place for the arbitrary notion of government. Pesetsky is also forced to posit conditions holding at SS. In particular, he is forced to assume that one part of the Case Filter and the binding conditions, which determine the distribution of PRO on his analysis, apply at SS, a position that is untenable in the minimalist framework, in which SS has no independent syntactic significance. Clearly, then, Pesetsky's analysis cannot be maintained in the framework adopted here.

The analysis is also problematic on empirical grounds. The most serious problem concerns constructions such as (3a), repeated as (62), and (14a), repeated as (63).

(62) John believed him to be crazy

(63) I want him to leave

Under Pesetsky's analysis the embedded-clause subject in both (62) and (63) is Case-licensed under government by the higher verb in the embedded-clause SpecIP. As a result, under Pesetsky's analysis it does not seem to be possible to account for the different behavior of the subject of the infinitival complement of *believe*- and *want*-class verbs with respect to the binding conditions and NPI licensing (see (16)–(18)). The contrast between (6b) and (20b) with respect to the possibility of ellipsis also remains unaccounted for. As shown above, the data in question are straightforwardly accounted for under the minimalist approach to Case licensing, according to which all structural Case marking takes place in a single configuration of Spec-head agreement, rather than the heterogeneous relation of government.[53]

Let us now examine more closely Pesetsky's and Ormazabal's claim that, contrary to standard assumptions, English ECM infinitivals are CPs. The evidence Ormazabal offers for this claim concerns *re*-affixation. Pesetsky's evidence, which I will consider first, is based on the impossibility of nominalizing *believe*-class verbs taking infinitival complements. Pesetsky notes that the fact that no grammatical output can be derived from the D-Structure (DS) form in (64a) (I use the term "D-Structure" only for expository purposes) follows from the CP analysis of ECM infinitivals, given Myers's generalization, which states that complex words that are derived through affixation of a phonologically null morpheme (zero-derived words) do not permit further affixation of derivational morphemes.[54]

(64) a. DS   (the) proof [to have John kissed Mary]
     b. SS   *John$_i$'s proof [t$_i$ to have t$_i$ kissed Mary]
     c. SS   *the proof [of John$_i$ to have t$_i$ kissed Mary]

Assuming that the infinitival complement of both *prove* (a *believe*-class verb) and *proof* is headed by a null complementizer that must undergo incorporation into the higher head because of its [+affix] status, (64) involves a configuration that Myers's generalization disallows: a derivational affix is attached outside a complex word of which the zero morpheme forms a part.

(65) [[[prove] C] Nominalizer]

Given the configuration in (65), Pesetsky argues that the inability of *believe*-class verbs' nominalizations to take infinitival complements follows from Myers's generalization. Since Pesetsky's analysis is crucially based on the CP status of ECM infinitivals, if (64b–c) could not be ruled out independently of Myers's generalization, their ungrammaticality would provide evidence that at least ECM infinitivals that function as nominal complements are CPs. However, Chomsky (1986b) argues that the reason why no grammatical output can be derived from DS forms such as (64a) is that the infinitival subject cannot be Case-marked, owing to a difference in the status of accusative and genitive Case in English. According to Chomsky, accusative Case is assigned structurally in English, and genitive Case is assigned inherently (i.e., under θ-role assignment). Thus, in (66) the noun *destruction* θ-marks *Rome*, as a result of which it can assign *Rome* genitive Case, which is realized through *of*-insertion in (66a) and as *'s* in (66b).[55]

(66) a. destruction of Rome

     b. Rome$_i$'s destruction t$_i$

Note now that, given Chomsky's (1986b) analysis of genitive Case assignment, both (64b) and (64c) are straightforwardly ruled out because *John* cannot be assigned genitive Case owing to the lack of a θ-relation between *proof* and *John*. Note also that Chomsky's theory of genitive Case assignment seems to be needed independently of (64b–c). It is easy to verify that the ungrammatical constructions in (67) are straightforwardly ruled out under Chomsky's analysis. However, it is not clear whether the constructions in question can be ruled out in the current framework if Chomsky's theory of genitive Case assignment is altogether dispensed with.[56]

(67) a. *John$_i$'s destruction of portraits t$_i$

     b. *its proof that Peter likes Mary

     c. cf. It was proven that Peter liked Mary

     d. *my hatred of it when it rains on Sunday

     e. cf. I hate it when it rains on Sunday

Under the Case analysis the possibility of nouns taking noncontrol infinitival complements is ruled out independently of the categorial status of ECM infinitivals and the morphological status of nouns with respect to zero derivation. It is in fact well known that, like DS forms such as (64a), DS forms such as (68a), which contains nondeverbal nouns, cannot yield a grammatical output.[57]

(68) a. DS   (the) thesis/sign [to be John a liar]

     b. SS   *John's$_i$ thesis/sign [t$_i$ to be t$_i$ a liar]

     c. SS   *the thesis/sign [of John$_i$ to be t$_i$ a liar]

Since, in contrast to *proof*, the nouns in (68) are not deverbal and thus do not contain a nominalizer affix, the fact that they cannot take a propositional infinitival complement cannot be explained by appealing to Myers's generalization. Even if the infinitival complement were to be headed by a null complementizer that must undergo affixation to the nouns, (68b–c) (unlike (64b–c)) would not involve a configuration that violates Myers's generalization. On the other hand, it is easy to verify that if, as argued by Chomsky, genitive Case (unlike accusative Case) is assigned inherently, the facts under consideration can be straightforwardly accounted for.[58]

    In conclusion, since (64b–c) are ruled out independently of Myers's generalization, their ungrammaticality does not provide support for the CP status of English ECM infinitives.

Ormazabal argues that certain facts concerning prefixation of verbs taking infinitival complements provide evidence for the CP analysis of ECM infinitivals, as well as the IP analysis of control infinitivals. He observes (attributing the observation to Samuel Jay Keyser) that adding a prefix to a verb that normally takes an ECM infinitival complement strips the verb of its ability to take such a complement. He also notes that, in contrast to ECM verbs, control verbs can undergo prefixation. He illustrates these observations with respect to the prefix *re*.

(69) a.   They discovered the problem
     b.   They discovered [the problem to be unsolvable]
     c.   They rediscovered the problem
     d.   *They rediscovered [the problem to be unsolvable]

(70) a.   He (re)persuaded me of my interest in the topic
     b.   He (re)persuaded me [PRO to do my job]

Ormazabal argues that the ungrammaticality of (69d) provides evidence that the infinitival complement of *discover* is headed by a null complementizer, specified as [+affix]. (Recall that for Ormazabal, all zero heads are affixes.) Keyser and Roeper (1992) propose that all English verbs contain an abstract clitic position and that the affix *re* occupies that position. Ormazabal argues that the null complementizer undergoing affixation into the higher verb competes with the affix *re* for the same position; hence the ungrammaticality of the construction. He further argues that the grammaticality of (70b) provides evidence that control infinitivals are IPs. If (70b) were headed by a null complementizer, which (being null) would have to be an affix, (70b) would be ruled out on a par with (69d).

However, it can be shown that the possibility of prefixing a verb taking an infinitival complement does not correlate with the categorial status of infinitival complements, a fact that renders Ormazabal's conclusions drawn by examining (69)–(70) invalid. Ormazabal himself notes that *want*-class verbs do not allow *re*-affixation (71). However, as shown by the examples in (72), the PRO infinitival complement of these verbs at least can be an IP; otherwise, these examples would be ruled out by the ECP.

(71) *Mary rewanted [PRO to go]

(72) a.   Mary wanted very much [PRO to leave]
     b.   What Mary wanted was [PRO to leave]
     c.   They preferred and we wanted [PRO to leave]
     d.   Mary wanted to finish school and Bill [PRO to get a job]

The ungrammaticality of (71) is unexpected under Ormazabal's analysis. Given that *want* can take an IP infinitival complement, we would expect it to be able to undergo *re*-affixation, just like *persuade* does and in contrast to *discover*. Ormazabal claims that the ungrammaticality of (71) is not problematic for his analysis, since the restriction against *re*-affixation with *want*-class verbs is more general; for example, the affixation is impossible even when *want* takes a DP/NP complement.

(73) *Mary rewanted a new analysis of the data

If *re*-affixation were uniformly excluded with *want*-class verbs, the conclusion Ormazabal draws from (69)–(70) could still be maintained. However, *want* seems to be just one case that is not representative of the whole class. (Similar examples of lexical incompatibilities with the prefix *re* are also found with other classes of verbs.) For instance, *arrange*, a *want*-class verb, is not incompatible with *re*.[59]

(74) John rearranged the meetings with Susan

However, when *arrange* takes an infinitival complement, *re*-affixation is disallowed.

(75) a. *John rearranged [PRO to meet Susan]
      b. cf. John arranged [PRO to meet Susan]

Apparently, although some *want*-class verbs can take an IP infinitival complement, they cannot undergo *re*-affixation when taking an infinitival complement. The data under consideration indicate that the impossibility of *re*-affixation cannot be used as evidence for the CP status of an infinitival complement. The ungrammaticality of (69d) then does not tell us anything about the categorial status of the infinitival complement of *discover*.

There is another problem with the C-incorporation analysis of the ungrammaticality of (69d). Recall that the analysis is based on the claim that the null C undergoing incorporation into the higher verb in (69d) competes with the prefix *re* for Keyser and Roeper's (1992) abstract clitic position. However, Keyser and Roeper show that *re* can cooccur with certain elements that occupy the abstract clitic position. To account for that, Keyser and Roeper argue that *re* is lexically inserted into the abstract clitic position and then moves away from it through a process of compound formation, vacating it for other elements. *Re* is then prevented from cooccurring only with elements that are lexically inserted into the abstract clitic position, but not with elements that undergo movement into the position. As a result, in order for the C-incorporation analysis of (69d) to be maintained, the putative null complementizer heading the embedded clause would actually have to be generated on the higher verb or, to be more precise, in the clitic position of the higher verb. The complementizer would then never be located within the embedded clause, whose head it is supposed to be, clearly an undesirable result.[60]

It should also be pointed out that, according to Keyser and Roeper, in contrast to the prefix *re*, verbal particles remain in the abstract clitic position. As a result, they are prevented from cooccurring both with the elements that are lexically inserted into the abstract clitic position and with the elements that are moved into the abstract clitic position. Given this, and given the claim that the landing site of C-affixation is the abstract clitic position, the C-affixation analysis would predict that particle verbs could not take propositional infinitival complements. This prediction is not borne out, however, as the grammaticality of Kayne's (1985) *He made John out to be a liar* and *He made out John to be a liar* illustrates. In light of the above discussion I conclude that the data concerning *re*-affixation do not provide evidence for the CP analysis of ECM constructions.

In summary, the arguments for the CP status of English ECM infinitivals given by Pesetsky and Ormazabal do not hold up. In chapter 3 I will present empirical evidence showing that the infinitival complement of English ECM verbs, such as *believe*, is in fact an IP, as is standardly assumed. The infinitival complement of *believe* will thus be shown to have the same categorial status as the infinitival complement of control verbs. Pending the discussion in chapter 3, I merely note here that the possibility of object shift, an example of A-movement, out of ECM infinitivals in fact suggests that ECM infinitivals are IPs, given that, as discussed in section 2.2, A-movement is not allowed to take place out of CPs. (See section 3.4 for more examples of the impossibility of A-movement out of CPs.)[61]

2.5 Conclusion

In this chapter I have provided evidence against c-selection for various types of infinitival clauses and against the standard binding-theoretic/ government account of the distribution of PRO, which I have argued is inferior to the Case-theoretic account on both conceptual and empirical grounds. I have shown that there is no need to impose either CP or IP status on any infinitival complement by appealing to c-selection. There is also no need to appeal to government to account for the distribution of PRO. I have argued that the systematic difference with respect to licensing of PRO and NP-trace in the subject position of ECM and control infinitivals follows ultimately from the s-selectional requirements of higher predicates. I have also argued that as long as CP status is not required by lexical properties independent of c-selection, control infinitivals not introduced by an overt complementizer must be IPs. This IP status is forced on these infinitivals by an economy principle. The relevant principle also imposes IP status on zero finite clauses.

Chapter 3
Wager-Class Verbs and French Propositional Infinitivals

3.1 Introduction

My goal in this chapter is to fill in the gaps left in chapter 2: that is, to provide an account of certain classes of infinitival complements that were not discussed there. In particular, I will examine syntactic properties of the infinitival complement of Pesetsky's (1992) *wager*-class verbs (Postal's (1974) DOC paradigm) and of French propositional infinitivals within the system developed in Bošković 1994b, which allows movement into θ-positions in certain well-defined configurations.[1]

Syntactic properties of the infinitival complement of *wager*-class verbs have been a serious problem ever since the appearance of Postal 1974, the first comprehensive discussion of this class of verbs in the literature; they have yet to receive a principled account in the principles-and-parameters framework. In some respects *wager*-class verbs behave like *believe*-class verbs. Thus, like the infinitival complement of *believe*-class verbs, the infinitival complement of *wager*-class verbs is interpreted as a Proposition. However, although, like *believe*, *wager*-class verbs allow passive raising (e.g., *John was wagered to be crazy*) and exceptionally Case-mark *wh*-traces (e.g., *Who did Peter wager to be crazy*), unlike *believe*, they cannot exceptionally Case-mark lexical NPs (e.g., **Peter wagered the students to be crazy*). This discrepancy between passive raising and ECM of lexical NPs is very surprising. Recall that, as discussed in chapters 1 and 2, ECM takes place through object shift, that is, A-movement to the higher-clause SpecAgr$_O$P. ECM is thus very similar to passive raising, which also involves A-movement to the Spec of an AgrP. It is very difficult to allow one while banning the other. To make the situation even more complicated, there are certain exceptions to the ban on ECM of lexical NPs with *wager*-class verbs. Thus, Postal (1974) notes that, as illustrated by *He* *alleged there to be stolen documents in the drawer*, *wager*-class verbs can exceptionally Case-mark expletives, and Pesetsky (1992) observes that *wager*-class verbs can even exceptionally Case-mark semantically contentful NPs when they θ-mark them (see section 3.2 for examples). Furthermore, Pesetsky (1992) notes that all the verbs that belong to this class assign the agent θ-role to their subject. The question now is whether the agentivity of the verbs in question is responsible for their curious behavior with respect to ECM and if it is, why.

The properties of *wager*-class verbs discovered by Postal (1974) and Pesetsky (1992) raise a serious problem for any analysis of infinitival complementation and still await a principled account. In sections 3.2 and 3.3 I will examine *wager*-class verbs with the aim of showing that their otherwise puzzling behavior with respect to ECM can be accounted for in a principled way given the view of DS and the θ-Criterion argued for in Bošković 1994b and certain assumptions concerning the representation of agentivity along the lines proposed by Hale and Keyser (1993). In section 3.4 I will examine another class of infinitival complements that has resisted a satisfactory account in the literature, namely, French propositional infinitivals. French propositional infinitivals behave in some respects like *wager*-class infinitivals. For example, like *wager*-class verbs, French verbs taking propositional infinitival complements cannot exceptionally Case-mark lexical subjects, but can exceptionally Case-mark *wh*-traces. However, as discussed in Bošković 1996b, the most serious problem that French propositional infinitivals raise for the Case-theoretic account of the distribution of PRO is that PRO is allowed in the subject position of these infinitivals in spite of their propositional interpretation (e.g., *Pierre croit PRO avoir convaincu son auditoire* 'Pierre believes to-have convinced his audience'). In section 3.4 I will provide a principled Case-theoretic account of the grammaticality of such constructions. I will also introduce new data concerning propositional infinitival complementation in French and show that they receive a principled analysis under the Case-theoretic account of the distribution of PRO, but remain a mystery under other accounts. These data will thus provide further evidence for the Case-theoretic account.

3.2   Infinitival Complementation and *Wager*-Class Verbs: The Agentive Hypothesis

Recall that under the Case-theoretic approach to the distribution of PRO, PRO is assumed to be marked for null Case, checked under Spec-head agreement with [+tense, −finite] I. Since the infinitival complement of *believe*-class verbs is specified as [−tense], constructions such as (1a) are ruled out because the Case PRO is marked for remains unchecked. In (1b), on the other hand, the infinitival I is marked as [+tense] and therefore can Case-check PRO.

(1) a. *John believes [PRO to be crazy]
    b. John tried [PRO to kiss Mary]

In chapter 2 it was shown that the possibility of ECM and passive raising out of *believe*-class verbs' infinitival complements and its impossibility out of control infinitival complements can be accounted for in a natural way without any additional stipulations given the Case-theoretic approach to the distribution of PRO. Assuming that exceptionally Case-marked NPs are Case-checked after undergoing object shift into the SpecAgr$_O$P of the superordinate clause, and given that the embedded-clause subject position in (2c–d), which contain a [+tense] infinitival, is a Case-checking position, (2c) and (2d) are ruled out by the Last Resort Condition, which prohibits movement from Case-checking to Case-checking positions. The Last Resort Condition is not violated in (2a–b), where the infinitival clause is specified as [−tense] and its SpecIP is therefore not a Case-checking position.

(2) a. John believed$_i$ [$_{Agr_O P}$ him$_j$ t$_i$ [$_{IP}$ t$_j$ to be crazy]]
    b. John$_i$ was believed [$_{IP}$ t$_i$ to be crazy]
    c. *John$_i$ was tried [$_{IP}$ t$_i$ to win]
    d. *John tried$_i$ [$_{Agr_O P}$ him$_j$ t$_i$ [$_{IP}$ t$_j$ to win]]

However, there are verbs that do not pattern with either *believe* or *try* with respect to ECM and licensing of PRO in the subject position of their infinitival complement. In this section I will examine one such class of verbs, which Pesetsky (1992) labels the "*wager*-class." Among the verbs belonging to this class are *admit, affirm, allege, announce, concede, maintain, scream, shout, wager,* and *whisper.* The defining characteristic of the verbs belonging to this class, noted by Pesetsky, is that they all assign the agent θ-role to their subject. This sets them apart from the *believe*-class, with which they share the property of taking a propositional clausal complement. According to Pesetsky, all agentive verbs taking a propositional infinitival complement belong to the *wager*-class (see in this respect note 2). As (3) illustrates, the temporal properties of the infinitival complement of *wager*-class verbs differ from those of the infinitival complement of *try*-class verbs.

(3) a. John was wagered by the press to be crazy

    b. Mary was admitted by the committee to have passed the test

In contrast to the infinitival complement in (1b), the infinitival complement in (3a–b) is clearly not specified with unrealized Tense. In fact, the infinitival complement of *wager*-class verbs is interpreted as a Proposition. Its temporal properties are the same as those of the infinitival complement of *believe*-class verbs. In other words, the infinitival complement of *wager*-class verbs is specified as [−tense]. Note that eventive predicates, which contain a temporal argument that must be bound by Tense in the absence of adverbs of quantification and the auxiliaries *have* and *be* (see section 2.2), cannot occur in the infinitival complement of *wager*-class verbs (e.g., **John was wagered to arrive late yesterday*). This also indicates that the infinitival complement of *wager*-class verbs is specified as [−tense]. (*Wager* patterns with *believe* (e.g., **John was believed to arrive late yesterday*), rather than *try* (e.g., *John tried to arrive late yesterday*), in the relevant respect.) Given this, it is not surprising that PRO is not allowed with *wager*-class verbs. Like (1a), (4a–b) are ruled out because PRO cannot be Case-checked.

(4) a. *John wagered [PRO to be crazy]

    b. *Mary admitted [PRO to have passed the test]

The impossibility of (5a–b) is, however, surprising.

(5) a. *John wagered Peter to be crazy

    b. *Mary admitted Peter to have passed the test

Since the embedded subject position in (5a–b) is not a Case-checking position, as in (2a) and in contrast to (2d) object shift in (5a–b) (i.e., movement of the embedded subject to the matrix SpecAgr$_O$P) is in accordance with the Last Resort Condition. Note that, as (6a–b) illustrate, *wager*, as well as a number of other verbs belonging to this class, clearly has the ability to check accusative Case. As a result, we cannot assume that (5a–b) are ruled out by the Case Filter.

(6) a. John wagered all his money on the Bulls

    b. Mary admitted her mistake

The ungrammaticality of (5a–b) thus seems to be a mystery. Pesetsky (1992) accounts for (5a–b) essentially by stipulating that verbs that assign the agent θ-role to their subject cannot assign Case via ECM (the agentive hypothesis).[2] As Pesetsky himself notes, this is merely a descriptive generalization that remains to be accounted for, rather than a principled solution. I propose to account for the generalization by appealing to Hale and Keyser's (1993) proposal that at least two VP shells must be projected with agentive verbs, the highest VP shell being headed by a null "agentive" V. I depart from their proposal in assuming that the higher agentive shell is projected only with true agentive verbs, but not with causative verbs (see note 2). In addition, I propose that both the agentive V and the main verb in agentive constructions are external θ-role assigners. True agentive subjects are thus θ-marked both in the SpecVP of the main verb and the SpecVP of the agentive verb. In other words, they are base-generated in the main-verb SpecVP, where they are θ-marked, and then move to the agentive SpecVP, where they also receive a θ-role. This is in accordance with the view of the θ-Criterion developed in Bošković 1994b, where I argued that movement into θ-positions is allowed in certain well-defined configurations. The case under consideration is in fact exactly the environment in which I argued independently in Bošković 1994b that movement into θ-positions is allowed to take place. In that work I examined constructions involving movement passing through a θ-position, which opens up the possibility that the movement is licensed by the Minimize Chain Links Principle (see chapter 4 for a detailed discussion of this principle). I showed that most constructions involving movement through a pure θ-(non-Case)position are still ruled out by independently needed principles of economy of derivation. One instance of movement into a pure θ-position was, however, not ruled out by the analysis developed in Bošković 1994b, namely, movement from a θ-marked SpecVP into a θ-marked SpecVP with no non-θ-marked Specs intervening between the θ-marked SpecVPs. (The relevant configuration thus involves a verb taking a bare VP complement.) I argued in Bošković 1994b that exactly in this context movement into or, to be more precise, through a pure θ-position is allowed to take place, and I provided several examples involving movement through a θ-position in the configuration in question. The representation of agentivity put forth here involves movement through a θ-position in exactly the same configuration.

Under the proposals made here, intransitive agentive constructions thus have the following structure:

(7) John$_i$ [$_{IP}$ t$_i$ V$_{ag}$ [$_{VP}$ t$_i$ laughed]]

Wager-class ECM constructions have the structure in (8). (For the moment I disregard the structure above the matrix VP.)

(8) *[$_{VP}$ John$_i$ V$_{ag}$ [$_{VP}$ t$_i$ wagered [$_{IP}$ Peter$_j$ to be t$_j$ crazy]]]

The question now is where the matrix Agr$_O$P projection, where the embedded subject is Case-checked, is located in (8).[3] The analysis of head movement presented by Li (1990) can help in determining the position of Agr$_O$P. Li extends the notions of θ- and non-θ-positions to cover heads as well as maximal projections and shows that head movement from a θ-assigning X^0 position to a non-θ-assigning X^0 position and back to a θ-assigning X^0 position is not allowed (see Bošković 1994b and Li 1990 for theoretical accounts of the descriptive generalization). Given Li's observation, the matrix Agr$_O$ cannot be located between the two VP shells. If it were, V-to-V$_{ag}$ movement would result in a θ–non-θ–θ X^0 movement, which, as Li convincingly demonstrates, is not allowed. The Agr$_O$P projection thus must dominate both VP shells.

(9) *[$_{Agr_OP}$[$_{VP}$ John$_i$ V$_{ag}$ [$_{VP}$ t$_i$ wagered [$_{IP}$ Peter to be crazy]]]]

Notice now that, given the structure in (9), the embedded subject cannot reach the matrix SpecAgr$_O$P in LF, as it must do in order to be Case-checked, without violating the Minimize Chain Links Principle. Chomsky's (1993) notion of equidistance as an escape hatch from the Minimize Chain Links Principle cannot resolve this problem. The following definitions are relevant to the notion of equidistance:

(10) a. The domain of a head α (= Dom(α)) is the set of nodes contained in the maximal projection of α that are distinct from and do not contain α.

   b. The minimal domain of α (= Min(α)) is the smallest subset K of α, such that for any member of Min(α) some member of K reflexively dominates it.

   c. α and β are equidistant from γ if they are in the same minimal domain.

Chomsky assumes that movement of Y to the first X^0 position above Y extends the minimal domain of Y. To be more precise, the domain is calculated for the whole chain (Y, t).

Returning now to (9), notice that the V-to-V$_{ag}$ movement and movement of the main verb+V_{ag} complex to Agr$_O$ make the higher SpecVP and SpecAgr$_O$P but not the lower SpecVP and SpecAgr$_O$P equidistant from the embedded-clause subject position. (5a–b) are thus ruled out either because the Case feature of the embedded subject remains unchecked or because the Minimize Chain Links Principle is violated. It is easy to verify that, given the notion of equidistance and LF movement of *believe* to the matrix Agr$_S$, which extends the domain of *believe*, the Minimize Chain Links Principle is not violated in (11), since the agentive VP shell is not projected with *believe*.[4]

(11) John$_i$ believes$_j$ [$_{Agr_O}$P Peter$_k$ t$_j$ [$_{VP}$ t$_i$ t$_j$ [$_{IP}$ t$_k$ to be t$_k$ crazy]]]

Recall now that, in contrast to ECM, passive raising is allowed with *wager*-class verbs.

(12) Peter$_i$ was wagered by John [t$_i$ to be t$_i$ crazy]

The contrast between (5a) and (12) is surprising since under current theoretical assumptions ECM and passive raising are very similar operations, both involving A-movement into the Spec of an AgrP. The otherwise surprising contrast between (5a) and (12), however, receives a straightforward account under the Minimize Chain Links Principle analysis. Note that there are no filled Specs intervening between *Peter* and its trace in (12). It seems plausible that the agentive VP shell is not present in (12), the element bearing the agent θ-role being θ-marked by *by* rather than V$_{ag}$. Alternatively, the agentive VP shell may be present in (12), the agentive θ-role being assigned to an X^0 element, essentially along the lines proposed by Baker, Johnson, and Roberts (1989). Either way, there are no filled Specs intervening between *Peter* and its trace in (12). Given this, it is easy to verify that, in contrast to A-movement to the matrix SpecAgr$_O$P in (5a), A-movement to the matrix SpecAgr$_S$P in (12) does not violate the Minimize Chain Links Principle. The contrast between (5a) and (12) thus receives a straightforward explanation under the analysis presented here.

More confirming evidence for this analysis is that it provides a straightforward account of a rather surprising fact concerning the relation between θ-role assignment and ECM with agentive verbs noted by Pesetsky (1992). Pesetsky observes that in some cases an agentive verb can exceptionally Case-mark a lexical NP, in particular, when it θ-marks the NP.[5] Consider (13).

(13) Congress declared March to be National Syntax Month

Pesetsky notes that the matrix verb in (13) affects the embedded subject. The act of declaring changes the property of March. March becomes National Syntax Month by virtue of the declaration. Pesetsky interprets this as indicating that the matrix verb θ-marks the embedded subject across the embedded-clause boundary.[6]

Postal's (1974) (14a–b), involving ECM with *estimate*, another agentive verb, also illustrate Pesetsky's point that ECM with agentive verbs is possible if the agentive verb θ-marks the NP it exceptionally Case-marks.

(14) a. Sue estimated Bill's weight to be 150 lbs
     b. *Sue estimated Bill to weigh 150 lbs

Apparently the embedded-clause subject, exceptionally Case-marked by *estimate*, must be some kind of measurement. (Here I am simplifying the actual generalization.) A similar restriction is found with "real" direct objects of *estimate*.

(15) a. Sue estimated Bill's weight
     b. *Sue estimated Bill

Pesetsky (1992) interprets the parallelism between (14) and (15) as indicating that there must be a θ-relation between *estimate* and the NP exceptionally Case-marked by *estimate*.[7]

Pesetsky's generalization that agentive verbs must θ-mark lexical NPs across a clausal boundary in order to be able to exceptionally Case-mark them is rather puzzling. It is also theoretically problematic, because it requires a relaxation of standard locality constraints on θ-role marking. I will show now that the generalization receives a principled account under the analysis presented here. Recall that the reason why Agr_OP has to be located above VP shells in (9) is that, in contrast to the V^0 of the VP shells, Agr_O is not a position from which θ-roles are assigned. As noted above, Li (1990) shows that X^0-movement from a θ-marking to a non-θ-marking and back to a θ-marking X^0 position is not allowed. Suppose, however, that a θ-role is assigned from the Agr_O position. Then there would be no reason why the Agr_OP projection could not be located between the two VP shells.[8] Now, Lasnik (1995a) argues that a V adjoined to Agr_O and an NP in $SpecAgr_OP$ are in a θ-licensing relation.[9] Given this, after *declare* moves to Agr_O in (13) and the embedded subject moves to $SpecAgr_OP$ to be Case-checked, *declare* and *March* are in a θ-licensing relation, and the embedded-clause subject can be θ-marked by the matrix verb. (The same holds for (14a).) Since, in contrast to the Agr_O position in (9), the Agr_O position is a θ-marking position in (13), it can freely intervene between the VP shells. (I leave open whether we are dealing here with primary or secondary θ-role assignment, and, for ease of exposition, I disregard the raising of the $Agr_O + declared$ complex to V_{ag}, which makes $SpecAgr_OP$ and $SpecV_{ag}P$ equidistant.)

(16) Congress$_i$ [$_{VP}$ t$_i$ V$_{ag}$ [$_{Agr_OP}$ March$_j$ Agr$_O$+declared$_k$ [$_{VP}$ t$_i$ t$_k$ [$_{IP}$ t$_j$ to be t$_j$ National Syntax Month]]]]]

It is easy to verify that under the analysis proposed here, and given Chomsky's (1993) notion of equidistance, the Minimize Chain Links Principle, which was violated in (5a–b), is not violated in (16). Pesetsky's observation that agentive verbs can exceptionally Case-mark lexical NPs only if they θ-mark them is thus accounted for. Notice also that, in contrast to what happens under Pesetsky's analysis, under the analysis presented here θ-marking of the embedded subject by the matrix verb in the constructions under consideration does not take place across a clausal boundary. It takes place within the first XP dominating the verb and is thus brought in line with standard assumptions concerning locality constraints on θ-role assignment.

A note is now in order concerning object shift in simple transitive agentive constructions such as (17).

(17) [$_{IP}$[$_{Agr_OP}$[$_{VP}$ John$_i$ V$_{ag}$ [$_{VP}$ t$_i$ kicked Peter]]]]

The direct object NP in (17) needs to reach SpecAgr$_O$P without violating the Minimize Chain Links Principle. Recall that in chapter 2 I adopted Saito's economy condition on chain links, derivable from the ban on superfluous steps, as a result of which positions that are immediately contained by the same maximal projection as X do not count as potential landing sites for X. The relevant definitions are repeated here as (18) (see section 2.3.1 and Bošković 1994b for evidence for (18)).

(18) a. A chain link must be at least of length 1.
   b. A chain link from A to B is of length *n* iff there are *n* "nodes" (X, X′, or XP, but not segments of these) that dominate A and exclude B.

One consequence of (18) is that the lower SpecVP in (17) does not count as a potential landing site for the direct object NP moving to SpecAgr$_O$P. As a result, LF object shift in (17) does not violate the Minimize Chain Links Principle. (Note that the LF movement of the V$_{ag}$+*kicked* complex to Agr$_O$ makes the highest SpecVP and SpecAgr$_O$P equidistant from the direct object position in (17).)

There are two alternative ways of ensuring that *Peter* in (17) finds itself in the matrix SpecAgr$_O$P without violating the Minimize Chain Links Principle. Under the alternative analyses we must assume that the V-to-V$_{ag}$ movement takes place overtly, an assumption that is not needed under the first analysis presented above. (Other authors arguing for VP shells also assume that V-movement within VP shells takes place overtly; see Hale and Keyser 1993, Larson 1988, and Koizumi 1993, 1995, among others.)

Under the analysis developed here, it may be possible to generate the Agr_OP projection between VP shells and insert and θ-mark the direct object NP in $SpecAgr_OP$ while the main verb is still located under Agr_O. Since under this analysis a θ-role is assigned from the head of the Agr_OP projection, V-to-V_{ag} movement does not violate Li's (1990) ban on head movement from θ-marking to non-θ-marking and back to θ-marking X^0 positions.[10]

(19) $John_i$ [$_{VP}$ t_i V_{ag}+$kicked_j$ [$_{Agr_OP}$ Peter t_j [$_{VP}$ t_i t_j]]]

The third way of accounting for the grammaticality of (17) is to allow *Peter* to be generated higher than *John*. It is easy to verify that, given the notion of equidistance, neither movement of *John* to $SpecV_{ag}P$ nor movement of *Peter* to $SpecAgr_OP$ violates the Minimize Chain Links Principle in (20).[11]

(20) [$_{IP}$ $John_i$ [V_{ag}+$kicked_k$]$_l$ [$_{Agr_OP}$ $Peter_j$ t_l [$_{VP}$ t_i t_l [$_{VP}$ t_j t_k t_i]]]]

Whichever of the three analyses of (17) considered here is adopted, *Peter* can be Case-checked without violating the Minimize Chain Links Principle.

Returning now to *wager*-class verbs, note that there are constructions in which agentive verbs can exceptionally Case-mark lexical NPs even when they do not θ-mark them. Thus, Postal (1974, 1993) notes that expletive *there* and *it* can be exceptionally Case-marked by agentive verbs (see (21a,c,d)). Howard Lasnik (personal communication) observes that referential pronouns can also be exceptionally Case-marked by *wager*-class verbs, as illustrated in (21f,h). (Noam Chomsky makes the same observation, as reported in Ura 1993b. (21a,c) are taken from Postal 1993 and (21d) from Ura 1993b.)

(21) a. Hc alleged there to be stolen documents in the drawer
     b. cf. *He alleged stolen documents to be in the drawer
     c. He acknowledged it to be impossible to square circles
     d. John wagered there to have been a stranger in that haunted house
     e. cf. *John wagered a stranger to have been in that haunted house
     f. Mary alleged him to have kissed Jane
     g. cf. *Mary alleged that man to have kissed Jane

   h. Mary never alleged him to be crazy

   i. cf. *Mary never alleged the students to be crazy

The elements that can be exceptionally Case-marked by an agentive verb even when a θ-marking relation between the agentive verb and the relevant elements is not established are all nonbranching and belong to the class of elements that Chomsky (1994) argues are at the same time X^0s and XPs.[12] In other words, they share properties of XPs and X^0s in that they can occur in both X^0 and XP positions; that is, they can undergo both XP- and X^0-movement. Given that *there*, *it*, and *him* in (21) can be located not only in XP but also in X^0 positions, they do not have to undergo movement to SpecAgr$_0$P in order to be Case-licensed. Baker (1988) argues that X^0 nominal elements can "pass" the Case Filter by undergoing incorporation into verbs and prepositions. It seems quite plausible that *there*, *it*, and *him*, all of which are analyzable as X^0s, satisfy the Case Filter in (21) by incorporating into the higher verb, a possibility that is not available to more complex, unambiguous XP elements such as *the students* in **John wagered the students to know French*.[13]

   There is also independent evidence for the incorporation analysis of (21f,h). (See section 4.4.1.2 for independent evidence for the incorporation analysis of *there* constructions in (21a,d).) Under the incorporation analysis, *him* in (21f,h) is essentially treated as a clitic.[14] Now, Kayne (1994) observes that clitics cannot be coordinated, as the following example from French illustrates. (See Kayne 1994 for evidence that some superficial counterexamples to this observation actually conform to it.)

(22) *Je le   et   la   rencontre tous les jours
     I   him and her meet   all   the days
     'I meet him and her every day'

Significantly, (21f,h) also become unacceptable if the pronoun is coordinated. Thus, (23a–b) seem to pattern with (21g,i) rather than (21f,h).

(23) a. *Mary alleged him and her to have kissed Jane

     b. *Mary never alleged him and her to be crazy

Under the incorporation/cliticization analysis of (21f,h), the ungrammaticality of (23a–b) reduces to the ungrammaticality of (22). The ungrammaticality of these constructions can be accounted for if coordinated phrases have a branching structure; that is, they are unambiguous XPs. Being XPs, they would not be allowed to undergo X^0-movement. A number of authors (see Collins 1987, Kolb and Thiersch 1991, and Munn 1987, 1993) have actually argued that *and* projects a phrase ("Boolean Phrase" (BP)) and takes the second conjunct as its complement, the first conjunct being located either in the Spec of the BP or adjoined to the BP. Since under this analysis the embedded-clause subject in (23a–b) cannot be analyzed as an X^0, in contrast to the embedded-clause subject in (21f,h), it cannot be Case-checked by incorporating into the higher verb. As discussed above, the option of undergoing Case checking in SpecAgr$_O$P is ruled out by the Minimize Chain Links Principle. The incorporation analysis thus accounts not only for the grammaticality of (21a,c,d,f,h) and the contrast between these constructions and (21b,e,g,i), but also for the contrast between (21f,h) and (23a–b).[15]

To summarize the discussion so far, we have seen that *wager*-class verbs do not allow PRO in the subject position of their infinitival complement, a consequence of the temporal properties of the complement. Furthermore, unless the exceptionally Case-marked subject is θ-marked by the higher verb, or analyzable as an X^0, *wager*-class verbs do not exceptionally Case-mark lexical NP subjects, although they freely allow passive raising, an operation that is very similar to ECM. Following Pesetsky's (1992) insight, the peculiar behavior of *wager*-class verbs with respect to ECM of lexical NPs and passive raising was attributed to their agentivity. I have provided a theoretical explanation of the fact that although they allow passive raising, agentive verbs cannot exceptionally Case-mark lexical NPs unless they θ-mark them or unless the NPs in question are analyzable as X^0s. The explanation is based on the Minimize Chain Links Principle and a theory of agentivity rooted in Hale and Keyser's (1993) proposal that agentive constructions contain a null agentive verb taking a VP complement, along with the view of DS and the θ-Criterion argued for in Bošković 1994b, on which movement into θ-positions is allowed in certain well-defined configurations. In addition to providing evidence for the proposals in Hale and Keyser 1993 and Bošković 1994b on which the theory of agentivity developed here is based, the current analysis, which provides a uniform account for several previously unexplained properties of *wager*-class verbs, also provides evidence for Lasnik's (1995a) claim that V adjoined to Agr$_O$ and NP in SpecAgr$_O$P are in a θ-licensing relation and for the existence of elements that share properties of both XPs and X^0s.

3.3   *Wh*-Extraction out of *Wager*-Class Infinitivals

One peculiar property of *wager*-class verbs still remains to be accounted for. As is well known, although *wager*-class verbs cannot exceptionally

Case-mark lexical NPs, they can exceptionally Case-mark *wh*-traces. Thus, (24) is grammatical.[16]

(24) Who$_i$ did John wager [t$_i$ to be t$_i$ crazy]

The question now is how the *wh*-phrase is Case-checked in (24). Note that, given the above discussion, movement of *who* to the matrix SpecAgr$_O$P should be ruled out by the Minimize Chain Links Principle for the same reason that movement of *Peter* to the matrix SpecAgr$_O$P is ruled out in (9). In his discussion of constructions such as (24), Kayne (1984) makes an influential proposal that the *wh*-phrase is assigned Case (or, in current terms, is Case-checked) in an Ā-position while undergoing *wh*-movement. This makes intervening A-Specs irrelevant in this example. There are several implementations of Kayne's insight in the literature (see Kayne 1984, Pesetsky 1992, and Ura 1993b). In this chapter I will adopt Ura's (1993b) analysis. (However, see section 4.4.2, where an alternative analysis is made available by adopting Chomsky's (1995) Move F theory.) Ura proposes that while undergoing *wh*-movement, the *wh*-phrase in (24) adjoins to the matrix Agr$_O$P, where it is Case-checked.[17] He suggests that, in contrast to *wh*-phrases undergoing *wh*-movement, lexical NPs such as *Peter* in (9) cannot be Case-checked in the Agr$_O$P-adjoined position, and he argues that this follows from economy principles. Consider (25). (For ease of exposition, only one VP shell will be represented in structures involving agentive verbs if the presence of the second VP shell does not crucially affect the argument.)

(25) a. wh$_i$ ... [$_{Agr_OP}$ t$'_i$ [$_{Agr_OP}$ Agr [$_{VP}$ V t$_i$]]] ...
    b. wh$_i$ ... [$_{Agr_OP}$ [$_{Agr_OP}$ t$'_i$ Agr [$_{VP}$ V t$_i$]]] ...
    c. ... [$_{Agr_OP}$ NP$_i$ [$_{Agr_OP}$ Agr [$_{VP}$ V t$_i$]]] ...
    d. ... [$_{Agr_OP}$[$_{Agr_OP}$ NP$_i$ Agr [$_{VP}$ V t$_i$]]] ...

Ura notes that, with respect to chain length, the *wh*$_i$-t$_i$ chain of (25a), where the *wh*-phrase is Case-checked in the Agr$_O$P-adjoined position, and (25b), where the *wh*-phrase is Case-checked in SpecAgr$_O$P, are equivalent. The t$'_i$-t$_i$ chain link in (25a) is longer than the t$'_i$-t$_i$ chain link in (25b), but the *wh*$_i$-t$'_i$ chain link in (25b) is longer than the corresponding chain link in (25a). Ura argues that since the *wh*$_i$-t$_i$ chains of (25a) and (25b) are equivalent with respect to chain length, both derivations in (25a–b) are available. On the other hand, as Ura notes, the NP$_i$-t$_i$ chain in (25c), where the NP is Case-checked in the Agr$_O$P-adjoined position, is longer than the NP$_i$-t$_i$ chain in (25d), where the NP is Case-checked in SpecAgr$_O$P. As a result, Ura argues, the availability of the derivation in

(25d) blocks the derivation in (25c) via economy of derivation. The option of undergoing Case checking in the Agr_OP-adjoined position is thus ruled out for lexical NPs such as *Peter* in (9) but not for *wh*-phrases undergoing *wh*-movement.

Note that if *who* remains in situ, (24) becomes ungrammatical.

(26) *Who wagered who to be crazy

If the embedded *who* were to undergo LF *wh*-movement in (26), it could be Case-checked in the same way as *who* in (24) and we would not be able to account for the contrast between (26) and (24). On the other hand, given Chomsky's proposal that *wh*-elements in situ do not undergo LF *wh*-movement, the ungrammaticality of (26) reduces to the ungrammaticality of (9). (26) thus provides evidence for Chomsky's claim that *wh*-phrases in situ, such as *who* in (26), undergo absorption in LF instead of *wh*-movement. (It also provides evidence that *who* is not a bare X^0.)

A question that arises now is why, in contrast to (24), (27a–b) are ungrammatical—that is, why we cannot use the same mechanism we used in (24) to get around the Case Filter in (27).

(27) a. *Who$_i$ did John try [t$_i$ to be crazy]
     b. *Who$_i$ did John demand [t$_i$ to be crazy]

Ura (1993b) suggests that control verbs are not Case checkers, so that the constructions in (27) are ruled out because the embedded-clause subject cannot be Case-checked. However, the grammaticality of (28a–b) provides evidence that the relevant verbs are clearly specified with the feature [+accusative].

(28) a. John tried something
     b. John demanded Peter's resignation

We are thus still faced with the question of why *wh*-movement from the subject position of the infinitival complement of *wager*-class verbs is acceptable, whereas *wh*-movement from the subject position of control verbs is not. The Case-theoretic account of the distribution of PRO provides a straightforward answer to this question. Recall that, in contrast to the infinitival SpecIP in (24), the subject position of the infinitivals in (27a–b) is a Case-checking position. Being specified as [+tense], the infinitival I in (27a–b) bears the null Case feature. If the embedded-clause subject undergoes Case checking in the matrix clause, (27a–b) can be ruled out because the Case feature of the embedded I remains unchecked. Whereas the contrast between (24) and (27a–b) receives a straightforward account under the Case-theoretic approach to the distribution of PRO, in light of the above discussion I see no principled way of accounting for it under the binding-theoretic account of the distribution of PRO. We thus have one more argument for the Case-theoretic approach to the distribution of PRO, argued for in chapter 2.

I should also point out here that the contrast between (24) and (27a–b) provides evidence that Case features of traditional Case assigners must be "discharged" or, to be more precise, checked. Note that the contrast in question cannot be accounted for by appealing to the Last Resort Condition, which rules out movement from Case-checking to Case-checking positions because it is superfluous, since adjunction to AgroP, necessary for Case checking of *wh*-phrases, is plausibly licensed independently by the Minimize Chain Links Principle. (This is even more apparent under the alternative analysis of the contrast between (24) and (27a–b) proposed in section 4.4.2.) On the other hand, as shown above, the contrast between (24) and (27a–b) can readily be accounted for if Case features of traditional Case assigners must be checked.[18]

I conclude here my discussion of *wager*-class infinitivals. In the next section I turn to French propositional infinitivals.

3.4 Infinitival Complementation in French

Kayne (1984) notes a systematic difference in Case marking and the occurrence of PRO between English and French infinitivals, which appears to raise a serious problem for the Case-theoretic account of the distribution of PRO. As (29) shows, in contrast to their English counterparts, French *believe*-class infinitivals allow PRO to appear in their subject position.

(29) a. Pierre croit [PRO avoir convaincu son auditoire]
       Pierre believes to-have convinced his audience
     b. Pierre a constaté [PRO avoir convaincu son auditoire]
       Pierre has noticed to-have convinced his audience

If, as argued by Martin (1992b), only [+tense, −finite] I can check null Case, which PRO is marked for, and if, like their counterparts in English, propositional infinitivals in French are specified as [−tense], (29a–b) should be ruled out under the Case-theoretic account because PRO cannot be Case-checked. In Bošković 1996b I suggest that the grammaticality of (29a–b) indicates that regardless of its Tense specification, nonfinite I can check null Case in French. In other words, what is needed for null Case checking in French is simply the presence of [−finite] I. (A similar proposal is made independently by Watanabe (1993).) The grammaticality of (29a–b) can then readily be accounted for.[19] This account is conceptually problematic, however, since it would be preferable to keep the source of null Case checking constant in English and French.

However, in contrast to English propositional infinitivals, the infinitival complement of French *croire*-class verbs can receive a nonhabitual interpretation even in the absence of an auxiliary or adverbs of quantification. Thus, in contrast to the corresponding constructions in English, (30a–e) are grammatical on the nonhabitual reading.[20]

(30) a. Je crois   rêver
         I   believe to-dream
         'I believe that I am dreaming'
     b. Anna croyait   arriver en retard hier   alors qu'en fait
         Anna believed to-arrive late   yesterday although in fact
         elle était à   l'heure
         she was   at the time
         'Anna believed that she arrived late yesterday although in fact she
         was on time'
     c. Je crois   réussir   l'examen demain
         I   believe to-succeed the exam tomorrow
         'I believe that I will pass the exam tomorrow'
     d. [There is no light in the room. Pierre is hitting somebody but is
         not sure who it is]
         Pierre croit   frapper un voleur
         Pierre believes to-hit   a   burglar
         'Pierre believes he is hitting a burglar'
     e. Pierre croyait   embrasser Marie
         Pierre believed to-kiss   Marie
         'Pierre believed he was kissing Marie'

Recall that, as discussed in section 2.2, in the absence of aspectual elements such as *have* and adverbs of quantification, on the nonhabitual reading eventive predicates are allowed only in clauses that are specified as [+tense]. The Tense is needed to bind the temporal argument of eventive predicates. Following Martin (1992b), the ungrammaticality of *John believed Peter to arrive late yesterday* was in fact interpreted in section 2.2 as evidence that the infinitival complement of *believe* is specified as

[−tense]. *John believed Peter to arrive late yesterday* is, then, ruled out because the temporal argument of the embedded eventive predicate remains unbound. Given this, the grammaticality of (30a–e) on the non-habitual reading should be taken as indicating that, in contrast to English propositional infinitivals, French propositional infinitivals are specified as [+tense]. The presence of PRO in (29)–(30) can then be straightforwardly accounted for without positing a parametric difference between English and French with respect to which elements function as null Case checkers, which was done in Bošković 1996b. In fact, the possibility of PRO in (29)–(30) confirms the Case-theoretic approach to the distribution of PRO. As shown above, French *believe*-class infinitivals differ from English *believe*-class infinitivals in that they are specified as [+tense]. As expected under the Case-theoretic approach to the distribution of PRO, on which the presence of [+tense] in an infinitival complement is necessary for licensing of PRO, French *believe*-class infinitivals also differ from their English counterparts in that they allow PRO in their subject position. I conclude, therefore, that the correlation between the possibility of PRO and temporal properties of infinitival complements, the pillar of the Case-theoretic account, holds not only in English but also in French, a language that at first sight appeared to be problematic for the Case-theoretic approach but upon closer scrutiny turns out to provide surprising evidence in its favor.[21]

Given that the subject position of the infinitival complement of *croire*-class verbs is a Case-checking position, the ungrammaticality of ECM and passive raising in (31) can be straightforwardly accounted for: the LF A-movement of *Marie* to SpecAgr$_O$P in (31a) and the SS A-movement of *Pierre* to SpecIP in (31b) violate the Last Resort Condition.[22]

(31) a. *Pierre a   cru   Marie avoir   acheté des   fraises
           Pierre has believed Marie to-have bought some strawberries

     b. *Pierre$_i$ a   été   cru   [t$_i$ avoir   acheté des   fraises]
           Pierre has been believed   to-have bought some strawberries

It is well known that ECM and passive raising are allowed with small clauses.

(32) a. Pierre a   jugé   Paul coupable
          Pierre has judged Paul guilty

     b. Paul$_i$ a   été   jugé   [t$_i$ coupable]
          Paul has been judged   guilty

It seems plausible that, in contrast to full clauses, small clauses lack the Tense node altogether. As a result, the embedded-subject position in (32a–b) is not a Case-checking position. Since the SS movement of *Paul* to SpecIP in (32b) and the LF movement of *Paul* to the matrix SpecAgr$_O$P in (32a) do not originate from Case-checking positions, (32a–b) are not ruled out by the Last Resort Condition. The lack of Tense, however, leads to ungrammaticality of constructions containing PRO in the subject position of small clauses. (33) is ruled out because PRO cannot be Case-checked.[23]

(33) *Pierre a   jugé   PRO coupable
     Pierre has judged   guilty

The Last Resort Condition provides an elegant account of the ungrammaticality of (31a–b), as well as the contrast between (31) and (32) and the contrast between (29) and (33). There is, however, evidence indicating that the Last Resort account cannot be maintained as is. It is well known that, in contrast to NP-movement, *wh*-movement from the subject position of the infinitival complement of *croire*-class verbs is allowed.

(34) Qui$_i$ Pierre croit-il   [t$_i$ avoir   acheté des   fraises]
     Who Pierre believes he   to-have bought some strawberries

The *wh*-phrase in (34) cannot be Case-checked in the embedded SpecIP, a null Case-checking position, since, as *Qui souhaite qui acheter des fraises* 'who wants who to buy strawberries' indicates, *wh*-phrases cannot bear null Case. However, the embedded-clause subject in (34) can be Case-checked in the same way as the embedded-clause subject in constructions such as *Who did John wager to be crazy*, discussed in section 3.3: namely, it can be Case-checked in an Ā-position while undergoing *wh*-movement. (See section 4.4.2 for an implementation of the Kayne-style analysis with respect to (34) based on the Move F theory.) Recall now that the derivation in which the *wh*-phrase in **Who did you try to kiss Mary* is Case-checked in the matrix Agr$_O$P-adjoined position is ruled out because on this derivation the null Case feature of the embedded I remains unchecked. Given this, the grammaticality of (34) indicates that, in contrast to SpecIP of English control infinitivals, SpecIP of French *croire*-class infinitivals is not obligatorily a Case-checking position; that is, null Case does not have to be discharged in French *croire*-class infinitivals. If this were not the case, (34) would be ruled out on a par with **Who did John try to kiss Mary*, because the null Case feature of the embedded I would remain unchecked. If we want to maintain the claim that [+tense, −finite] I has a null Case feature, which must be checked, we are led to the conclusion that French propositional infinitivals can contain either a [+tense] or a [−tense] I. The presence of a [+tense] I results in the licensing of PRO in the subject position of the infinitival. In fact, PRO is the only possibility on the [+tense] I option, since the presence of any other element in the Spec position of a [+tense] infinitival would leave the null Case feature of the infinitival I unchecked. The construction in (34), in which the subject position of the infinitival clause is filled by a *wh*-trace, instantiates the option in which the infinitival I is specified as [−tense]. The analysis presented here then makes the following prediction: when a propositional infinitival in French is unambiguously specified as [+tense], PRO but not *wh*-trace will be licensed in its subject position. Recall now that the infinitival complements in (30), which contain an eventive predicate in the absence of an auxiliary or adverbs of quantification, must be specified as [+tense]; otherwise, the temporal argument of the embedded clause would remain unbound. We then predict that, in contrast to what happens in (34), *wh*-movement will not be possible from the subject position of the infinitival complements in (30) on the nonhabitual reading. As (35a,c,e) show, the prediction is borne out. Notice also that, as expected, (35a,c,e) contrast with (35b,d,f), where the embedded clause does not have to be specified as [+tense], since the auxiliary can bind the temporal argument of the embedded clause (see section 2.2).

(35) a. *Qui crois-tu   rêver
         Who believe you to-dream
         'Who do you believe to dream'

     b. cf. Qui crois-tu   avoir   rêvé
            Who believe you to-have dreamt
            'Who do you believe to have dreamt'

     c. *Qui Anna croyait-elle arriver   en retard hier
         Who Anna believed she to-arrive late   yesterday
         'Who did Anna believe to arrive late yesterday'

     d. cf. Qui Anna croyait-elle être   arrivé en retard hier
            Who Anna believed she to-be arived late   yesterday
            'Who did Anna believe to have arrived late yesterday'

     e. *Qui Pierre croit-il   frapper un voleur
         Who Pierre believes he to-hit   a   burglar
         'Who does Pierre believe to hit a burglar'

   f. cf. Qui Pierre croit-il   avoir   frappé un voleur
           Who Pierre believes he to-have hit   a   burglar
           'Who does Pierre believe to have hit a burglar'

Since, in contrast to the infinitivals in (34) and (35b,d,f), the infinitivals in (35a,c,e) are unambiguously specified as [+tense], their I must bear a null Case feature. As a result, although the *wh*-phrase in (35a,c,e) can be Case-checked in the same way as the *wh*-phrase in (34) and (35b,d,f) (see sections 3.3 and 4.4.2), (35a,c,e) are still ruled out because the null Case feature of the embedded-clause I remains unchecked. The contrast between (35b,d,f) and (35a,c,e) thus receives a straightforward account under the Case-theoretic approach. In fact, it is difficult to see how the contrast in question can be accounted for in a principled way unless the Case-theoretic account of the distribution of PRO is accepted.

The only alternative account of the facts under consideration that I am aware of is provided by Déprez (1989), who discusses (35a–b). Déprez proposes an analysis in which, in order for constructions such as (35b) to be acceptable, overt Aux-to-C movement, an operation that is attested in Italian, must take place.[24] Déprez makes the assumption that in French, as in Italian, auxiliaries but not main verbs can undergo movement to C in infinitival clauses, and she attributes the ungrammaticality of (35a) to the fact that Aux-to-C movement fails to occur. There are several problems with this analysis, one of which is that, unlike in Italian, Aux-to-C movement, crucial for the grammaticality of (35b) on Déprez's analysis, is not otherwise attested in French. However, the most serious problem is raised by the fact that *wh*-movement from the subject position of French infinitival complements is in fact possible in the absence of an auxiliary, contrary to what is predicted on Déprez's account. Thus, for example, (35c) improves if the embedded eventive predicate is replaced by a stative predicate. ((36) seems to have the same status as (35d).)

(36) Qui Anna croyait-elle plaire   à Pierre
     Who Anna believed she to-please to Pierre
     'Who did Anna believe to please Pierre'

Since, as in (35a,c,e), Aux-to-C movement cannot take place in (36), the construction is incorrectly ruled out under Déprez's analysis. However, its grammaticality can readily be accounted for under the analysis presented here. Since, unlike eventive predicates, stative predicates do not have an event variable, in contrast to what is found in (35a,c,e), where [+tense] I must be present to bind the event variable of the embedded verbs,

[+tense] I does not have to be present in the infinitival complement in (36). As a result, null Case does not have to be checked in the embedded-clause subject position.

Note that the presence of adverbs of quantification also improves the ungrammatical constructions in (35). For example, (37) contrasts with (35c).

(37) ?Qui Anna croyait-elle arriver   toujours en retard
     Who Anna believed she to-arrive always   late
     'Who did Anna believe to always arrive late'

The contrast between (35c) and (37) is unexpected under Déprez's analysis since, as in (35c), Aux-to-C movement clearly cannot take place in (37). On the other hand, the contrast can be straightforwardly accounted for under the Case-theoretic analysis. As discussed in chapter 2, like Tense and aspectual auxiliaries, adverbs of quantification can serve as binders for the temporal argument of eventive predicates. Then, unlike in (35c), [+tense] I does not have to be present in the infinitival complement of *croire* in (37), as a result of which, again unlike in (35c), null Case does not have to be discharged by the embedded I in (37). The contrast between (35a,c,e) and (36)–(37) (in light of the grammaticality of (30a–e)) confirms that the possibility of licensing a *wh*-trace in the subject position of a propositional infinitival in French depends on the presence versus absence of Tense in the infinitival complement, rather than the possibility of Aux-to-C movement, as expected under the analysis presented here but not under Déprez's (1989) analysis. (The contrasts in (39), discussed below, also remain unaccounted for under Déprez's analysis, but receive a straightforward account under the analysis presented here.)

Let us return now to (31). Given that, as shown above, the SpecIP position of French propositional infinitivals is not obligatorily a null Case-checking position, the Last Resort account of the ungrammaticality of (31a–b) cannot be maintained. If the I of the infinitival complement is specified as [−tense], an option that is available and on which the embedded SpecIP in (31a–b) is a Caseless position, there is nothing wrong with respect to the Last Resort Condition and Case theory in (31a–b). Like English constructions such as *Peter believed Mary to have bought strawberries* and *Peter was believed to have bought strawberries*, (31a–b) involve A-movement from a non-Case-checking position to a Case-checking position, in accordance with the Last Resort Condition. This is actually a desirable result, since constructions such as (31a–b) are ruled out independently of the Last Resort Condition and Case theory. This has to do with the fact that there is evidence that the infinitival complement of *croire*-class verbs is a CP, to which I will immediately return. Given this, (31a–b) are ruled out because A-movement of the embedded-clause subject into the matrix clause, motivated by Case checking, violates the ban on A-movement crossing CP boundaries, derivable from the economy principles (see section 2.2.1). Consider the following constructions involving dislocated infinitival complements:

(38) a.   Pierre croit   avoir   convaincu ses amis
          Pierre believes to-have convinced his friends
    b.   *Avoir   convaincu ses amis,   Pierre le croit
          to-have convinced his friends Pierre it believes
    c.   Il a   toujours souhaité revenir   mourir en France
          he has always   desired to-return to-die in France
    d.   Revenir mourir en France, il l'a   toujours souhaité
          to-return to-die in France he it has always   desired

(38b) shows that the infinitival complement of *croire*—and the same holds for all *croire*-class verbs—cannot be dislocated. The infinitival complement of "classical" control verbs such as *souhaiter*, on the other hand, can be dislocated (38d). (The observation illustrated by (38a–d) was first made by Huot (1981).) The grammaticality of (38d) indicates that nothing goes wrong with respect to control theory in (38b). (38b) can be straightforwardly accounted for if the infinitival complement of *croire* is a CP. Given this, (38b) is ruled out because the null complementizer heading the infinitival complement of *croire* is not properly governed.[25] As noted above, given that the infinitival complement of *croire*-class verbs is a CP, (31a) and (31b) are ruled out because the SS A-movement of the embedded-clause subject to SpecAgr$_S$P in (31b) and the LF A-movement of the embedded-clause subject to SpecAgr$_O$P in (31a) violate the ban on A-movement out of CPs.[26] Notice also that the grammaticality of (38d) provides evidence that the infinitival complement of the "classical" control verb *souhaiter* is an IP. This can be accounted for under the analysis presented in chapter 2, which allows control infinitivals to be IPs.[27]

   Returning now to passive raising and ECM (i.e., LF object shift out of French propositional infinitivals), notice that under the analysis presented here we would expect constructions such as (31a–b) to be even worse if we force the infinitival complements to be unambiguously specified as [+tense], which can be done by using eventive predicates without an auxiliary in the embedded clause. This is so because, in addition to violating the ban on A-movement out of CPs, passive raising and ECM out of [+tense] infinitivals leave the null Case feature of the infinitival I unchecked. As (39) shows, the prediction is borne out. (39a,c), involving an unambiguously [+tense] infinitival complement, are indeed worse than (39b,d), where the infinitival complement can be specified as [−tense].

(39) a. **Anna croyait   Pierre arriver   en retard hier
         Anna believed Pierre to-arrive late   yesterday

     b. *Anna croyait   Pierre être   arrivé   en retard hier
         Anna believed Pierre to-be arrived late   yesterday

     c. **Pierre était cru   arriver   en retard hier
         Pierre was believed to-arrive late   yesterday

     d. *Pierre était cru   être   arrivé en retard hier
         Pierre was believed to-be arrived late   yesterday

This provides further confirmation of the Case-theoretic approach to the distribution of PRO.

In summary, in this section I have examined certain differences between English and French *believe*-class infinitivals. I have argued that, in addition to differing with respect to the possibility of PRO, English and French *believe*-class infinitivals differ with respect to their Tense specification. The Case-theoretic account of the distribution of PRO provides a uniform account of the differences between English and French *believe*-class infinitivals. The data discussed in this section thus provide further evidence for this approach to the distribution of PRO. I have shown that several previously unnoticed facts concerning propositional infinitival complementation in French receive a straightforward account under the Case-theoretic approach, whereas they remain a mystery if this approach is not adopted. The French data in question indicate that extraction from the subject position of infinitival complements is sensitive to the Tense specification of these complements. This is expected under the Case-theoretic account of infinitival complementation and the distribution of PRO, but not under alternative accounts.

Chapter 4

Existential Constructions, A-Movement, and Infinitival Complementation

4.1 Introduction

In this chapter I examine syntactic properties of existential constructions. To be more precise, I use infinitival complements as a probe for investigating the properties of expletive *there* constructions with respect to Case theory and economy principles. Working within the expletive replacement analysis of existential constructions, I show that certain data concerning infinitival complementation provide clear tests for determining the Case properties of the associate of *there* and identifying the driving force for LF replacement of the expletive, issues that have been a subject of considerable debate. I also show that these data have important theoretical consequences for the economy principles that go beyond accounting for the syntactic properties of existential constructions. Among other things, they shed light on the general question of what drives applications of the operation Move α and the issue of whether or not lowering operations are allowed.

The chapter is organized as follows. In section 4.2 I briefly sum up the most recent analyses of existential constructions and identify the major issues that are still under debate. In section 4.3 I examine the relevance of infinitival complementation for existential constructions, in particular, the questions of what drives LF replacement of the expletive and whether or not the associate of the expletive is Case-marked prior to the replacement. In section 4.4 I explore theoretical consequences of the analysis proposed in section 4.3 for the traditional ECM construction, quantifier float in infinitival complements, and *wh*-movement out of *wager*-class infinitivals. In section 4.5 I examine constraints relevant to A-movement and A-positions and attempt to eliminate some of the redundancies that applications of the constraints induce. Section 4.6 is the conclusion.

4.2   Existential Constructions and the Expletive Replacement Hypothesis

In order to account for agreement facts in *there* constructions, as well as the chainlike relation between the expletive and its associate NP, Chomsky (1986b) proposes that the indefinite NP in (1a) moves to SpecIP in LF, replacing the expletive. (1a), then, has the same LF representation as (1b).

(1) a. There is likely to be someone in the garden
    b. Someone is likely to be in the garden

Chomsky (1991) slightly modifies this analysis by proposing that the associate of *there* adjoins to the expletive in LF.[1]

In addition to the well-known facts concerning agreement and chainlike locality constraints on the relation between expletive *there* and its associate, discussed at length in Chomsky 1986b, 1991, the expletive adjunction/replacement analysis also has sound theoretical motivation. Chomsky (1993) argues that because expletive *there* receives no semantic interpretation, constructions involving freestanding *there* cannot be interpreted coherently, an inadequacy that can be overcome by adjunction to the expletive.

Two main issues associated with the expletive adjunction analysis concern the Case marking of the associate NP and the motivation for adjunction to the expletive. There are two main views concerning these issues. Chomsky (1986b, 1991, 1993) assumes that the verb *be* is not a Case assigner; as a result, the associate NP is located in a Caseless position prior to expletive replacement. Adjunction to the expletive is then motivated by the Case marking of the associate. On this analysis adjunction to *there* is in accordance with the principle called Greed (Chomsky 1993), which requires that α move only to satisfy a requirement on α. Thus, on Chomsky's analysis (2) is ruled out by Greed.

(2) *There seems to someone that Peter likes Mary

Since the indefinite NP *someone* is already located in a Case-checking position, it does not need to undergo NP-movement to satisfy its own requirements. Greed then prevents it from adjoining to *there*, an operation that would satisfy an interpretive requirement on the expletive. Since the associate of *there* is located in a Caseless position in (1a), adjunction to the expletive is motivated by the Case checking of the associate and therefore is in accordance with Greed.

However, Lasnik (1995a) points out several problems that arise on Chomsky's analysis. He notes that this analysis crucially depends on an extension of the core X-bar relation of Spec-head agreement to the notion of *checking domain*. This is necessary since on Chomsky's analysis an NP adjoined to an element located in SpecIP must still be allowed to undergo Case checking by I. Chomsky's extension of the core notion of Spec-head agreement raises a serious conceptual question since it prevents us from reducing Case-checking configurations to Spec-head agreement or, more generally, X-bar-theoretic relations. In this respect, it is similar to the preminimalist notion of government.

Lasnik (1995a) also points out an inconsistency in Chomsky's analysis. In Chomsky's (1993) system the effects of the Extended Projection Principle (EPP) follow from the fact that the N feature of Tense is strong. Since strong features are illegitimate PF objects, the N feature of Tense must be checked in the overt syntax. If it were to remain present at PF, the derivation would crash. Chomsky also crucially assumes that when the N feature of Tense is checked, it disappears. In constructions such as (1a), *there* checks the strong N feature of Tense, which disappears after checking. Lasnik notes that, as a result, the N feature of Tense, responsible for nominative Case checking, is not present in LF when the associate of *there* adjoins to the expletive. The Case feature of the associate thus remains unchecked. To account for the problems raised by Chomsky's analysis, following Belletti (1988) and Lasnik (1992), Lasnik (1995a) argues that the verb *be* is a partitive Case assigner and that the associate NP is Case-marked by *be* prior to adjunction to the expletive in (1a). He proposes that expletive *there* is an LF affix that must be adjoined to by an NP bearing partitive Case at LF. (Chomsky (1993) actually also assumes that *there* is an LF affix, though his exact position is somewhat different from Lasnik's.) Lasnik considers this to be a morphological requirement on the expletive, which drives adjunction of the associate to the expletive. On Lasnik's analysis (2) is ruled out because, not bearing partitive Case, *someone* is not a proper host for the LF affix *there*. The same holds for (3a–c), which, as noted by Lasnik, remain unaccounted for under Chomsky's (1993) analysis, since the associate is located in a Caseless position prior to LF adjunction to the expletive. LF adjunction of the associate can then be driven by Case checking on Chomsky's account. (STRIKE differs from *strike* in that it has no Case features. Lasnik notes that Chomsky's analysis does not account for the nonexistence of such verbs.)

(3) a. *There STRIKES someone that John is in the garden
    b. *There [$_{VP}$ someone laughed]
    c. *John wanted there someone dead

On Lasnik's analysis LF adjunction to the expletive is driven by the need to overcome a morphological inadequacy of the expletive rather than the associate.

In summary, there are two major points of disagreement between the proposals in Chomsky 1993 and Lasnik 1995a.[2] The first concerns whether or not *be* is a Case assigner. Chomsky argues that *be* does not have the ability to assign Case and Lasnik argues that it does.[3] The second concerns motivation for adjunction to the expletive. According to Chomsky, adjunction is driven by a morphological inadequacy of the associate. On Lasnik's analysis, on the other hand, adjunction is driven by a morphological inadequacy of the expletive. Chomsky's analysis is consistent with Greed, which requires that α move only to satisfy a requirement on α. Lasnik's analysis, on the other hand, requires a relaxation of Greed to allow movement that is motivated by an inadequacy of the target. Lasnik refers to this relaxed version of Greed as "Enlightened Self-Interest." Enlightened Self-Interest allows movement to be driven either by an inadequacy of the moved element or by an inadequacy of the target. In the following sections I will discuss the points of disagreement between Chomsky's (1993) and Lasnik's (1995a) proposals. I will examine certain data concerning infinitival complementation and argue that they provide evidence that, in agreement with Lasnik's proposal and contra Chomsky's, *be* is a Case assigner. The data will, however, provide empirical evidence for Chomsky's Greed and against Lasnik's Enlightened Self-Interest. I will then propose a way of reconciling the seemingly conflicting assumptions that *be* is a Case assigner and that expletive adjunction obeys Greed with the expletive replacement hypothesis.

4.3 Infinitival Complementation and Existential Constructions

4.3.1 Case Assignment in Existential Constructions
In this section I will show that certain properties of infinitival complements of *wager*-class verbs provide a rather straightforward test for determining how the associate of *there* is Case-marked, an issue that remains to be settled conclusively.

A property of *wager*-class verbs that is of interest here is that, with the exception of a few constructions where the exceptionally Case-marked NP is θ-marked by the matrix verb, *wager*-class verbs cannot exceptionally Case-mark lexical NPs. Thus, constructions such as (4) are ungrammatical. As argued in section 3.2, they are ruled out either because the embedded-clause subject is not Case-checked or because they violate the Minimize Chain Links Principle.

(4) a. *He alleged stolen documents to be in the drawer
    b. *John wagered a stranger to have been in that haunted house

However, as originally noted by Postal (1974) and discussed in section 3.2, the counterparts of (4) with *there* are grammatical.[4]

(5) a. He alleged there to be stolen documents in the drawer
    b. John wagered there to have been a stranger in that haunted house

Note first that the indefinite NPs in (5) cannot be exceptionally Case-marked in the matrix SpecAgr$_O$P. Even if the indefinite NPs were to replace *there* in LF, their movement to the matrix SpecAgr$_O$P, motivated by Case marking, would be blocked for the same reason it is blocked in constructions such as (4a–b), discussed in section 3.2. In fact, if, as argued by Chomsky (1993), *be* is not a Case assigner, there seems to be no way for the indefinite NPs in (5a–b) to be Case-marked, and the constructions are incorrectly predicted to be strongly ungrammatical. Apparently *be* is the only source of Case marking for the indefinite NPs in (5a–b).[5] Given the above discussion, I conclude that, as argued by Lasnik (1995a) and contra Chomsky's (1993) proposal, *be* has the ability to assign Case and that the associate of *there* is Case-marked prior to undergoing adjunction to the expletive; as a result, we can maintain the assumption that all structural Case marking takes place under Spec-head agreement. (Lasnik (1995a) argues that inherent Case assignment also takes place under Spec-head agreement. According to Lasnik, *be* Case-marks the associate of *there* after it raises to Agr$_O$ and the associate moves to SpecAgr$_O$P (see note 55, chapter 2).) This conclusion also leads me to accept Lasnik's (1995a) claim that the associate of *there* must bear partitive Case, which, as discussed above, is also empirically well motivated.

To summarize, I have shown in this section that constructions involving *wager*-class verbs provide a test for determining how the associate of *there* is Case-marked, one of the two central issues that arise on the expletive replacement analysis of existential constructions, which has been a subject of considerable debate. In particular, on the basis of properties of *wager*-class infinitivals, I have argued, following Belletti (1988) and Lasnik (1992,

1995a), that the associate of *there* is Case-marked by *be*. In the next section I turn to the second major issue that arises on the expletive replacement analysis of existential constructions, namely, what drives LF adjunction to the expletive.

4.3.2 What Motivates A-Movement?

In this section I will examine more closely the question of what drives the operation Move α, Greed or Enlightened Self-Interest, my ultimate goal being to determine the driving force behind expletive replacement. I will argue that certain facts concerning infinitival complementation provide evidence that Greed is empirically superior to Enlightened Self-Interest. More precisely, I will show that A-movement from Case-checking to non-Case-checking positions is not allowed, and I will argue that the impossibility of such A-movement can readily be accounted for if Greed but not Enlightened Self-Interest, is adopted.

Consider first the following constructions:

(6) a. *John$_i$ seems t$_i$ is ill
    b. *John$_i$ seems to t$_i$ that Peter is ill

If *John* is Case-marked by the embedded I in (6a) and *to* in (6b), movement to the higher SpecIP results only in the satisfaction of the EPP, which is interpreted as a formal inadequacy of I in the minimalist system. Since the movement of *John* is motivated by overcoming an inadequacy of the target but not the moved element, it is ruled out by Greed but not by Enlightened Self-Interest. However, (6a–b) do not necessarily provide evidence for Greed. As noted by Martin (1992a) and discussed in section 2.2, given that *John* is Case-checked prior to movement to the matrix SpecIP, both (6a) and (6b) can be ruled out independently of Greed because the Case feature of the matrix I remains "undischarged" or, to be more precise, unchecked. (There is apparently some redundancy between Greed and the requirement that Case features of traditional Case assigners be checked, elimination of which is one of the goals of section 4.5.) Certain facts concerning A-movement within infinitival complements, however, provide evidence in favor of Greed.

The first piece of evidence concerns the Brody 1993/Bošković 1994b BELIEVE-class verbs, that is, verbs that assign subject θ-role, do not check accusative Case, and take a propositional infinitival complement. In Bošković 1994b I suggested that *remark* belongs to this class of verbs. However, it seems to me now that *conjecture* is a better candidate for most speakers. (*Predestine* seems to behave like *conjecture* in all relevant respects.) As (7) shows, *conjecture* takes a propositional complement. However, the propositional complement cannot be realized as an NP.

(7) a. John has conjectured that Mary would arrive early

  b. *John has conjectured something/it

Given the theory of Case and selection proposed by Pesetsky (1982b) and adopted in this book, the ungrammaticality of (7b) indicates that *conjecture* is not a Case checker. The question that arises now is whether it can take (l-select in Pesetsky's (1992) terms) an infinitival complement. Most instances of *conjecture* taking an infinitival complement are ruled out for independent reasons. Recall that, as argued in section 2.2, control infinitivals cannot be interpreted as Propositions. Given this, being a propositional verb, *conjecture* cannot take a control infinitival complement (see (8a)). Traditional ECM infinitivals, which can be interpreted as Propositions, cannot occur in the complement position of *conjecture* either (see (8b)), because the subject of the infinitival cannot be Case-checked, *conjecture* not being able to check Case.

(8) a. *John has conjectured [PRO to like Mary]

  b. *John has conjectured [Mary to like Peter]

The last environment that can be used to determine whether *conjecture* can take (i.e., l-select) an infinitival complement involves passive infinitives. Under some theories passivization is in principle ruled out with [−accusative] verbs. However, passivizing a [−accusative] verb taking a clausal complement generally does not give a very bad result. Thus, passivization of *remark* (a verb that is specified as [−accusative], as indicated by the fact that it can take a propositional complement but does not allow the proposition to be realized as an NP) is somewhat degraded, but not fully unacceptable.

(9) a. John remarked that Mary would arrive early

  b. *John remarked something/it

  c. ?It was remarked that Mary would arrive early

Notice now that passivization improves (8b), since it eliminates the traditional Case Filter violation from the construction, *Mary* being Case-checked in the matrix SpecIP.

(10) ?Mary has been conjectured to like Peter

The construction is still somewhat degraded, however. Its slightly marginal status can be attributed to the fact that it involves passivization of a [−accusative] verb taking a clausal complement. In fact, (10) seems to have more or less the same status as (9c) and ?*It has been conjectured that Peter likes Mary*. What is important here is that (10) is clearly better than constructions involving a violation of l-selectional requirements of verbs. As shown by (11a–b), involving a verb that l-selects a finite but not an infinitival complement, and (11c–d), involving a verb that l-selects an infinitival but not a finite complement, violations of this type of l-selectional requirement lead to much stronger unacceptability than the unacceptability displayed by (10).[6]

(11) a. *John announced [(for) (Peter) to be crazy]
     b. cf. John announced [that Peter was crazy]
     c. *Mary wants very much [that Peter will graduate]
     d. cf. Mary wants very much [(for) Peter to graduate]

Therefore, we can conclude that *conjecture* can take an infinitival complement. As shown above, it assigns subject θ-role, s-selects Proposition, and does not assign Case. In other words, it belongs to the BELIEVE-class.[7]

Given the above discussion, consider (12).

(12) *John has BELIEVED/conjectured [$_{IP}$ stolen documents$_i$ to be t$_i$ in the drawer]

Notice first that since the subject position of the infinitival complement of BELIEVE-class verbs is not a null Case-checking position, (12) cannot be ruled out on a par with **John tried [stolen documents$_i$ to be t$_i$ in the drawer]*, which can be ruled out because the null Case feature of the embedded irrealis Tense remains undischarged (see section 3.3). In fact, given that *stolen documents* can be Case-marked by *be*, there is no violation with respect to Case theory in (12). Then the question is why there are no verbs that allow the configuration in (12) or, if *conjecture* is indeed a BELIEVE-class verb, why (12) is ungrammatical. However, notice that, given that *stolen documents* is Case-marked by *be*, movement of *stolen documents* to the embedded SpecIP is driven merely by the need to satisfy the EPP, that is, to check the N feature of the embedded I. The movement thus satisfies a formal property of the target, but not the moved element. In other words, it is consistent with Enlightened Self-Interest but not with Greed. (12) is thus straightforwardly ruled out if we adopt Greed. On the other hand, it is not at all obvious how (12) can be ruled out if we adopt Enlightened Self-Interest.

Consider also the following constructions:

(13) a. *I have BELIEVED/conjectured John$_i$ to seem [$_{IP}$ t$_i$ [$_{VP}$ t$_i$ likes Mary]]
      b. *I have BELIEVED/conjectured there$_i$ to seem [$_{IP}$ t$_i$ is someone in the garden]

The embedded-clause subject in (13a–b) can be Case-checked without movement to the higher embedded SpecIP. In fact, it must be, or the Case feature of the most embedded I will remain unchecked. As in (12), movement to the embedded SpecIP is motivated merely by a need to satisfy the EPP. The ungrammaticality of the constructions indicates that satisfying the EPP cannot serve as a driving force for movement. This is consistent with Greed, which requires that every movement be driven by an inadequacy of the moved element, but not with Enlightened Self-Interest, which allows movement to be driven by a formal inadequacy of the target.

The constructions in (14) also favor Greed over Enlightened Self-Interest.

(14) a. *I have BELIEVED/conjectured Peter$_i$ to seem to t$_i$ [that John is in the garden]
      b. *I have BELIEVED/conjectured Peter$_i$ to strike t$_i$ [that John is in the garden]

(14a–b) remain unaccounted for if we adopt Enlightened Self-Interest, since movement of *Peter* to the higher embedded-clause subject position satisfies a morphological inadequacy of the higher embedded-clause I. On the other hand, both (14a) and (14b) are straightforwardly ruled out if we adopt Greed, because in neither (14a) nor (14b) is movement of *Peter* driven by a morphological inadequacy of *Peter* itself.

The same point can be made with respect to (15).

(15) *John has BELIEVED/conjectured [PRO$_i$ to be illegal [$_{IP}$ t$_i$ to [$_{VP}$ t$_i$ park there]]]

After being Case-checked in the lowest SpecIP, a null Case-checking position, PRO in (15) moves to the higher SpecIP to satisfy the EPP. The movement is in accordance with Enlightened Self-Interest but not Greed. The construction is thus straightforwardly ruled out if we adopt Greed but not if if we adopt Enlightened Self-Interest.[8]

These facts concerning the infinitival complement of BELIEVE-class verbs indicate that A-movement from Case-checking to non-Case-checking positions is disallowed, a prohibition that can readily be accounted for if we adopt Greed.[9]

The following constructions involving the passive form of "regular" *believe*-class verbs also show that A-movement from Case-checking to non-Case-checking positions is not allowed and thus provide more evidence for Greed:[10]

(16) a. *[$_{IP}$[$_{IP}$ John$_i$ to seem [$_{IP}$ t$_i$ [$_{VP}$ t$_i$ likes Mary]]]$_j$ is believed t$_j$]

    b. *[$_{IP}$[$_{IP}$ Peter$_i$ to seem to t$_i$ that John is in the garden]$_j$ is believed t$_j$]

    c. *[$_{IP}$[$_{IP}$ Stolen documents$_i$ to be t$_i$ in the drawer]$_j$ is believed t$_j$]

    d. *[$_{IP}$[$_{IP}$ PRO$_i$ to be illegal [$_{IP}$ t$_i$ to [$_{VP}$ t$_i$ park there]]]$_j$ is believed t$_j$]

The NPs undergoing NP-movement to the higher embedded-clause subject position in (16a–d) can be Case-checked prior to undergoing NP-movement, so that there is nothing wrong with respect to Case theory in (16a–d). Given this, it is not clear how (16a–d) can be ruled out if Enlightened Self-Interest is adopted. (Notice that infinitival clauses can function as subjects of finite clauses, as illustrated by *To park there is illegal*.) On the other hand, like the constructions in (12)–(15), all the constructions in (16) are straightforwardly ruled out by Greed, because they involve A-movement driven merely by an inadequacy of the target.

The following constructions involving infinitival complements of nominalizations of *believe*-class verbs illustrate the same point:

(17) a. *the belief [$_{IP}$ John$_i$ to seem [$_{IP}$ t$_i$ [$_{VP}$ t$_i$ likes Mary]]]

    b. *the belief [$_{IP}$ Peter$_i$ to seem to t$_i$ that John is in the garden]

    c. *the belief [$_{IP}$ stolen documents$_i$ to be t$_i$ in the drawer]

    d. *the belief [$_{IP}$ PRO$_i$ to be illegal [$_{IP}$ t$_i$ to [$_{VP}$ t$_i$ park there]]]

The NPs undergoing movement into the higher infinitival SpecIP position can be Case-checked prior to movement. As a result, nothing goes wrong with respect to Case theory in (17a–d). However, given that the NPs in question are Case-marked prior to undergoing A-movement, movement to the infinitival SpecIP is motivated merely by a need to satisfy the EPP, an inadequacy of the target. (17a–d) are thus straightforwardly ruled out by Greed, but remain problematic if Enlightened Self-Interest is adopted.[11] I conclude, therefore, that Greed is empirically superior to Enlightened Self-Interest.[12]

To sum up, the facts concerning the infinitival complement of *wager*-class verbs examined in section 4.3.1 provide evidence that, as argued by Lasnik (1995a) and contra Chomsky's (1993) proposal, *be* is a Case assigner. However, the facts concerning A-movement within infinitival complements of BELIEVE-class verbs, as well as passives and nominalizations of *believe*-class verbs, discussed in this section, provide evidence for Chomsky's Greed and against Lasnik's Enlightened Self-Interest. The expletive replacement/adjunction analysis thus seems to be in rather desperate straits. One possible approach is to reject the expletive replacement hypothesis altogether. Since in the minimalist system this move would have serious consequences for the Full Interpretation and the theory of agreement, which would have to be considerably complicated to account for agreement facts in existential constructions, I will not pursue it here. Let us therefore see how the conclusions reached above can be reconciled with the expletive replacement hypothesis.

As discussed above, the associate of *there* in (5a–b) must be Case-marked by *be* prior to LF adjunction to the expletive. However, given Greed, being Case-marked, it is not allowed to adjoin to the expletive at LF and we thus seem to be left with a freestanding LF affix *there*.[13] There is, however, one way of associating *there* and the indefinite NP in (5a–b) through adjunction that is consistent with Greed. I propose that instead of the indefinite NP raising to adjoin to *there*, *there* lowers and adjoins to the indefinite NP.[14] Given Lasnik's claim that *there* is an LF affix that must be attached to an NP bearing partitive Case, the proposal amounts to claiming that *there* undergoes affix hopping in LF. Since the lowering of *there* is motivated by overcoming a morphological inadequacy of *there*, it is consistent with Greed. It takes place to satisfy the requirement that *there* be affixed to an NP bearing partitive Case. I assume that either affix hopping of *there* does not leave a trace or the trace can be deleted since no principle of the grammar requires *there* to leave a trace.[15] Nothing, then, goes wrong if *there* adjoins to the indefinite NP in (5a–b), and as a result *there* and the indefinite NP end up in the right configuration at LF without violating Greed.

Note that the view of lowering operations taken here is compatible with Chomsky's (1995) system, where lowering is in principle ruled out in the overt syntax but not in LF. Chomsky suggests that lowering is ruled out in the overt syntax because of linear ordering requirements, which are irrelevant in LF, the component in which I propose expletive *there* undergoes lowering. It is worth noting in this context that since lowering is ruled out in the overt syntax, the existence of a PF counterpart of *there* (i.e., a PF affix expletive that would undergo overt lowering from SpecIP to its host) is excluded.

It seems natural to extend the affix-hopping analysis to constructions such as (1a), an extension that enables us to maintain the assumption that all structural Case marking takes place under Spec-head agreement. (Recall that under Chomsky's (1993) analysis this assumption cannot be maintained.) Under the affix-hopping analysis, the fact that the associate of *there* agrees with the matrix verb in (1a) can be accounted for in the same way as in Lasnik 1995a, where it is proposed that the apparent agreement of the associate with the main verb in (1a) is a result of a constraint on affixation. Lasnik proposes that *there* is freely generated with any set of φ features. Furthermore, he proposes that an affix and its host cannot disagree in φ features. Given this, the associate must have the same φ features as *there*, which undergoes Spec-head agreement with the matrix I. The agreement between the matrix verb and the associate of *there* follows straightforwardly.

In summary, in order to reconcile the conclusions reached above— namely, that *be* is a Case assigner and that Greed holds—with the expletive adjunction analysis, I have proposed that *there*, an LF affix that must be associated with a partitive NP, undergoes LF affix hopping in accordance with Greed. Having demonstrated how the affix-hopping analysis works and established its theoretical validity, in the next section I will present evidence that supports it.

4.3.3 Evidence for the Affix-Hopping Analysis

4.3.3.1 Interpretation of the Associate of *There* I will first show that the affix-hopping analysis provides a straightforward explanation for well-known facts concerning the interpretation of the associate of *there*, which have long posed a problem for the expletive adjunction analysis. As mentioned in note 1, it is well known that the associate of *there* is interpreted at LF in its SS position and not in the SpecIP position that is occupied by *there* at SS, as would be expected if the associate were to adjoin to *there* in LF. Let us reconsider (1), repeated here as (18).

(18) a. There is likely to be someone in the garden
     b. Someone is likely to be in the garden

In (18b) *someone* can take either wide or narrow scope with respect to *likely*. In (18a), on the other hand, *someone* must take narrow scope.

Given the natural assumption that LF rather than SS determines scope, this is unexpected under the LF raising-to-*there* analysis, since on this analysis all the elements that are c-commanded by *someone* in the LF representation of (18b) are also c-commanded by *someone* in the LF representation of (18a) (see note 1). On the other hand, under the LF lowering-of-*there* analysis, in which *someone* remains in the embedded clause in the LF representation of (18a), the facts under consideration are straightforwardly accounted for. Since, unlike in (18b), in (18a) *someone* does not c-command *likely* and *likely* does c-command *someone* at LF, *someone* must take narrow scope with respect to *likely*.

The same point can be made with respect to (19).

(19) a. *There seems to himself to be someone in the garden
   b. Someone seems to himself to be in the garden
   c. *There seems to his$_i$ father to be someone$_i$ in the garden
   d. Someone$_i$ seems to his$_i$ father to be t$_i$ in the garden
   e. *Before his$_i$ father left, there was someone$_i$ in the room
   f. Before his$_i$ father left, someone$_i$ was in the room
   g. *There seems to any European team to be no NBA team beatable
   h. No NBA team seems to any European team to be beatable

Assuming that binding theory applies at LF (see Chomsky 1993), under the raising-to-the-expletive analysis we would expect Condition A to be satisfied in (19a), as in (19b). Also, since under the raising-to-the-expletive analysis (19c,e) have the same LF representation in all relevant respects as (19d,f), we would not expect to detect any weak crossover effects in (19c,e), apparently an incorrect prediction. We also incorrectly predict that the negative polarity item (NPI) can be licensed in (19g), as in (19h). The ungrammaticality of (19a,c,e,g) thus raises a serious problem for the raising-to-the-expletive analysis. On the other hand, under the affix-hopping-of-*there* analysis, the indefinite NPs in (19a,c,e,g) remain in their SS position at LF, so that the constructions in question are straightforwardly ruled out because the relevant NPs do not c-command the anaphor in (19a), the pronoun in (19c,e), and the NPI in (19g). The facts concerning the interpretation of the associate of *there* thus favor the expletive-lowering analysis over the associate-raising analysis.

4.3.3.2 Antecedent-Contained Deletion and Existential Constructions
Certain data concerning antecedent-contained deletion also favor the affix-hopping analysis.[16] The phenomenon of antecedent-contained deletion,

illustrated in (20), has received a great deal of attention in the literature (see Sag 1976, May 1985, Baltin 1987, Diesing 1992, Lasnik 1993, Takahashi 1993, Hornstein 1994, among others).

(20) John beat everyone that Bill did [$_{VP}$ e]

Assume that constructions involving VP-deletion are interpreted by copying a nonelided VP into the deleted VP. In (20) the only VP available for copying is the matrix VP. However, since the matrix VP contains the deleted VP, copying the matrix VP into the deleted VP would lead to a regress. In other words, it would create another null VP (e.g., *John beat everyone that Bill beat everyone that Bill did*). To avoid infinite regress, the deleted VP must somehow be removed from the matrix VP prior to copying. Hornstein (1994), Lasnik (1993), and Takahashi (1993) note that the regress problem can be straightforwardly solved in the minimalist framework.[17] Given the standard minimalist assumption that all Case checking takes place under Spec-head agreement, the direct object NP in (20), which contains a null VP, must move in LF to SpecAgr$_O$P to be Case-checked. After LF movement of the direct object NP, the matrix VP can be copied into the null VP without causing regress. (I assume that it suffices to copy the trace of the matrix verb into the null VP to derive a well-formed structure.)

(21) [$_{IP}$ John beat$_i$ [$_{Agr_O}$P[$_{NP}$ everyone that Bill did [$_{VP}$ e]]$_j$ t$_i$ [$_{VP}$ t$_i$ t$_j$]]]

Given this much background, consider the following instances of antecedent-contained deletion involving existential and ECM constructions, noted by Hornstein (1994):

(22) a.   There is no one electable
      b.   John [$_{Agr_O}$P[$_{VP}$ expected [$_{IP}$[$_{NP}$ no one that I did [$_{VP}$ e]] to be electable]]]
      c.   *John [$_{Agr_O}$P[$_{VP}$ expected [$_{IP}$ there to be [$_{NP}$ no one that I did [$_{VP}$ e]] electable]]]

In (22b) the embedded-clause subject moves to the matrix SpecAgr$_O$P in LF, thus making it possible for the matrix VP to be copied into the null VP without causing regress. As noted by Hornstein (1994), on the associate-raising analysis we would expect a similar derivation to be available in (22c). On both Chomsky's (1993) and Lasnik's (1995a) analyses, the *there + no one that I did* complex is located in the matrix SpecAgr$_O$P in the LF representation of (22c). As a result, as in (22b), the matrix VP can be copied into the null VP in (22c) without causing an interpretive regress. The contrast between (22b) and (22c) thus remains unaccounted for under the associate-raising analysis of expletive replacement. However, it receives a straightforward account under the affix-hopping analysis. On this analysis the indefinite NP does not undergo LF movement. Rather, *there* undergoes affix hopping in LF by adjoining to the indefinite NP. Since the indefinite NP remains within the matrix VP at LF, the matrix VP cannot be copied into the null VP without causing an interpretive regress. The ungrammaticality of (22c) is thus straightforwardly accounted for. The facts concerning antecedent-contained deletion discussed above thus favor the analysis presented here over Chomsky's (1993) and Lasnik's (1995a) analyses of existential constructions.

4.3.3.3 Agreement with Conjoined NPs in Existential Constructions

Certain facts concerning conjunct agreement in *there* constructions provide more evidence for the affix-hopping analysis. It is well known that in constructions involving conjoined indefinite subjects the verb agrees with the whole conjunct rather than with one of the NPs forming the conjunct.

(23) a. A man and a woman are in the house
     b. *A man and a woman is in the house
     c. A man and five women are in the house
     d. *A man and five women is in the house
     e. Four men and a woman are in the house
     f. *Four men and a woman is in the house

However, as noted by Munn (1993) and Sobin (1994), in *there* constructions involving conjoined NPs, the verb agrees with the first conjunct. Agreement with the whole conjoined phrase or the second conjunct is degraded.[18]

(24) a. There is a man and a woman in the house
     b. *There are a man and a woman in the house
     c. There is a man and five women in the house
     d. *There are a man and five women in the house
     e. There are four men and a woman in the house
     f. *There is four men and a woman in the house

Under Chomsky's (1993) analysis we would expect the whole conjoined phrase to adjoin to *there* in LF, adjunction being driven by Case checking of the NPs forming the conjunct. As a result, as Sobin (1994) notes, under this analysis we would expect to find the same pattern of agreement in constructions involving overt and covert preposing of conjoined indefinite NPs. Both the contrast between (23b) and (24a) and the contrast between (23d) and (24c) are thus totally unexpected on this analysis. These contrasts are also mysterious under Lasnik's (1995a) analysis. Recall that on Lasnik's analysis the associate of *there* is Case-marked by *be*. As a result, the traditional Case Filter is not violated if only the first conjunct is adjoined to *there* in the LF representation of (24), which also gives the correct agreement pattern. However, the movement violates the Coordinate Structure Constraint (e.g., *A man is and five women in the house*). I will now show that under the affix-hopping analysis these facts can readily be accounted for.

It is well known that the first conjunct in a coordinate structure behaves as if it is higher than the second conjunct. This is illustrated by the lack of weak crossover effects in (25a), which contrasts with (25b), as well as by the Condition C effect in (25c), which contrasts with (25d).

(25) a. [Every father]$_i$ and his$_i$ son went fishing on Sunday
     b. cf. ?*His$_i$ son and [every father]$_i$ went fishing on Sunday
     c. John's$_i$ dog and he$_i$/him$_i$ went hunting
     d. cf. *He$_i$ and John's$_i$ dog went hunting

To account for the well-known structural asymmetries between the first and second conjuncts, a number of authors have argued for the existence of a Boolean Phrase (BP), headed by conjunctions, which allows the first conjunct to be located in a structurally higher position than the second conjunct. (The periods in (26) indicate that the second conjunct can be more deeply embedded within BP than shown in (26).)

(26) [$_{BP}$ NP [$_{B'}$ B ... NP]]
     (Munn 1987, Collins 1987, Kolb and Thiersch 1991)

Recall now that under the analysis adopted here *there* must be adjoined to an NP bearing partitive Case and the movement must be consistent with Greed. It seems natural to assume that the LF affixal property of *there* must be satisfied in the most economical way, that is, through the shortest movement possible. Assuming that (26) is the structure of coordinate NPs, the most economical way of satisfying the morphological property of *there* in (24) is to adjoin *there* to the first conjunct, which is the closest partitive-Case-bearing NP to the expletive.[19] Given Lasnik's requirement that an affix and its host cannot disagree in ϕ features, it follows straightforwardly that, unlike what happens in constructions involving preposed conjoined indefinites, in *there* constructions the verb agrees only with the first conjunct. The facts concerning V-agreement in *there* constructions thus also favor the analysis presented here over Chomsky's and Lasnik's analyses.

To summarize the discussion in section 4.3.3, on the basis of facts concerning the interpretation of the associate, antecedent-contained deletion, and first conjunct agreement, I have shown that the LF affix-hopping analysis of existential constructions is empirically superior to Chomsky's (1993) and Lasnik's (1995a) associate-raising analyses. In the next section I will digress briefly from existential constructions to discuss constructions involving expletive *it*. I will show that my analysis of expletive *there* constructions can readily be extended to expletive *it* constructions.

4.3.4   *It* and Expletive Replacement

Consider the following constructions:

(27) a. *It is someone in the garden
     b. cf. It seems that someone is in the garden

Given that *be* is a Case assigner, the indefinite NP in (27a) can be Case-marked by *be*. Expletive *it* can be Case-marked under Spec-head agreement with I. The traditional Case Filter is thus satisfied in (27a). To account for the ungrammaticality of (27a), as well as the contrast between (27a) and (27b), Lasnik (1995b) suggests that, like expletive *there*, expletive *it* is an LF affix, which must be adjoined to by an appropriate host at LF. (Shlonsky (1987) and Tanaka (1995) also propose expletive replacement analyses for expletive *it*. Such an analysis is also hinted at in Chomsky 1991.) Notice that if, as suggested by Chomsky (1993), the LF affix status of expletive *there* is a result of its lack of semantic import, which prevents it from being freestanding at LF, we would actually expect expletive *it* to also be an LF affix. Expletive *it* does not seem to have any more semantic import than expletive *there*, and as a result we would expect that constructions involving freestanding expletive *it* cannot be interpreted coherently. I therefore assume that, like *there*, expletive *it* is an LF affix. Following Lasnik's proposal concerning the LF affix status of *there*, I assume that the LF affix status of *it* is a result of a morphological requirement. It is tempting to think that, given the standard minimalist assumption that semantic considerations such as uninterpretability of freestanding expletives cannot drive movement, the morphological requirement on expletive *there* and *it* has developed in order to provide a proper driving force for expletive replacement/adjunction. I assume that, just like *there*, expletive *it* undergoes LF affix hopping in accordance with Greed. It must still be determined which elements can serve as hosts for the LF affix *it*. Recall that *there* must be attached to an NP, in particular, an NP bearing partitive Case. It seems clear that the associate of expletive *it* must be a clause, a requirement that suffices to rule out (27a). However, as in the case of *there*, the LF requirement on expletive *it* must be slightly more specific. In particular, I assume that the associate of expletive *it* must be a clause specified as [+tense]. Recall that, as argued by Stowell (1982) and discussed in section 2.2, in addition to finite clauses, some nonfinite clauses are specified as [+tense]. Given the Case-theoretic approach to the distribution of PRO, the possibility of PRO in an infinitival clause can in fact serve as a diagnostic for determining the Tense specification of the clause. Infinitives having PRO in their subject position are specified as [+tense]. Infinitives containing an NP-trace in their subject position, on the other hand, are specified as [−tense]. Given this, the infinitive in *It was arranged PRO to leave* but not in *$*It_i$ was believed t_i to be someone in the garden* can serve as a host for the LF affix *it*.[20]

McCloskey (1991), however, argues against the expletive replacement analysis of *it* constructions, which I adopt here in a slightly revised form of affix hopping. McCloskey's argument is based on agreement differences between expletive constructions with *there* and *it*. However, I will show that *it* constructions do not differ from *there* constructions in the relevant respect, as expected under the unified analysis of expletive constructions argued for above.

As (28a–b) show, when a clause functions as a sentential subject, or when it is extraposed, with *it* filling the subject position, the verb is inflected for third person singular.

(28) a. That John will resign seems likely
      b. It seems likely that John will resign

Since it is not quite clear whether the verb agrees with the clause or simply has default agreement features in (28a), the third person singular inflection on the verb in (28b) does not say anything conclusive about whether the expletive-associate relation is formed between the extraposed clause and *it* in (28b). To determine whether *it* is subject to expletive replacement by a clause, McCloskey (1991) examines constructions involving coordinated sentential subjects. He observes that coordinated sentential subjects sometimes do and sometimes do not trigger plural agreement. In particular, when coordinated clauses are compatible (i.e., denote a single complex state of affairs), they do not trigger plural agreement, as shown in (29a). On the other hand, when coordinated clauses are contradictory (i.e., denote a plurality of distinct states of affairs or situation-types), they trigger subject agreement, as shown in (29b).

(29) a. That the position will be funded and that Mary will be hired now seems/??seem likely
     b. That he'll resign and that he'll stay in office seem at this point equally possible

McCloskey notes that when the coordinated clauses in (29b) are extraposed, they do not trigger plural agreement.

(30) It seems/*seem at this point equally possible that he'll resign and that he'll stay in office

McCloskey argues that the contrast between (29b) and (30) indicates that, in contrast to indefinite NPs and *there* in constructions such as (31a–b), clauses and expletive *it* do not agree in ϕ features. The next logical step is to conclude that the expletive replacement analysis is not appropriate for expletive *it* constructions.

(31) a. There is/*are someone in the garden
     b. There are/*is some men in the garden

The conclusion is too hasty, however. Notice that (29)–(30), which are intended to illustrate the lack of agreement in expletive *it* constructions, involve a coordinated associate; this is not the case in (31a–b), which illustrate the presence of agreement between the expletive and its associate in expletive *there* constructions. I would like to suggest that this and not the *it* versus *there* distinction is responsible for the contrast in the agreement patterns between (30) and (31a–b). That the presence versus absence of coordination rather than the *it/there* distinction is indeed responsible for this contrast is confirmed by the fact that, as discussed above, even in expletive *there* constructions the verb does not agree with conjoined associate NPs.

(32) There is/*are a man and five women in the garden

Apparently agreement with conjoined "associates" fails in both *there* and *it* constructions. The impossibility of plural agreement on the verb in (30) then cannot be used to argue that expletive *it* and expletive *there* constructions should be analyzed differently. In other words, the ungrammaticality of (30) on the plural specification of the verb does not provide evidence that the expletive replacement analysis cannot be extended to expletive *it* constructions. Recall now that in *there* constructions such as (32) the verb actually agrees with the associate. In particular, it agrees with the first conjunct. I would like to suggest that the same holds for (30). I take *That he'll resign seems possible* to indicate that the first conjunct of the conjoined clause in (30) on its own triggers third person singular agreement on the verb. Given this, if, like (32), (30) displays first conjunct agreement with the associate, we would expect the verb to display singular agreement. The analysis of first conjunct agreement in (32) can readily be extended to (30).[21] Given the minimalist assumption that every requirement must be satisfied in the most economical way (i.e., through the shortest movement possible), and given that [$_{BP}$ CP [$_{B'}$ B CP]] is the structure of coordinated clauses (see section 4.3.3.3 for discussion of coordination), the most economical way of satisfying the LF affixal requirement of expletive *it* in (30) is to adjoin it to the first conjunct, which is the closest [+tense] clause to the expletive. (Note that, being a BP, the whole conjoined phrase does not qualify as a proper host for the LF affix *it*, which must attach to a clause.) Since both *it* and the clause are specified as third person singular, Lasnik's (1995a) requirement that an affix and its host cannot disagree in φ features is satisfied.[22]

It is worth noting here that, as observed by an anonymous reviewer, Greed was the major obstacle for a uniform treatment of expletive *there* and expletive *it* constructions for Chomsky (1993), the problem being that there is no need for expletive replacement in expletive *it* constructions under Chomsky's analysis. The Greed problem is solved with the affix-hopping analysis, and expletive *there* and expletive *it* constructions receive a uniform treatment.

4.3.5 Feature Movement Analyses of Existential Constructions

Before concluding my discussion of expletive constructions, in this section I will discuss two recent analyses of existential constructions based on Chomsky's (1995) theory of feature movement, namely, those of Chomsky (1995) and Lasnik (1995b), and compare them with the analysis proposed above.

It is a standard assumption in the minimalist framework that all movement is driven by the need for formal features to be checked. Chomsky (1995) notes that a natural consequence of this assumption is that, all else being equal, the operation Move should apply to features and not to syntactic categories, and he argues that this is indeed the case. However, overt movement, which feeds PF, still needs to carry whole categories under the natural assumption that lexical items with "scattered" features are uninterpretable/unpronounceable at PF and cause the derivation to crash. Since the considerations of PF interpretability are not relevant to LF movement, the operation Move applies only to features in LF. Chomsky argues that in LF, formal features move to heads bearing matching features. He furthermore argues that whenever the operation Move F affects a formal feature, it carries all formal features of the relevant element and not just one particular feature. Chomsky (1995) and Lasnik (1995b) apply this Move F theory to existential constructions, restating expletive replacement in terms of LF feature adjunction to heads. According to Chomsky and Lasnik, in the LF representation of (33a) the formal features of the indefinite NP adjoin to Agr_S. (I am adapting Chomsky's analysis to the system adopted here. In particular, I am keeping Agr phrases. My modifications do not affect the gist of Chomsky's analysis.)

(33) a. There is a man in the garden
      b. $[_{Agr_S P}$ There FF(a man)$_i$+is$_j$+Agr$_S$ t$_j$ t$_i$ in the garden]

There are two major differences between Chomsky's and Lasnik's analyses of existential constructions that have a bearing on the phenomena discussed in this chapter. According to Chomsky, expletive *there* has neither Case nor agreement features. The set of features that undergoes LF adjunction to Agr_S thus checks both the agreement and the Case features of Agr_S/Tense. The associate of the expletive then cannot be Case-checked prior to LF feature movement. (Chomsky thus rejects the partitive Case assignment hypothesis.)

Lasnik, on the other hand, argues that *there* has a Case feature, so that the formal features adjoined to Agr_S check only agreement features. The associate of the expletive is Case-checked by *be*.[23] Another important difference between Chomsky's and Lasnik's feature movement analyses of existential constructions concerns the content of features undergoing adjunction to Agr_S. According to Chomsky, formal features carried by the movement contain the referential content necessary for them to serve as binders, controllers, and so on. Lasnik, on the other hand, is more strict in his interpretation of the term "formal features." According to Lasnik, referential and quantificational properties, which are crucially involved in phenomena such as binding, control, and scope, are not determined by formal features, which undergo LF movement in (33).

Rather, they are determined by the semantic features that are left behind by movement of formal features.

Here I should note that the LF affix-hopping analysis of expletive constructions can readily be restated in terms of feature movement. In fact, expletive *there* would be affected by the operation Move in essentially the same way regardless of whether Move is stated in terms of features or in terms of categories. Recall that Chomsky (1995) proposes that whenever the operation Move F affects a formal feature, it carries all formal features of the relevant element and not just one particular feature. Since, according to Chomsky, expletives such as *there* have formal but not semantic features (here I am ignoring phonological features, which are stripped off at Spell-Out and therefore are not present in LF), if Move F applies to any formal feature of *there*, it would actually affect the whole content of the expletive; that is, it would move the whole expletive. (Recall also that Chomsky leaves open the possibility that lowering exists in LF.)

Returning now to Chomsky's (1995) and Lasnik's (1995b) Move F analyses of existential constructions, let us examine how they fare with respect to the data discussed in section 4.3.3, which favor the affix-hopping analysis over Chomsky's and Lasnik's category-raising analyses of *there* constructions. Consider first the following contrast involving antecedent-contained deletion:

(34) a. *John [$_{Agr_oP}$[$_{VP}$ expected [$_{IP}$ there to be [$_{NP}$ no one that I did [$_{VP}$ e]] electable]]]

     b. cf. John [$_{Agr_oP}$[$_{VP}$ expected [$_{IP}$[$_{NP}$ no one that I did [$_{VP}$ e]] to be electable]]]

     c. cf. John [$_{Agr_oP}$[$_{VP}$ expected [$_{NP}$ no one that I did [$_{VP}$ e]]]]

Recall that in constructions such as (34b) LF object shift of the embedded-clause subject removes the embedded-clause subject from the matrix VP, which then can be copied into the deleted VP without causing infinite regress. Since under Chomsky's (1993) and Lasnik's (1995a) analyses of existential constructions the *there + no one that I did* complex is located in the matrix SpecAgr$_o$P at LF, we would also expect that the matrix VP could be copied into the elided VP in (34a) without causing infinite regress, which is apparently not the case. However, as shown above, the ungrammaticality of (34a) can readily be accounted for under the LF affix-hopping analysis. The same holds for Chomsky's (1995) and Lasnik's (1995b) analyses, since under these analyses only the formal features of the associate of *there* move to the matrix clause, leaving the elided VP internal to its antecedent. The problem with this account of the ungrammaticality of (34a) is that it extends to (34b) and (34c), incorrectly predicting both constructions to be ungrammatical. Under the Move F analysis, LF object shift affects only formal features and thus cannot remove the semantic content of the embedded-clause subject in (34b) and the matrix object in (34c) outside the matrix VP, a prerequisite for freeing the null VP from its antecedent. To account for the contrast between (34a) and (34b–c), Lasnik (1995b) argues that object shift takes place overtly in English.[24] Since under the Move F theory considerations of PF well-formedness require that overt movement operate on whole categories and not merely on features, if object shift in (34b) and (34c) takes place overtly, it completely removes the null VPs from the matrix VP. The contrast between (34a) and (34b–c) thus can be accounted for under the Move F analysis of existential constructions if object shift takes place overtly in English, an assumption that is accepted by Lasnik (1995b), but not by Chomsky (1995). ((34b–c) thus seem to be incorrectly ruled out under Chomsky's analysis. In all fairness, it should be noted that Chomsky does not discuss antecedent-contained deletion.) However, the assumption that object shift takes place overtly in English is not unproblematic. Whereas, as will be discussed in section 4.4, there seem to be no obstacles to the overt object shift analysis of ECM constructions, the overt object shift analysis of standard transitive constructions, such as (34c), is problematic. Thus, Branigan (1992) argues that if the direct object NP in (35a) is located in SpecAgr$_o$P at SS, we would expect extraction out of the object NP to exhibit the Subject Condition effect, since it would take place in essentially the same configuration as extraction out of subject NPs. This is also true under the minimalist accounts of the Subject Condition effect offered in the literature. (See Kitahara 1994a,b, Ormazabal, Uriagereka, and Uribe-Etxebarria 1994, Takahashi 1994, and Uriagereka 1996.) As (35b) shows, the expectation is not borne out.

(35) a. I saw [friends of John]
     b. Who did you see [friends of t]

(For a more detailed discussion of the issues concerning the level at which object shift takes place in English and for additional arguments against overt object shift in English simple transitive constructions, see section 4.4.)

Now consider the facts concerning the interpretation of the associate of *there* discussed in section 4.3.3.1. Recall that the associate of *there* is interpreted in the position it occupies at SS, and not in the position where the expletive is located, as expected under the affix-hopping analysis but not under Chomsky's (1993) and Lasnik's (1995a) raising-to-the-expletive analyses. The facts concerning the interpretation of the expletive can also be accounted for under Lasnik's (1995b) LF feature movement analysis of existential constructions. Since under Lasnik's analysis only formal features of the associate (which, according to Lasnik, do not have the referential and quantificational content necessary for them to serve as binders or affect scope relations) move in LF, the associate is interpreted within the clause it occupies at SS. Under Lasnik's analysis, in spite of the LF formal feature movement of the associate, referential and quantificational features, which Lasnik assumes are semantic in nature, are still located at LF within the clause the associate occupies at SS, which accounts for the facts concerning the interpretation of the associate discussed in section 4.3.3.1. However, as in the case of the facts concerning antecedent-contained deletion, Lasnik's analysis of the facts concerning the interpretation of the associate of *there* crucially depends on the assumption that object shift always takes place overtly in English. If object shift were to take place covertly, under Lasnik's analysis the referential content of the direct object NP and the embedded-clause subject in (36a–d) would remain in the SS position of the elements in question. (36a–b) would then incorrectly be ruled out as Condition A violations, on a par with (19a) and (44a), and (36c–d) would incorrectly be ruled in, since the Condition C violation would be eliminated.[25]

(36) a. The DA questioned Peter and Mary during each other's trials
     b. The DA proved [Peter and Mary to be guilty] during each other's trials
     c. *The DA questioned her$_i$ during Mary's$_i$ trial
     d. *The DA proved [her$_i$ to be guilty] during Mary's$_i$ trial

Let us turn now to Chomsky's (1995) feature movement analysis of existential constructions. Recall that Chomsky assumes that formal features of the associate, which undergo raising in LF, contain the referential content necessary for them to serve as binders. (Overt object shift is, then, not necessary to account for (36a–d) under Chomsky's analysis.) Chomsky does not make any explicit claims concerning the quantificational properties of the associate. However, judging by his analysis of simple transitive and ECM constructions, where he claims that object shift takes place covertly, the quantificational properties must also be determined by formal features, which undergo LF movement. The assumption raises an obvious problem with respect to the facts concerning the interpretation of the associate. However, Chomsky presents an account of the ungrammaticality of constructions such as (19a), discussed in section 4.3.3.1, which he claims to be compatible with his assumption. He argues that anaphors undergo LF feature movement through adjunction to Agr_S. Given the LF feature movement of the anaphor and the LF feature movement of the associate, the relevant portion of (19a) has either the structure in (37a) or the structure in (37b).

(19) a. *There seems to himself to be someone in the garden

(37) a. *There $[_{Agr_S}$ himself [FF(someone)] ...
     b. *There $[_{Agr_S}$ FF(someone) [himself] ...

Chomsky suggests that neither (37a) nor (37b), with the anaphor and FF(*someone*) adjoined to the same head, is a legitimate binding-theoretic configuration for FF(*someone*) to serve as an antecedent for the anaphor. According to Chomsky, in order for the relevant binding relationship to be established when the bindee is adjoined to Agr_S, the associate must be located in $SpecAgr_SP$, as it is in (19b), the relevant part of which is given in (38). (Recall that in Chomsky's system sets of formal features adjoined to Agr_S can serve as binders. The problem with (37a–b) then must be that the anaphor is "too close" to the binder.)

(38) $[_{Agr_SP}$ Someone $[_{Agr_S}$ himself] ...

Note, however, that object-oriented anaphors raise a problem for Chomsky's analysis if Lasnik (1993) is right in arguing that object-oriented anaphors such as *themselves* in (39) undergo LF anaphor movement via adjunction to Agr_O.

(39) I asked them about themselves

Since the direct object NP undergoes LF feature movement to Agr_O in Chomsky's system, the anaphor and its antecedent end up adjoined to the same node at LF. Since (40) involves the same configuration in all relevant respects as (19a), (39) then seems to be incorrectly ruled out in Chomsky's system, on a par with (19a).

(40) I asked $[_{Agr_O}$ themselves [FF(them)] ...

Even if we disregard the problem raised by object-oriented anaphors, Chomsky's analysis seems to make a wrong prediction with respect to constructions such as (19c–d), discussed in section 4.3.3.1.

(19) c. *There seems to his$_i$ father to be someone$_i$ in the garden

      d. Someone$_i$ seems to his$_i$ father to be t$_i$ in the garden

It seems safe to assume that, in contrast to pure anaphors, *his* does not have to adjoin to Agr$_S$ in LF. If *his* remains in its SS position at LF, FF(*someone*), adjoined to Agr$_S$ at LF, is in a legitimate configuration to serve as a binder for *his* in Chomsky's (1995) system. As a result, both the weak crossover effect in (19c) and the contrast between (19c) and (19d) remain unaccounted for under Chomsky's (1995) LF feature movement analysis of expletive replacement. The same holds for the contrast between (19e) and (19f), discussed in section 4.3.3.1. Chomsky's analysis of (19a–b), which crucially depends on the anaphor status of the element entering into a relation with the associate of *there*, also fails to extend to the scope and NPI-licensing facts considered in section 4.3.3.1. I see no obvious way of accounting for the contrast between (18a) and (18b) with respect to the scope interpretation of the indefinite NP and the contrast between (19g) and (19h) with respect to NPI licensing under Chomsky's feature movement analysis.

(18) a. There is likely to be someone in the garden

      b. Someone is likely to be in the garden

(19) g. *There seems to any European team to be no NBA team beatable

      h. No NBA team seems to any European team to be beatable

In fact, upon closer scrutiny even the contrast between (19a) and (19b) remains unaccounted for.

(19) a. *There seems to himself to be someone in the garden

      b. Someone seems to himself to be in the garden

To account for the ungrammaticality of double *there* constructions such as (41), Chomsky (1995) argues that the N feature of the associate must raise to the D element *there* as an instantiation of Longobardi's (1994) N-to-D movement analysis.[26]

(41) *There$_1$ seems there$_2$ to be someone in the garden

According to Chomsky, given that the N feature of the associate raises to *there$_2$*, the construction is ruled out because *there$_1$* remains intact at LF. The N feature raising-to-*there* analysis also accounts for the ungrammaticality of (42) with expletive *there*, which otherwise seems to remain unaccounted for in Chomsky's system.

(42) *John laughed there

Recall now that whenever a formal feature is affected by the operation Move in Chomsky's system, Move must carry all formal features of the relevant element. As a result, when the N feature of the associate adjoins to the expletive in constructions such as (19a), all formal features of the associate, which carry the referential content of the associate, adjoin to *there*. The structure of the relevant portion of (19a) then must be (43) rather than (37a) or (37b), as argued by Chomsky.

(43) $[_{\text{AgrsP}}$ FF(someone) + there $[_{\text{Agrs}}$ himself] ...

Since the illicit configuration for anaphor binding shown in (37a–b) is not present in (43), Condition A seems to be incorrectly predicted to be satisfied in (19a), just as it is in (19b). In fact, given that the N feature of the associate must adjoin to the expletive, an adjunction that is needed to account for the ungrammaticality of *there* object (see (42)) and double *there* (see (41)) constructions in Chomsky's (1995) system, the associate of *there* is for all practical purposes always adjoined to *there*. As a result, all the problems concerning the data in (18) and (19) that arise under the more traditional category-raising analyses of Chomsky (1993) and Lasnik (1995a) also arise under Chomsky's (1995) Move F analysis. In fact, there is no real difference between the two analyses.

As pointed out by Howard Lasnik (personal communication), Chomsky's feature movement analysis also fails to account for the contrasts in (44). ((44a–b) are from Lasnik and Saito 1991 and (44e–f) from Lasnik 1995b.)

(44) a. *The DA proved [there to have been two men at the scene] during each other's trials

b. The DA proved [two men to have been at the scene] during each other's trials

c. *The DA proved [there to be someone$_i$ at the scene] during his$_i$ trial

d. The DA proved [someone$_i$ to be at the scene] during his$_i$ trial

e. *The DA proved [there to be no one at the scene] during any of the trials

f. The DA proved [no one to be at the scene] during any of the trials

The indefinite NP in (44b) serves as a binder for an anaphor; in (44d) it binds a pronoun; and in (44f) it licenses an NPI. In Chomsky's system the indefinite NP in all the constructions in (44) is located in the same position at LF: namely, its formal features are adjoined to Agr_O at LF. As a result, since (44a) and (44b), (44c) and (44d), and (44e) and (44f) have the same structure in all relevant respects, it does not seem to be possible to account for the contrasts in (44) under Chomsky's analysis. Under his analysis we would expect all the constructions in (44) to have the same grammaticality status.[27]

In summary, whereas Lasnik's (1995b) feature movement analysis accounts for the interpretation of the associate of *there*, given the problematic assumption that object shift always takes place overtly in English, Chomsky's (1995) feature movement analysis fails to account for the interpretation of the associate and thus faces the same problem as his (1993) and Lasnik's (1995a) analyses.[28] Recall that the facts in question can be straightforwardly accounted for without any additional assumptions under the affix-hopping analysis.

Let us now turn to the last piece of evidence in favor of the affix-hopping analysis and against the traditional associate-to-*there* raising analysis that I gave in section 4.3.3.3, namely, the phenomenon of first conjunct agreement. As far as I can see, the facts concerning first conjunct agreement cannot be accounted for in a principled way under either Chomsky's (1995) or Lasnik's (1995b) feature movement analysis of existential constructions. Both the contrast between (23b) and (24a) and the contrast between (23d) and (24c) are unexpected under these analyses for essentially the same reasons they are unexpected under the more traditional category-raising analyses of Chomsky (1993) and Lasnik (1995a) (see the discussion in section 4.3.3.3). Since the facts under consideration receive a straightforward account under the affix-hopping analysis, the phenomenon of first conjunct agreement in existential constructions favors the LF affix-hopping analysis over the LF feature-raising analyses of existential constructions.

Having discussed how the LF feature movement analyses fare with respect to the data examined in section 4.3.3, I will now briefly discuss several other problems that arise under these analyses, but not under the affix-hopping analysis.

Lasnik (1995b) points out one additional problem that arises under Chomsky's feature movement analysis. He observes that under this analysis we would expect (45) to be grammatical.

(45) *There [$_{VP}$ someone laughed]

Recall that Chomsky assumes that *there* does not check Case. Given that *there* is Caseless, nominative Case should be available for the indefinite

NP in (45). If *someone* is Case-checked through LF adjunction to Agr_S, it is not clear how (45) can be ruled out in Chomsky's system.

Let us now turn to Lasnik's (1995b) analysis. Lasnik himself points out that constructions such as (46a–b) raise a problem for his analysis, which dispenses with the requirement that the associate of *there* bear partitive Case. (The requirement actually seems to be unstatable in Lasnik's (1995b) system.)

(46) a. *There seems to a strange man Peter likes Mary
     b. *There seems a woman likes Peter

Following Chomsky (1995), Lasnik assumes that the agreement features of I, which are not involved in the interpretation, must undergo checking and disappear after they are checked. The agreement features of NPs, which are involved in the interpretation, do not have to be checked and, if they do undergo checking, they do not disappear. As a result, one NP may check agreement features of more than one element. Lasnik also assumes that expletive *there* has Case but not agreement features. *There* thus cannot check the agreement features of the matrix I in (46). Since Lasnik adopts Enlightened Self-Interest rather than Greed, the agreement features of the indefinite NP should be available for checking the agreement features of the matrix I in (46a–b). The question then is why the constructions are bad. To account for the ungrammaticality of (46a–b), Lasnik essentially reinstates Greed by proposing that only NPs whose Case features are not checked are available for A-movement. Since the Case features of the indefinite NPs are checked in the overt syntax, the indefinite NPs are not allowed to adjoin to the matrix Agr_S in LF. The constructions are then ruled out because the agreement features of the matrix Agr_S remain unchecked. Note that in Lasnik's system both Enlightened Self-Interest and a version of Greed are needed. Under the analysis I have pursued only Greed is needed; this parsimony provides a conceptual argument in favor of my analysis. The conceptual argument aside, the grammaticality of (47) raises a serious empirical problem for Lasnik's analysis of (46).

(47) There is a man in the garden

In Lasnik's system *a man* in (47) is Case-marked by *be*. As a result, it seems that it should be prevented from adjoining to Agr_S by the ban on A-movement of NPs whose Case features are checked. (47) should then be ruled out on a par with (46a–b), because the agreement features of Agr_S

remain unchecked. However, Lasnik observes that the Case for which the indefinite NP in (47) is marked, namely, partitive Case, has semantic import and therefore must survive to the LF interface level. In Chomsky's (1995) terms, partitive Case is a [+interpretable] feature. Lasnik takes advantage of the fact that [+interpretable] features do not disappear after checking. Since the Case of the indefinite NP in (47) is not checked off after entering into a checking relation with *be*, the NP is allowed to adjoin to Agr$_S$ in LF, thus checking the agreement features of Agr$_S$. However, Chomsky (1995) argues that not only can [+interpretable] features survive feature checking, they are also legitimate LF objects even when they do not undergo checking at all. The intuitive guiding idea here is that if a feature is unaffected by checking, it does not have to be checked at all. According to Chomsky, features with semantic import can undergo checking as many times as necessary, including more than once and less than once. From his treatment of agreement features of nouns, it appears that Lasnik (1995b) adopts Chomsky's view of [+interpretable] features (i.e., features that because of their semantic import must be present at the LF interface level). Returning now to the partitive Case feature, a feature with semantic import according to Lasnik, we would expect the feature in question not only to survive checking, but also to be a legitimate LF object even when it does not enter into a checking relation. This opens a Pandora's box. We should always be able to take an NP bearing partitive Case from the lexicon, insert it into a Caseless position, and leave it in a Caseless position throughout the derivation. The traditional Case Filter is thus essentially rendered inoperative, and constructions such as (48a–c), which under standard assumptions are ruled out because the indefinite NPs cannot be Case-checked, are incorrectly predicted to be grammatical.

(48) a. *John remarked something
     b. *John inquired something
     c. *John's proof something

It is worth noting here that the distinction between features that are affected by checking (i.e., features that must be checked and disappear after checking) and features that are unaffected by checking (i.e., features that do not disappear after checking and can undergo checking as many times as necessary) plays a very important role in both Chomsky's (1995) and Lasnik's (1995b) systems. However, it is not clear that there is a principled criterion for distinguishing these two classes of features. (For relevant discussion, see also Lee 1994.) As noted above, Chomsky (1995) argues that the semantic import of a feature determines whether or not it is affected by checking. According to Chomsky, features that are involved in the interpretation, such as categorial features, ϕ features of nouns, and the [+wh] feature, are not affected by checking. ϕ features of verbs and Case features (with the exception of partitive Case in Lasnik's (1995b) analysis), on the other hand, are not involved in the interpretation and are affected by checking. However, there are examples of [−interpretable] features that are unaffected by checking (i.e., are able to enter into a checking relation both more than once and less than once).[29] The traditional gender feature of Serbo-Croatian nouns is one such example. Like nouns in numerous other languages, most Serbo-Croatian nouns are assigned traditional gender arbitrarily. Thus, the noun *abortus* 'abortion' is masculine, and *kita*, a word denoting the masculine sexual organ, is feminine. *Žrtva* 'victim' is feminine regardless of whether it refers to a male or a female. Note also that *mesec* 'moon' and *sto* 'table' are masculine, whereas the corresponding French words, *lune* and *table*, are feminine. The difference in traditional gender between Serbo-Croatian and French 'moon' and 'table' has no semantic effect. We thus seem to be dealing here with a purely grammatical feature without semantic import. In Chomsky's (1995) terms, we are dealing with a [−interpretable] feature. As a result, we would not expect this feature to be able to enter into multiple feature checking. Also, we would not expect it to survive to the LF interface level, since, according to Chomsky (1995), [−interpretable] features must be eliminated. However, the data in (49) show that the expectation is not borne out.

(49) a. Žrtva   i   dete   su   otišli
        victim-FEM and child-NEUT are-3PL left-MASC.PL
        'The victim and the child left'
     b. Žrtve   su   bile   otišle
        victims-FEM are-3PL been-FEM.PL left-FEM.PL
        'The victims had left'

Consider first the number feature. Constructions such as (49b) are generally taken to indicate that the number of nouns, a natural agreement feature that has semantic import and is therefore specified as [+interpretable], can enter into multiple checking (see Chomsky 1995 and Lasnik 1995b). Constructions such as (49a), which contain a coordinate NP whose individual conjuncts fail to agree with the verbal elements, are taken to indicate that the number feature of Serbo-Croatian nouns does not have to be checked (see Lasnik 1995a). Note, however, that the arbitrary grammatical feature of gender, which has no semantic import, patterns with the natural agreement feature of number in all relevant respects. (49b) thus indicates that, like number, the gender feature of Serbo-Croatian nouns can undergo multiple checking. (49a), involving a coordinate NP with conjuncts that disagree in the gender feature, indicates that the gender feature of Serbo-Croatian nouns does not have to be checked. (49a) thus seems to contain a feature without semantic import that survives to the LF interface level, a state of affairs that also raises a problem for Full Interpretation, according to which only elements with semantic import can be present at LF.

The data discussed above thus seem to indicate that the feature [+/−interpretable], defined in terms of semantic import at the LF interface level, cannot serve as a criterion for distinguishing features that are affected by checking and those that are not, a distinction that plays an important role in the LF feature movement theories of Chomsky (1995) and Lasnik (1995b). The relevant criterion remains to be formulated; until this is done, the conceptually undesirable option of simply stipulating that some features are and some features are not affected by checking will have to be invoked.

To summarize the discussion in this section, I have examined Chomsky's (1995) and Lasnik's (1995b) LF feature movement analyses of existential constructions. I have shown that a number of facts that receive a straightforward account under the affix-hopping analysis remain unaccounted for under the LF feature movement analyses. The affix-hopping analysis thus appears to be superior to the LF feature movement analyses on empirical grounds. (Recall that the affix-hopping analysis can also be stated in terms of LF feature movement and that Chomsky (1995) leaves room for the possibility of LF lowering.)

4.3.6 Conclusion: Expletive Replacement

In the preceding sections I have provided evidence that the verb *be* is a partitive Case assigner and that Greed holds. I have reconciled the seemingly conflicting conclusions with the expletive replacement hypothesis by adopting Chomsky's and Lasnik's proposal that *there* is an LF affix and proposing that *there* undergoes LF affix hopping to overcome its morphological inadequacy. LF affix hopping of *there* is clearly consistent with Greed. I have also provided evidence that the affix-hopping analysis is empirically superior to both Chomsky's (1993) and Lasnik's (1995a) associate category-raising analyses and Chomsky's (1995) and Lasnik's

(1995b) LF feature movement analyses. I have extended my version of the expletive replacement analysis of *there* constructions to expletive *it* constructions. Having now concluded my discussion of existential constructions, in the following sections I will tie up some loose ends of the proposed analysis. In particular, I will explore some questions raised by adopting Greed.

4.4   More on Greed: ECM Constructions

As shown in section 4.3.2, certain facts concerning NP-movement in infinitival complements provide strong evidence for Greed. I have argued that a number of constructions remain unaccounted for unless Greed is adopted. Therefore, I take it that the empirical validity of Greed is established. In this section I will examine some constructions that appear to be problematic for Greed and show that upon closer scrutiny they are not only unproblematic but in fact provide additional support for Greed. The discussion will center around the traditional ECM construction, which, according to Lasnik (1995a), raises a serious problem for Greed.

Before I discuss the ECM construction, however, a note is in order concerning constructions such as (50).

(50) John$_i$ seems [$_{IP}$ t$_i$ to be t$_i$ crazy]

In order for the EPP to be satisfied in (50), *John* must move through the embedded SpecIP on its way to the matrix SpecIP. I assume that movement through the embedded SpecIP is driven by the Minimize Chain Links Principle, which requires that every chain link be as short as possible. The whole movement of *John* to the matrix SpecIP is motivated by the Case checking of the moved element and is therefore in accordance with Greed, which requires that every instance of the operation Form Chain be motivated by satisfying morphological requirements of the element undergoing the operation (see Chomsky 1994 for more examples of grammatical constructions in which formation of a particular chain link is not driven by Greed, but is nevertheless required by the Minimize Chain Links Principle).[30] The grammaticality of (50) can thus be accounted for rather straightforwardly. The traditional ECM construction, however, seems to raise a problem.

(51) John believes the students to be crazy

Under standard minimalist assumptions, *the students* in (51) is Case-checked after undergoing movement to the matrix SpecAgr$_O$P. However, at SS it is located in the embedded SpecIP. Since the embedded SpecIP is a Caseless position, movement to it is not motivated by Case checking of *the students* and a violation of Greed seems to have taken place. Yet the construction is grammatical. (Since the infinitival SpecIP is the final landing site of the operation Form Chain, movement to it is not required by the Minimize Chain Links Principle.) On standard assumptions, (51) thus represents an instance of grammatical movement—or, to be more precise, of Form Chain—that is driven merely by satisfying the EPP (i.e., checking the strong N feature of the infinitival I). (The ungrammaticality of *John believes to be the students crazy* provides evidence that the N feature of [−tense, −finite] I is strong.) However, recall that, as shown by the constructions examined in section 4.3.2, movement motivated solely by satisfying the EPP is not allowed. Given this, the grammaticality of (51) indicates that movement of *the students* is driven by something other than the EPP. In fact, a number of authors (see Authier 1991, Johnson 1991, Koizumi 1993, Lasnik 1995b, Runner 1995, and Ura 1993b, among others) have argued that the movement is driven by the Case checking of the embedded-clause subject and that the relevant NP is in fact located in the matrix SpecAgr$_O$P, a Case-checking position, at SS. (Authier (1991) and Johnson (1991) state this in somewhat different terms without using Agr$_O$P.) I will now show that nothing in the minimalist framework prevents object shift from taking place overtly in ECM constructions. In fact, I will show that in the minimalist system overt object shift is forced in constructions such as (51).[31] Having established the theoretical basis for overt object shift in ECM constructions, I will then discuss empirical evidence that the embedded-clause subject in (51) is actually located in the matrix SpecAgr$_O$P at SS.

4.4.1   Overt Object Shift in ECM Constructions

It is a standard assumption that overt object shift in (52) is blocked by the principle called "Procrastinate," which favors covert over overt movement by requiring that movement take place as late as possible.

(52) John likes Mary

However, Procrastinate does not block all overt movement. Movement can take place overtly in spite of Procrastinate if it is necessary for convergence. Thus, on Chomsky's (1993) analysis *John* in (53) moves overtly from SpecVP to SpecIP in spite of Procrastinate because if the movement does not take place, the strong N feature of I, an illegitimate PF object, enters PF and the derivation crashes.

(53) [$_{IP}$ John$_i$ already [$_{VP}$ t$_i$ left]]

Note now that in (51) *the students* should be allowed to move overtly to the matrix SpecAgr$_O$P in spite of Procrastinate for the same reason *John* moves overtly to SpecIP in (53). If the overt movement to SpecAgr$_O$P in (51) does not take place, the derivation crashes, either because Greed is violated (if *the students* moves to the embedded SpecIP) or because the strong N feature of the embedded I enters PF, that is, because the EPP is violated (if *the students* remains in its base-generated position within VP).[32] On the other hand, if *the students* moves overtly to SpecAgr$_O$P, the derivation converges, since the Minimize Chain Links Principle forces the exceptionally Case-marked NP to pass through the embedded SpecIP on its way to SpecAgr$_O$P. Overt movement to SpecAgr$_O$P in (51) thus takes place in spite of Procrastinate for essentially the same reason that movement to SpecIP takes place overtly in (53), namely, to ensure convergence.[33] However, we still need to account for the fact that although the exceptionally Case-marked NP in (51) is located in the matrix SpecAgr$_O$P at SS on the analysis adopted here, it is not allowed to linearly precede the matrix verb (e.g., **John the students believes to be crazy*). In Chomsky's (1993) system main verbs in English remain in situ at SS and undergo successive-cyclic head movement to Agr$_S$ in LF, their overt movement being blocked by Procrastinate. However, given that movement can take place overtly to ensure convergence, the verb in (51) would be allowed to undergo overt movement if the movement were necessary for convergence. I propose that this is exactly what happens. Given that, as argued in Chomsky 1994 and Bošković 1995a, violations of the Minimize Chain Links Principle result in nonconvergence,[34] the matrix verb in (51) in fact has to undergo head movement to ensure that object shift of the exceptionally Case-marked NP to the matrix SpecAgr$_O$P across the matrix subject, located in SpecVP, and matrix subject movement to SpecIP across the shifted exceptionally Case-marked NP, located in SpecAgr$_O$P, do not violate the Minimize Chain Links Principle, a violation that would result in nonconvergence. Thus, the derivation in (54), where the matrix verb remains in situ, crashes as a result of two Minimize Chain Links Principle violations: object shift across the subject trace and movement of the subject across the shifted object.

(54) *[$_{Agr_SP}$ John$_i$ [$_{Agr_OP}$ the students$_j$ [$_{VP}$ t$_i$ believes [$_{IP}$ t$_j$ to be t$_j$ crazy]]]]

Given Chomsky's notion of equidistance, these violations can be circumvented if the matrix verb undergoes overt head movement, which extends the relevant minimal domains (see (10) in chapter 3 for relevant definitions). As a result, since overt V-movement in (54) is necessary in order for the derivation to converge, it is allowed to take place in spite of Procrastinate. In fact, given that Procrastinate allows overt movement only insofar as it is needed to ensure convergence, the matrix verb will move to the *first* X^0 position (T^0, Laka's (1990) Σ^0, or even some lower head position in the split-I framework) above Agr_O; this V-movement ensures that movements to SpecAgrP take place without causing the derivation to crash, given equidistance.[35]

(55) $[_{AgrsP}$ John$_i$ $[_{XP}$ t$_i$ believed$_k$ $[_{Agr_OP}$ the students$_j$ t$_k$ $[_{VP}$ t$_i$ t$_k$ $[_{IP}$ t$_j$ to be t$_j$ crazy]]]]]]

4.4.1.1 Quantifier Float in Infinitival Complements   In this section I will show that movement to a Case-checking SpecAgrP may take place overtly in control infinitivals for exactly the same reason as in ECM infinitivals; this will provide evidence for the analysis of ECM constructions proposed above. Consider the following constructions:

(56) a. *The diplomats tried all to like Yeltsin
     b. ?The diplomats tried to all like Yeltsin

Sportiche (1988) argues that the ungrammaticality of (56a) and the grammaticality of (56b) indicate that PRO, which the quantifier *all* is associated with (adjoined to on Sportiche's analysis), must remain in its base-generated position within VP in the overt syntax. Martin (1992b) reaches the same conclusion on the basis of certain facts concerning expletive insertion in control infinitivals. As Martin observes, in the minimalist system this can be interpreted as indicating that the N feature of English infinitival I that assigns null Case is weak and therefore does not have to be eliminated before Spell-Out. In other words, the EPP holds at LF in control infinitivals. Procrastinate then precludes the possibility of overt movement of PRO to the embedded SpecIP in (56a), where the position of the quantifier indicates that PRO has undergone SS movement outside VP under Sportiche's (1988) analysis of quantifier float. Bearing this in mind, consider the following construction:[36]

(57) ?The protesters tried $[_{IP}$ all PRO$_i$ to be/get $[_{AgrP}$ t$_i$ $[_{VP}$ arrested t$_i$]]]

Although in both (56a) and (57) the quantifier *all* precedes *to*, (57) is better than (56a). The position of the quantifier in (57) indicates that, unlike in (56a), PRO is allowed to move overtly to its Case-checking SpecIP in (57) in spite of Procrastinate. The overt movement of the embedded subject in (57) can be accounted for in the same way as the overt movement of the embedded subject in (55), given Lasnik's (1995a) proposal that the complement of the passive *be* (the same should hold for *get*) is actually a small clause with a functional head, namely, the passive morpheme, which has a strong N feature that must be checked in the overt syntax. In other words, its Spec is subject to the EPP. (See Haegeman 1985 for a similar proposal. I assume that PassP is immediately dominated by an AgrP.) If PRO moves to $SpecAgr_{Pass}P$ to check the strong N feature and remains there at SS, the construction is ruled out by Greed. Since, like SpecIP in (55), $SpecAgr_{Pass}P$ in (57) is not a Case-checking position, NP-movement to this position cannot be motivated by satisfying a requirement of the moved element. The only way for the derivation in (57) to converge, then, is for PRO to undergo Case checking in the highest infinitival SpecIP at SS instead of LF. The Minimize Chain Links Principle will then force PRO to move through $SpecAgr_{Pass}P$, checking the strong N feature of Pass. The contrast between (56a) and (57) is thus accounted for. PRO in (57) is forced to move overtly to its Case-checking position in spite of Procrastinate because if the movement does not take place, the derivation crashes either because Greed is violated (if PRO moves only to the lowest SpecAgrP) or because a strong N feature enters PF, that is, because the EPP is violated (if PRO remains in its base-generated position within VP at SS). Procrastinate, which bans overt movement unless it is necessary for convergence, is thus satisfied. Overt Case checking of PRO in (57) thus takes place for exactly the same reason as overt Case checking of *the students* in (55) and confirms the analysis of (55) proposed above. The data in (56)–(57) are particularly interesting in that the position of floating quantifiers provides a footprint of the path taken by the derivation.[37]

Interestingly, quantifier float is allowed in (58a), in contrast to (58b).

(58) a. I believe the students all to have left
　　 b. *I believe the students all (sincerely)

Given Sportiche's (1988) analysis of quantifier float, on which floating quantifiers can be associated with traces, the possibility of quantifier float in (58a) can be accounted for straightforwardly on the overt object shift analysis. The quantifier can be left behind in the embedded subject position after *the students* undergoes overt object shift (i.e., moves to the matrix Spec-Agr_OP from the embedded subject position). The possibility of quantifier float in (58a) may in fact provide evidence for the overt object shift analysis. However, the argument is not conclusive, since it goes through only if *to* is located under the highest X^0 position within the infinitival clause, a rather plausible assumption; otherwise, the quantifier could be left behind in an intermediate Spec on the way to the highest Spec in the infinitival clause.[38]

To summarize the discussion so far, I have shown that there is sound theoretical motivation for overt object shift and V-movement in ECM constructions. I have argued that the movements in question take place to ensure convergence. I have also provided initial evidence for the overt object shift analysis. In the following sections I will present additional empirical evidence for overt object shift and V-movement in ECM constructions. I will also argue that in simple transitive constructions the accusative NP and the verb remain in situ at SS, a behavior that is consistent with the analysis developed so far.

4.4.1.2 Adverb Placement in ECM Constructions In principle, there is an easy way to determine whether exceptionally Case-marked subjects are located in the higher clause at SS, namely, by placing a higher-clause adverbial between an exceptionally Case-marked subject and the infinitival clause whose SpecIP this subject occupies prior to object shift. The test has been used by a number of authors arguing for overt object shift in English ECM constructions (see Authier 1991, Johnson 1991, Koizumi 1993, Ura 1993b, and also Postal 1974 under a somewhat different set of assumptions). Unfortunately, the relevant data are not as clear as one would want them to be. I believe that processing difficulties—namely, a garden path caused by the possibility of analyzing an exceptionally Case-marked NP followed by a matrix adverbial as being the direct object of the matrix verb—are a strong interfering factor. (In this respect, see Frazier's (1978) Minimal Attachment Strategy.) The possibility of analyzing the adverb as belonging to the lower clause is a potential source of another garden path. In spite of all of this, some of the relevant examples sound quite good, which is difficult to explain if exceptionally Case-marked subjects stay in SpecIP at SS.

(59) a. I've believed John for a long time now to be a liar (Kayne 1985)
      b. I can prove Bob easily to have outweighed Martha's goat
      c. I have found Bob recently to be a liar (Postal 1974)

The data in (59) thus favor the overt object shift analysis.

Interestingly, as observed by Kayne (1985), in contrast to exceptionally Case-marked lexical NPs, exceptionally Case-marked expletives cannot precede higher-clause adverbials.

(60) *I've believed there for a long time now to be no solution to this problem (Kayne 1985)

Under my analysis, in which object shift takes place overtly in ECM constructions so that the infinitival SpecIP can be filled without violating Greed, the ungrammaticality of (60), as well as the contrast between (59a–c) and (60), can readily be accounted for. It seems plausible that *there* in (60) is inserted directly into the infinitival SpecIP. Since lexical insertion is not subject to Greed for reasons discussed by Chomsky (1994), the EPP is then satisfied in the infinitival clause without violating Greed. As a result, since there is no reason to overtly Case-check the infinitival subject in (60), movement of *there* into the higher clause is straightforwardly ruled out by Procrastinate. However, this analysis does not extend to (61), where *there* is inserted into the most embedded SpecIP. In order for the higher SpecIP to be filled without violating Greed, *there* then must overtly undergo Case checking in the higher clause.[39]

(61) *I've believed there$_i$ for a long time now [$_{IP}$ t$_i$ to be likely [$_{IP}$ t$_i$ to be no solution to this problem]]

The contrast between (59a) and (61) can be accounted for under the analysis of ECM with *there* presented in section 3.2. As I argued in that section, being a nonbranching element and therefore analyzable as an X^0, *there* can be exceptionally Case-marked by incorporating into the higher V. Given the natural assumption that every feature must be checked in the most economical way (i.e., through the shortest movement possible), *there* would actually have to be checked through incorporation into the higher verb in ECM constructions, since the incorporation results in shorter movement than object shift to SpecAgr$_O$P. After the incorporation takes place, (61) has the structure shown in (62).

(62) I$_j$'ve for a long time now [$_{VP}$ t$_j$ believed + there$_i$ [$_{IP}$ t$_i$ to be likely t$_i$ to be no solution to this problem]]

Recall now that in (59a) the matrix verb must move overtly from its base-generated position, crossing the adverb, which I assume is adjoined to the matrix VP, in order for the embedded-clause subject to move to SpecAgr$_O$P and the higher subject to move to SpecIP without violating the Minimize Chain Links Principle. In (62), on the other hand, there is no need for the higher verb to move overtly, since the Minimize Chain Links Principle is not violated without the movement. In other words, the construction converges even without the movement. As a result, overt movement of the higher verb, necessary to derive (61), is blocked by Procrastinate.[40] The contrast between (59a) and (60)–(61) is thus accounted for under the overt object shift analysis. Under the covert object shift analysis, on the other hand, it remains a mystery.[41]

Under the analysis presented here, Kayne's (1985) observation that *there* cannot be exceptionally Case-marked in V+particle constructions can also be accounted for, given some rather natural assumptions. ((63a–d) are from Kayne 1985.)

(63) a. *They're trying to make there out to be no solution to this problem
    b. cf. They're trying to make John out to be a liar
    c. *They're trying to make out there to be no solution to this problem
    d. cf. (?)They're trying to make out John to be a liar

Assume that, as argued by Kayne (1985) and Den Dikken (1995), among others, the sequence following *make* in (63a–d) forms a small clause, whose subject position must be filled overtly to satisfy the EPP. (Den Dikken argues that the small clause is headed by the particle.) Assume, furthermore, that the particle of the small clause must incorporate into the verb. I assume that the incorporation can take place either overtly, as in (63d), or covertly, as in (63b), which can be accounted for if the feature driving the incorporation can be either strong or weak. (For particle incorporation analyses, see also Déchaine 1993, Den Dikken 1995, and Van Riemsdijk 1978, among others.) As discussed in section 2.4, Keyser and Roeper (1992) propose that all English verbs have an abstract clitic position and argue that particles occupy that position. (Under the analysis suggested here, they move into the abstract clitic position.) Suppose now that the abstract clitic position serves as the landing site for incorporation into English verbs. Given that *there* is inserted into the embedded infinitival SpecIP, or possibly the most embedded SpecVP (see note 40), *there* also has to incorporate into *make* in (63a–d) to satisfy the EPP (check the strong N feature) in the particle's small clause without violating Greed. Since the landing site of the incorporation is by hypothesis the abstract clitic position, both (63a) and (63c) are ruled out because they contain two elements competing for the same position.[42] Thus, in (63a) *out* is prevented from moving into the abstract clitic position since the position is already filled by *there*. (63c) can be accounted for in essentially the same way.[43] The fact that *there* cannot occur in V+particle ECM constructions thus receives a principled account under the *there* incorporation analysis.

In summary, I have argued in this section that certain facts concerning adverb placement in ECM constructions provide evidence for overt object shift in these constructions. I have also provided additional evidence for the *there*-incorporation analysis.

4.4.1.3   Coordination of ECM Infinitives   In Bošković 1997 I show that the grammaticality of constructions involving coordinated ECM infinitives also favors the overt object shift analysis of ECM constructions over the covert movement analysis.

(64) a. John believes Peter to be crazy and Mary to be smart
      b. John believed Peter to have played football and Mary to have played basketball

Under the standard minimalist analysis, the matrix verb is located in its base-generated position in the SS representation of (64a–b) and the embedded-clause subjects are located in the infinitival SpecIP. In LF they undergo movement to the matrix $SpecAgr_OP$, motivated by Case checking. Under this analysis (64a–b) can only be analyzed as involving infinitival IP-coordination. (For ease of exposition I omit BP, projected by the conjunction.)[44]

(65) a. John [$_{Agr_OP}$[$_{VP}$ believes [[$_{IP}$ Peter to be crazy] and [$_{IP}$ Mary to be smart]]]]
      b. John [$_{Agr_OP}$[$_{VP}$ believed [[$_{IP}$ Peter to have played football] and [$_{IP}$ Mary to have played basketball]]]]

To derive legitimate LF structures under the standard covert movement analysis, the infinitival subjects in (65a–b) must undergo LF Case licensing in $SpecAgr_OP$. Given the structures in (65), one of the infinitival subjects can be Case-checked by moving to the matrix $SpecAgr_OP$ in LF. However, the movement violates the Coordinate Structure Constraint, which bans movement out of one conjunct in a coordinate structure (see Ross 1967 and Williams 1978, among others). Furthermore, the subject of the other infinitival clause cannot be Case-checked at all, so that the construction is also ruled out via Case theory. The standard minimalist analysis of ECM constructions, in which all relevant action takes place covertly, thus fails to account for the grammaticality of (64a–b). (As shown in Bošković 1997, the same holds for Chomsky's (1995) covert V-movement + Move F analysis of ECM constructions.) On the other hand, the constructions receive a straightforward account under the overt object shift analysis, in which exceptionally Case-marked NPs move overtly to SpecAgr$_o$P, with the higher verb undergoing overt movement to the first head position above Agr$_o$P. Under this analysis (64) can be analyzed as involving Agr$_o$P coordination, with the matrix subject and the verb undergoing overt across-the-board extraction from the matrix Agr$_o$P. In (66a–b) and (66c–d) I give structures before and after the relevant movements take place, respectively.

(66) a. John [[$_{Agr_oP}$[$_{VP}$ believes [$_{IP}$ Peter to be crazy]]] and
       [$_{Agr_oP}$[$_{VP}$ believes [$_{IP}$ Mary to be smart]]]]

   b. John [[$_{Agr_oP}$[$_{VP}$ believes [$_{IP}$ Peter to have played football]]] and
       [$_{Agr_oP}$[$_{VP}$ believes [$_{IP}$ Mary to have played basketball]]]]

   c. John$_i$ believes$_j$ [[$_{Agr_oP}$ Peter$_k$ t$_j$ [$_{VP}$ t$_i$ t$_j$ [$_{IP}$ t$_k$ to be crazy]]] and
       [$_{Agr_oP}$ Mary$_l$ t$_j$ [$_{VP}$ t$_i$ t$_j$ [$_{IP}$ t$_l$ to be smart]]]]

   d. John$_i$ believes$_j$ [[$_{Agr_oP}$ Peter$_k$ t$_j$ [$_{VP}$ t$_i$ t$_j$ [$_{IP}$ t$_k$ to have played
       football]]] and [$_{Agr_oP}$ Mary$_l$ t$_j$ [$_{VP}$ t$_i$ t$_j$ [$_{IP}$ t$_l$ to have played
       basketball]]]]

It is easy to verify that the problems that arise under the standard minimalist LF movement account of (64a–b) do not arise under the overt movement analysis. The grammaticality of (64a–b) thus provides evidence that the overt object shift/V-movement analysis is superior to the LF object shift/V-movement analysis of ECM constructions.[45]

4.4.1.4 Pseudocleft Constructions The ungrammaticality of pseudocleft constructions such as (67a) provides another argument for overt object shift with ECM constructions.[46]

(67) a. *What John believed was [$_{IP}$ *Peter*$_i$ to [$_{VP}$ t$_i$ know French]]
   b. cf. What John believed was [$_{CP}$ that [$_{IP}$ Peter$_i$ [$_{VP}$ t$_i$ knew
       French]]]

Under the overt object shift analysis, the ungrammaticality of (67a) is readily accounted for. The construction is ruled out because the exceptionally Case-marked subject, given in italics, did not undergo overt object shift. More precisely, under my analysis the construction is ruled out by Greed. Recall that ECM subjects must undergo overt object shift so that the subject position of ECM infinitivals can be filled without violating Greed, movement through the infinitival SpecIP being licensed by the Minimize Chain Links Principle. In (67a) the movement stops in the infinitival SpecIP. Since the formation of the chain headed by the NP located in the infinitival subject position is not motivated by an inadequacy of the moved element, the construction is ruled out by Greed. On the other hand, it is not clear how the ungrammaticality of (67a) can be accounted for under the covert object shift analysis. Notice first that, as shown in section 2.2.4.1, pseudoclefting is not in principle ruled out with infinitival complements, as illustrated by *What the terrorists tried was to hijack an airplane.* The only candidate for ruling out (67a) under the covert object shift analysis seems to be Case theory. In particular, (67a) might be ruled out because the embedded-clause subject cannot be Case-checked. The initial plausibility of this analysis is immediately undermined by the grammaticality of (68).

(68) What John likes is *that cake you made last year*

The grammaticality of (68) indicates that the NP following *to be*, given in italics, can be Case-checked. Given that the relevant NP in (68) can be Case-checked, I see no reason why the NP following *to be* in (67a) cannot be Case-checked. It does not seem possible to find a principled way of Case checking the italicized NP in (68) that would not be available for Case checking the italicized NP in (67a). In Bošković, in press b, I argue that the post-*be* phrases in the constructions under consideration are located within the *wh*-clause; that is, they are complements of the verbs contained in the *wh*-clause, at LF. Given that the binding conditions apply at LF and that NPI licensing takes place at LF, evidence for this claim is provided by (69a–c).

(69) a.   What John likes is pictures of himself
      b.   *What he$_i$ likes is John's$_i$ picture
      c.   What John didn't buy was any pictures of Fred

Given (69), I argue in Bošković, in press b, that the focus constituent following *be* is located within the *wh*-clause at LF, more precisely, in the complement position of the *wh*-clause verb. (For discussion of exactly how this is achieved, see Bošković, in press b, and the discussion immediately below.) The italicized NPs in (67a) and (68) can then be Case-checked within the *wh*-clause in LF after undergoing LF object shift.

One may argue, however, that the Case of the embedded finite clause verb in the constructions under consideration is checked by *what*. However, in Bošković, in press b, I argue that pseudocleft *what* or, to be more precise, the chain headed by *what* is a surface anaphor in the sense of Hankamer and Sag (1976), replaced in LF by the post-*be* phrase. Since, as a result of the replacement, *what* is not present in the LF representation of pseudocleft constructions, it does not have to be Case-checked. That pseudocleft *what* does not have to be Case-checked is confirmed by the fact that it can appear in Caseless positions. Consider (70a–i).

(70) a. What they hoped was that Mary would arrive on time
     b. *They hoped Mary's arrival/something
     c. cf. They hoped that Mary would arrive on time
     d. What John remarked was that Mary would arrive on time
     e. *John remarked Mary's arrival/something
     f. cf. John remarked that Mary would arrive on time
     g. What they inquired was what the time was
     h. *They inquired the time
     i. cf. They inquired what the time was

Given Pesetsky's (1982b) approach to selection and Case marking, argued for in this book, (70b–c), (70e–f), and (70h–i) should be taken as indicating that *hope*, *remark*, and *inquire* are not Case checkers. The grammaticality of (70a,d,g) then provides evidence that pseudocleft *what* does not have to be Case-checked, which is expected if it is not present in the output of LF, as argued in Bošković, in press b.[47] Since *what* in (67a) and (68) does not have to be Case-checked, the accusative Case of the verb in the *wh*-clause is available for Case-checking the italicized NPs.

The contrast between (68) and constructions such as (71) confirms that the post-*be* NP is Case-checked by the verb of the pseudocleft clause, in which case (71) is ruled out via Case theory. It is not at all clear how (71) can be ruled out in light of the facts in (70a–c) if the post-*be* NP is Case-checked independently of the pseudocleft verb.

(71) *What they hoped was Mary's arrival

The following data are particularly enlightening in this respect.

(72) a. *I wondered the time
     b. I asked the time

(73) a. ?*What John wondered was the time
     b. What John asked was the time

As shown by Pesetsky (1982b), the contrast between (72a) and (72b) provides evidence that *ask* but not *wonder* is a Case-checking verb. As a result, (72a) is ruled out because *the time* cannot be Case-checked. No problems arise with respect to Case theory in (72b), where *the time* is Case-checked by *ask*. Notice now that the contrast in (73) parallels the contrast in (72). The contrast between (73a) and (73b) suggests that the post-*be* NP depends on the *wh*-clause verb for Case checking. If the NP could be Case-checked in the post-*be* position, we would expect both (73a) and (73b) to be acceptable. If, on the other hand, the *wh*-clause verb is the only source of Case checking for the post-*be* NP, the contrast between (73a) and (73b) can be accounted for in the same way as the contrast between (72a) and (72b). (For more evidence that the post-*be* NP is Case-checked within the *wh*-clause, see Bošković, in press b.)

Given that the italicized NPs in (67a) and (68) can be Case-checked as discussed above, I see no principled way of ruling out (67a) under the standard covert object shift analysis of ECM constructions. On the other hand, under my analysis, in which object shift must take place overtly in ECM constructions to avoid violating Greed, (67a) is straightforwardly ruled out by Greed.[48]

Recall now that under the analysis adopted here the direct object in simple transitive constructions remains in its base-generated position at SS. Unlike in *John believes the students to be crazy*, in *John believes Mary* there is no reason to violate Procrastinate by moving either the direct object NP or the verb overtly. Neither Greed nor the Minimize Chain Links Principle is violated if the verb and the NP following it remain in their base-generated positions. In other words, the construction converges even if the direct object NP and the verb remain in situ. Overt movement of the elements in question is, then, blocked by Procrastinate.

Returning to pseudocleft constructions, notice that, given that the direct object NP in (68) is Case-checked only after LF movement within the *wh*-clause, which in turn indicates that the Agr_O that Case-checks it is located within the *wh*-clause, the grammaticality of the construction provides evidence that, in contrast to accusative NPs in ECM constructions, accusative NPs in simple transitive constructions do not undergo overt object shift. The contrast between (67a) and (68) is thus straightforwardly accounted for under the current analysis, in which object shift takes place overtly in English in ECM but not simple transitive constructions. On the other hand, it is difficult to see how the contrast can be accounted for if object shift always takes place covertly, or if it always takes place overtly.

4.4.1.5 The Subject Condition Effect

As noted in the previous section, under the analysis presented here accusative NPs undergo overt object shift in ECM but not simple transitive constructions. Unlike in (74b), in (74a) both the accusative NP and the verb remain in situ at SS.

(74) a. I [$_{VP}$ saw a picture of John]

b. I believe$_i$ [$_{AgroP}$[a picture of John]$_j$ t$_i$ [$_{VP}$ t$_i$ [$_{IP}$ t$_j$ to be on sale]]]

Given this, the only empirical argument against overt object shift in English given in the literature does not raise a problem for the analysis developed here. As discussed in section 4.3.5, Branigan (1992) argues that if the direct object NP in (74a) were located in SpecAgr$_O$P at SS, we would expect extraction out of the object NP to exhibit the Subject Condition effect, since it would take place in essentially the same configuration as extraction out of subject NPs, located in SpecAgr$_S$P at SS. This expectation is not borne out. (Recall that, as noted in section 4.3.5, minimalist accounts of the Subject Condition effect given in the literature (Kitahara 1994a,b, Ormazabal, Uriagereka, and Uribe-Etxebarria 1994, Takahashi 1994, and Uriagereka 1996) would assign (75) the status of a Subject Condition violation if object shift takes place overtly, but not if it takes place covertly.)

(75) Who$_i$ did you see [a picture of t$_i$]

Branigan's problem does not arise with the overt object shift analysis of ECM constructions, since extraction out of exceptionally Case-marked NPs is rather degraded.

(76) ?*Who$_i$ did you believe [a picture of t$_i$] to be on sale

The facts concerning *wh*-extraction are thus compatible with the overt object shift analysis of ECM constructions. However, they provide evidence that object shift does not take place overtly in simple transitive constructions, which is consistent with the analysis presented here.[49]

4.4.1.6 Superiority and Object Shift   Certain facts concerning the Superiority Condition provide more evidence that simple transitive and ECM constructions differ with respect to when object shift of the accusative NP takes place.

The Superiority Condition requires that, given two *wh*-phrases in situ, the one that is structurally higher undergo *wh*-movement. It is responsible for the contrast in (77).

(77) a.   Whom did you persuade t to buy what

b. ?*What did you persuade whom to buy t

For our purposes the formulation of the Superiority Condition in (78) will suffice.

(78) A multiple question is well-formed in English only if at S-structure there is a *wh*-phrase that does not c-command the variable of the *wh*-phrase moved into the target Spec of CP. (Watanabe 1992, 274)

I leave it open here what the descriptive generalization in (78) could follow from. For relevant discussion, see Bošković, in press a, Cheng and Demirdache 1990, Kitahara 1993b, Lasnik and Saito 1992, Pesetsky 1982b, and Watanabe 1992, among others. (I show in Bošković, in press a, that (78) can be reformulated as a derivational constraint, thus eliminating the reference to SS. However, to avoid unnecessary complications, I will adopt (78) here. Note that Watanabe (1992) refers to "the trace of the *wh*-phrase" instead of "the variable of the *wh*-phrase" in (78).)

Now consider the following multiple questions:

(79) a. When did John buy what
     b. What did John buy when

It is standardly assumed that adverbs such as *when* in (79a–b) are generated in a higher position than direct objects (see also note 25). Following proposals in Bošković, in press a, I assume that *when* in (79a–b) is base-generated right-adjoined to VP. Given this, (79a–b) have the following structure prior to *wh*-movement:

(80) John$_i$ [$_{VP}$[$_{VP}$ t$_i$ [$_{V'}$ bought what]] when]

Given (80), it is not surprising that *when* can move to SpecCP without violating the Superiority Condition, since *when* is located in a structurally higher position than *what*. As a result, the variable bound by *when* is not c-commanded by *what*. What is surprising is that *what* can move to SpecCP without violating the Superiority Condition although *what* is c-commanded by *when* in its base-generated position. However, in Bošković, in press a, I show that crosslinguistically, accusative *wh*-phrases undergoing $\bar{\text{A}}$-movement to a position higher than SpecAgr$_O$P pass through SpecAgr$_O$P on their way to their final landing site regardless of the strength of the N feature of Agr$_O$.[50] I argue that movement to SpecAgr$_O$P provides an escape hatch from the Superiority Condition in constructions such as (79b). After movement to SpecAgr$_O$P, *what* is higher than *when* and therefore can undergo *wh*-movement without violating the Superiority Condition. As shown in (81), the variable bound by *what*, located in SpecAgr$_O$P, is not c-commanded by *when*.[51]

(81) What$_i$ did John$_j$ buy$_k$ [$_{AgroP}$ t$_i$ t$_k$ [$_{VP}$[$_{VP}$ t$_j$ [$_{V'}$ t$_k$ t$_i$]] when]]

Given that *what* passes through SpecAgr$_O$P on its way to SpecCP, (79b) in fact abstractly has the same structure as (82).

(82) Who$_i$ t$_i$ seems to whom t$_i$ to be t$_i$ crazy

In both (79b) and (82) the *wh*-phrase that moves to SpecCP is generated in a structurally lower position than the *wh*-phrase that remains in situ. It moves to an A-position that is higher than the *wh*-phrase in situ and then undergoes *wh*-movement from that position. Movement to an A-position thus provides an escape hatch from the Superiority Condition in both (79b) and (82).

If movement to SpecAgr$_O$P is responsible for the grammaticality of (79b), we would expect ECM subjects to pattern with direct objects in the relevant respect; that is, we would expect ECM subjects to be able to undergo *wh*-extraction in constructions containing an in situ *when* modifying the higher clause. As noted in Bošković, in press a, the prediction is borne out.[52]

(83) Whom$_i$ did John$_j$ prove$_k$ [$_{AgroP}$ t$_i$ t$_k$ [$_{VP}$[$_{VP}$ t$_j$ t$_k$ [$_{IP}$ t$_i$ to be t$_i$ guilty]] when]]

Given that *whom* starts with *wh*-movement from the matrix SpecAgr$_O$P, which is higher than the VP-adjoined position where *when* is generated, it is not surprising that (83) does not violate the Superiority Condition. What is surprising is that, in contrast to what we find in (79a), if we move the adverb instead of the accusative NP to SpecCP in (83), we get a degraded sentence.

(84) ?*When did John prove whom to be guilty

The question now is why, in contrast to *when* in constructions with accusative direct objects, *when* in constructions with accusative ECM subjects cannot undergo *wh*-movement. The relevant facts are straightforwardly explained if movement to SpecAgr$_O$P must take place overtly in ECM constructions, but not in simple transitive constructions. Given that *when* in the constructions under consideration is adjoined to the root VP, the exceptionally Case-marked subject will always be higher than *when* prior to *wh*-movement, so that it will have to move to SpecCP. The result is (83) but not (84). Since *who* c-commands the variable bound by *when*, (84) violates the Superiority Condition.

(85) ?*When$_i$ did John$_l$ prove$_j$ [$_{Agr_oP}$ whom$_k$ t$_j$ [$_{VP}$[$_{VP}$ t$_l$ t$_j$ [$_{IP}$ t$_k$ to be t$_k$ guilty]] t$_i$]]

As for simple transitive constructions, since the accusative NP in such constructions does not move overtly to SpecAgr$_O$P, it is lower than the adverb. As a result, nothing goes wrong with respect to the Superiority Condition if the adverb moves to SpecCP, the variable bound by the adverb being higher than the *wh*-phrase in situ.

(86) When$_i$ did John$_j$ [$_{VP}$[$_{VP}$ t$_j$ [$_{V'}$ buy what]] t$_i$]

The contrast between (79a) and (84) thus receives a principled explanation given that ECM subjects, but not direct objects, must undergo object shift overtly.

4.4.1.7 Object Shift in Auxiliary + Participle Constructions I have argued above that in ECM constructions such as *John believes Mary to be sick* the embedded-clause subject moves overtly to the matrix SpecAgr$_O$P, with the matrix verb moving to the first head position above Agr$_O$, the precise identity of which I left open. A question now arises concerning the possibility of overt object shift in auxiliary+participle constructions such as (87).

(87) John has believed Mary to be sick

Given the system developed in this chapter, we would clearly expect such constructions to involve overt object shift and V-movement. In chapter 5 I show that in Serbo-Croatian there is an X^0 position above Agr$_O$P to which participles obligatorily move in the overt syntax. In Bošković 1994c I show that even in simple transitive constructions such as (88), the direct object NP can be located in SpecAgr$_O$P at SS, the participle being located outside Agr$_O$P.

(88) Jovan je poljubio$_i$ [$_{Agr_oP}$ Mariju$_j$ t$_i$ [$_{VP}$ t$_i$ t$_j$]]
    Jovan is kissed   Maria
    'Jovan kissed Maria'

I will sum up here the arguments for the structure in (88) given in Bošković 1994c.

Following the work of Avery Andrews, Pesetsky (1989) observes that scope interactions of adverbs can be accounted for if structures involving stacked adverbs are articulated rather than flat. Consider (89a–b), taken from Pesetsky 1989.

(89) a.   John [[[knocked on the door] intentionally] twice]
           twice > intentionally
     b.   (?)John [intentionally [twice [knocked on the door]]]
           intentionally > twice

In (89a), where the adverbs are right-adjoined, *twice* must have scope over *intentionally*. The sentence can only refer to two instances of intentional knocking. On the other hand, in (89b), where the adverbs are left-adjoined, *intentionally* must have scope over *twice*. There was only one intention, which was to knock twice. The judgments concerning the relative scope of adverbs thus provide evidence about the direction of adverb adjunction. Given this, they can serve as a probe for determining whether elements base-generated within VP have moved outside the VP. Consider the following Serbo-Croatian constructions:

(90) a.   Jovan je namerno   dva put oborio Petra
           Jovan is deliberately twice   failed Peter
           namerno > dva put
     b.   Jovan je oborio Petra namerno   dva put
           Jovan is failed Peter deliberately twice
           'Jovan failed Peter deliberately twice'
           namerno > < dva put

In (90a) the first adverb must have scope over the second adverb. (90b), on the other hand, is ambiguous: both the reading on which *dva put* has scope over *namerno* and the reading on which *namerno* has scope over *dva put* are available. Whereas on the former reading the adverbs are right-adjoined, on the latter reading they must be left-adjoined. Given this, on the latter reading both the participle and the object must have moved outside the VP across the adverbs. Before we examine the landing site of the movements, note that the English counterpart of (90b) is unambiguous.

(91) John failed Peter deliberately twice
     twice > deliberately

The fact that, in contrast to (90b), (91) is unambiguous suggests that in English simple transitive constructions the main verb and the object NP following it remain within VP at SS. This conclusion is fully in accordance with the current analysis, in which object shift takes place overtly in English ECM constructions but not simple transitive constructions. The data discussed above can in fact be interpreted as providing further evidence that object shift does not take place overtly in English simple transitive constructions. (I show immediately below that Serbo-Croatian (90b), which differs from (91) with respect to scopal interaction of adverbs, involves overt object shift.)

Returning now to Serbo-Croatian (90b), where both the main verb and the direct object can be located outside the VP, there is evidence that the object is located in an A-position, which indicates that we are dealing here with overt object shift. It is well known that parasitic gaps are licensed only by elements in Ā-positions. (92a) shows that Serbo-Croatian allows parasitic gaps. Given this, the inability of the object in (92b) (which, as shown above, may have moved outside the VP) to license a parasitic gap suggests that the object is not located in an Ā-position.

(92) a. Jovan je Petra oborio a da nije ni   ispitao
         Jovan is Peter failed   without even examining
         'Jovan failed Peter without even examining him'
     b. *Jovan je oborio Petra a da nije ni ispitao

Quantifier float data confirm this conclusion. Sportiche (1988) proposes an analysis of quantifier float on which floating quantifiers are associated with traces of movement (see section 4.4.1.1). Déprez (1989) shows convincingly that A-movement, but not Ā-movement, can float quantifiers. Given this, the possibility of quantifier float on the relevant reading in (93) provides evidence that the object is located in an A-position.[53]

(93) Jovan je oborio studente sve
     Jovan is failed   students all
     'Jovan failed the students all'

The grammaticality of (93) together with the ungrammaticality of (92b) indicates that Serbo-Croatian direct objects following participles may undergo overt A-movement. As in Bošković (1994c), I assume that the landing site of this movement is SpecAgr$_O$P.

The data discussed above provide evidence that object shift is in principle possible in auxiliary + participle constructions, which must be the case if constructions such as *John has believed Mary to be sick* are to be derived in the current system. It is worth noting here that object shift in Serbo-Croatian constructions such as (88) does not raise any problems with respect to the Minimize Chain Links Principle, given Chomsky's (1993) notion of equidistance. Recall that Chomsky argues that in order for an object to move to SpecAgr$_O$P across a subject, base-generated in SpecVP, and in order for the subject to move to SpecAgr$_S$P across the shifted object, the verb must move to a head position above Agr_O. Notice now that, given the above discussion, Serbo-Croatian (88) can be derived as shown in (94).

(94) a. je $[_{XP}[_{Agr_OP}[_{VP}$ Jovan poljubio Mariju]]]

     b. je $[_{XP}[_{Agr_OP}$ poljubio$_i$ $[_{VP}$ Jovan t_i Mariju]]]

     c. je $[_{XP}[_{Agr_OP}$ Mariju$_j$ poljubio$_i$ $[_{VP}$ Jovan t_i t_j]]]

     d. je $[_{XP}$ poljubio$_i$ $[_{Agr_OP}$ Mariju$_j$ t_i $[_{VP}$ Jovan t_i t_j]]]

     e. Jovan$_k$ je $[_{XP}$ t_k poljubio$_i$ $[_{Agr_OP}$ Mariju$_j$ $[_{VP}$ t_k t_i t_j]]]

It is easy to verify that the Minimize Chain Links Principle is not violated in (94), given equidistance.[54]

Turning now to English, I assume that English patterns with Serbo-Croatian with respect to participle movement in auxiliary+participle constructions, which makes overt object shift possible, the only difference between English and Serbo-Croatian with respect to participle movement being that in English auxiliary+participle constructions the participle generally undergoes movement in LF rather than in the overt syntax. In (87), however, the participle moves overtly since the movement is necessary for the derivation to converge; that is, it is necessary in order to make it possible for overt object shift of *Mary* and movement of *John* to SpecAgr$_S$P to take place without violating the Minimize Chain Links Principle.[55]

To summarize the discussion in section 4.4.1, I have argued that ECM and simple transitive constructions in English differ with respect to the possibility of overt object shift and V-movement. I have argued that in ECM constructions the accusative NP undergoes overt object shift and the higher verb moves overtly to the first head position above Agr_O to ensure convergence or, to be more precise, to satisfy Greed, which I argued is superior to Enlightened Self-Interest, the EPP, and the Minimize Chain Links Principle. In simple transitive constructions, on the other hand, there is no need for the accusative NP and the verb to undergo overt movement. As a result, they remain in their base-generated positions in overt syntax in accordance with Procrastinate.

4.4.2 *Wh*-Movement out of *Wager*-Class and French Propositional Infinitivals

In this section I will briefly demonstrate that the interaction of Greed and the Minimize Chain Links Principle opens up a new way of analyzing certain contrasts between A- and Ā-movement with respect to Case theory, discussed in section 3.3. The discussion below will provide more evidence for Greed.

4.4.2.1 *Wh*-Extraction and *Wager*-Class Infinitivals Revisited   Consider again the following contrast:

(95) a. Who did you allege to know French
      b. *You alleged the students to know French

In section 3.3. I argued that contructions such as (95b) are ruled out through interaction of Case theory and the Mininimize Chain Links Principle. Essentially following Hale and Keyser (1993), I argued that at least two VP shells must be projected with agentive verbs, as a result of which the embedded-clause subject in (95b) cannot reach the matrix SpecAgr$_O$P, as it must do in order to be Case-checked, without violating the Minimize Chain Links Principle. As for (95a), in section 3.3 I adopted Ura's (1993b) analysis, in which the *wh*-phrase is Case-checked while undergoing *wh*-movement in the Agr$_O$P-adjoined position, thus escaping the Minimize Chain Links Principle violation. Ura (1993b) suggests that the option of undergoing Case checking in the Agr$_O$P-adjoined position is ruled out in (95b) via economy of derivation because a more economical derivation exists in which the embedded-clause subject moves to SpecAgr$_O$P. As discussed in section 3.3, since the embedded-clause subject in (95a) must move further than the higher-clause Agr$_O$P-adjoined position for independent reasons, the principles of economy of derivation do not rule out the option of undergoing Case checking in the Agr$_O$P-adjoined position for the embedded-clause subject in (95a).

There are several problems with this analysis, however. First, it crucially depends on extending the Case-checking configuration for NPs from Spec-head agreement to the position adjoined to the maximal projection of a head, a result that raises a conceptual question. Second, the relevant notion of economy of derivation needs to be sharpened considerably in order to rule out the option of undergoing Case checking in the Agr$_O$P-adjoined position for the NP in (95b), since under Ura's analysis SpecAgr$_O$P and the Agr$_O$P-adjoined position apparently belong to the same minimal domain, namely, that of Agr$_O$. (For another problem, see note 34.) In this section I will present an alternative analysis of the contrast between (95a) and (95b) under which the problems noted above do not arise.

Consider first (95a). Let us assume that *wh*-movement in (95a) proceeds successive cyclically, respecting the Minimize Chain Links Principle and leaving behind traces or, in the minimalist system, copies. If, as argued by Manzini (1994), the Minimize Chain Links Principle forces movement to proceed through the domain of each head, the *wh*-phrase in (95a) will have to either adjoin to the maximal projection of each head or move through its Spec. Given this, both the movement to the embedded-clause SpecIP and the movement to the matrix VP-adjoined position in (95a) are licensed by the Minimize Chain Links Principle.[56] The fact that they are not needed to overcome a formal inadequacy of the element undergoing movement is thus irrelevant.[57]

(96) Who$_i$ did you$_j$ [$_{Agro}$P[$_{VP}$ *who*$_i$ [$_{VP}$ t$_j$ V$_{ag}$ [$_{VP}$ t$_j$ allege [$_{IP}$ *who*$_i$ to *who*$_i$ know French]]]]]]

In LF the accusative Case of the chain headed by *who* must be checked. (Recall that although SpecAgr$_O$P is filled overtly in English in some cases, English Agr$_O$ does not have a strong N feature, so that object shift does not necessarily have to take place overtly in English.) As discussed above, Chomsky (1995) proposes that, in contrast to what happens overtly, in LF features rather than syntactic categories undergo movement, the proposal being a natural consequence of the minimalist assumption that movement is driven by feature checking. Given this assumption, all else being equal, we would expect the operation Move to apply to features and not to syntactic categories. Whereas overt movement still needs to affect whole categories under the natural assumption that lexical items with "scattered" features are unpronounceable, Move applies only to features in LF, where the considerations of PF interpretability are irrelevant. Chomsky argues that in LF formal features adjoin to the heads bearing matching features. Now consider (96) in light of the Move F theory. In order to satisfy the minimalist version of the Case Filter, the Case feature of the *wh*-chain in (96) must adjoin to Agr$_O$, which has the relevant feature of V adjoined to it. Mamoru Saito (personal communication) suggests that the Case feature of the copy in the VP-adjoined position adjoins to Agr$_O$ in LF, thus satisfying the Case Filter.[58]

Note that we need to allow for the possibility of movement out of copies independently of the construction under consideration. Thus, to account for the grammaticality of (97a) under the LF anaphor movement theory, LF movement of the anaphor—which, like every LF movement, must be an instance of feature movement—would have to take place out of a copy that is higher than the position in which the embedded-clause object appears in the LF representation of (97b). In fact, assuming that

John, the antecedent of the anaphor, is located within the matrix Agr_OP projection at LF, the anaphor feature movement would probably have to take place out of the copy adjoined to the matrix VP and land in the Agr_O-adjoined position, as in the case of (96).[59]

(97) a. ??[Which picture of himself$_i$]$_j$ did Mary [$_{Agr_OP}$ Agr_O [$_{VP}$*which picture of himself$_i$*]$_j$ [$_{VP}$ ask John$_i$ whether she should sell [*which picture of himself$_i$*]$_j$]]]

   b. cf. *Mary asked John$_i$ whether she should sell some picture of himself$_i$

Let us turn now to (95b), whose structure without movement of *the students* is given in (98).

(98) You$_i$ [$_{Agr_OP}$[$_{VP}$ t$_i$ V_{ag} [$_{VP}$ t$_i$ alleged [$_{IP}$ to [$_{VP}$ the students know French]]]]]]

There are three derivations to consider here. On one derivation *the students* moves to the embedded SpecIP in the overt syntax. In LF the Case feature of *the students* adjoins to the higher Agr_O, thus satisfying the Case Filter. This derivation is ruled out, however, because the overt movement of *the students* to the embedded SpecIP violates Greed. The Minimize Chain Links Principle, which can license intermediate movements even when they are not driven by an inadequacy of the element undergoing movement, is irrelevant here since SpecIP is the final landing site of the overt movement of *the students*. There are, however, two other derivations that also satisfy the Case Filter but do not violate Greed. On one derivation *the students* remains in its base-generated position at SS. Feature movement driven by Case checking then takes place in LF. This derivation is ruled out because it violates the EPP, since the embedded SpecIP remains empty at SS. In addition, the LF feature movement from the base-generated position of *the students* to the matrix Agr_O may violate locality conditions on movement.[60] The last derivation to consider, which satisfies the EPP as well as Greed, involves overt movement to SpecAgr$_O$P. Since in English object shift does not have to take place before LF, this derivation appears to violate Procrastinate, which requires that movement take place as late as possible. However, as discussed above with respect to "classical" ECM constructions, overt movement is allowed here in spite of Procrastinate since it is needed for convergence, namely, in order to fill the embedded-clause SpecIP, thus satisfying the EPP without violating Greed. However, as discussed in section 3.2, this derivation violates the

Minimize Chain Links Principle, since the element undergoing overt object shift skips two A-Specs. (I will continue to use the symbol "t" in the cases where no LF movement takes place out of copies.)

(99) *You$_j$ alleged$_k$ [$_{Agr_OP}$ the students$_i$ t$_k$ [$_{V_{ag}P}$ t$_j$ t$_k$ [$_{VP}$ t$_j$ t$_k$ [$_{IP}$ t$_i$ to [$_{VP}$ t$_i$ know French]]]]]

Given the above discussion, I conclude that the structure in (98) cannot yield a legitimate output. The contrast between (95a) and (95b) is thus accounted for. An advantage of the account presented in this section over Ura's (1993b) analysis is that we no longer need to assume that direct object elements can be Case-checked in the Agr$_O$P-adjoined position. We can also dispense with the technically problematic mechanism used by Ura (1993b) to allow Case checking in the Agr$_O$P-adjoined position for *wh*-phrases and to rule it out for non-*wh*-phrases. The option of undergoing Case checking in the Agr$_O$P-adjoined position can in fact be eliminated altogether.

There is, however, one more configuration concerning Case marking of *wh*-phrases extracted out of the complement of *wager*-class verbs that remains to be discussed. Suppose we embed a finite clause containing a BELIEVE-class verb taking an infinitival complement under *wager* and have the subject of the infinitival complement undergo *wh*-movement. This configuration is to be compared with the one in which no embedding under *wager* takes place.

(100) a. Who did John wager that Peter BELIEVED to know French
      b. Who did Peter BELIEVE to know French

Recall that since BELIEVE-class verbs are not Case checkers, configurations such as (100b) are ruled out because the *wh*-phrase cannot be Case-checked. Notice now that under the Move F analysis of the saving effect of *wh*-movement with respect to Case theory, we would expect that embedding (100b) under *wager* should lead to improvement. Assuming that *wh*-movement of *who* leaves a copy in the matrix VP-adjoined position, the *wh*-phrase could be Case-checked through feature movement of the copy to the matrix Agr$_O$, as discussed with respect to (96). Admittedly, the relevant judgments are delicate. However, my informants do detect the expected improvement if BELIEVE is replaced by a verb that I argued above belongs to this class, namely, *conjecture*. Thus, they found (101a) to be somewhat better than (101b). (I ignore irrelevant pieces of structure.)[61]

(101) a. ??Who$_i$ did John [$_{AgroP}$[$_{VP}$ t$_i$ [$_{VP}$ wager that Peter conjectured [$_{IP}$ t$_i$ to t$_i$ know French]]]]

b. *Who$_i$ did Peter [$_{AgroP}$[$_{VP}$ t$_i$ [$_{VP}$ conjecture [$_{IP}$ t$_i$ to t$_i$ know French]]]]

Note that the contrast in (101) provides evidence for Kayne's (1984) proposal that *wh*-phrases undergoing *wh*-movement from the subject position of an infinitival embedded under a *wager*-class verb are Case-marked through an intermediate trace. Under no theory of Case marking would *wager* be able to Case-mark the trace in SpecIP in (101a).[62]

On the basis of constructions such as (102a–b), however, Pesetsky (1992) argues that in order for an infinitival *wh*-subject to be Case-checked by *wager*, the infinitival in question must be the complement of *wager*.

(102) a. *Who$_i$ did you [$_{AgroP}$[$_{VP}$ t$_i$ [$_{VP}$ wager that it$_j$ seems [$_{IP}$ t$_i$/t$_j$ to t$_i$ know French]]]]

b. *Who$_i$ does it$_j$ seem [$_{IP}$ t$_i$/t$_j$ to t$_i$ know French]

I agree with Pesetsky that embedding (102b) under *wager* does not improve the construction. However, given the above discussion, we cannot attribute the ungrammaticality of (102a) to Case theory since *who* in (102a) can be Case-checked in the same way as *who* in (95a) and (101a), namely, through LF feature movement from the copy of *who* left in the matrix VP-adjoined position. This is desirable, since the construction is in fact ruled out independently of Case theory. Recall that expletive *it* must be associated with a clause specified as [+tense]. This requirement is not satisfied in (102a) and the construction is ruled out because "expletive replacement" fails. (102a) is thus ruled out for the same reason as *It is someone in the garden* and *It$_i$ was believed t$_i$ to be someone in the garden*, discussed in section 4.3.4.[63]

4.4.2.2 *Wh*-Movement and French Propositional Infinitivals Returning now to the contrast between (95a) and (95b), notice that the Move F analysis of that contrast can readily be extended to the following one from French:

(103) a. Qui croyais-tu   [$_{CP}$ aimer   Anne]
       Who believed you   to-love Anne
       'Who did you believe to love Anne'

b. *Tu croyais [$_{CP}$ Pierre aimer   Anne]
       you believed   Pierre to-love Anne

The *wh*-phrase in (103a) moves successive cyclically to the matrix SpecCP, leaving behind intermediate copies, including the ones shown in (104). The intermediate movements are licensed by the Minimize Chain Links Principle.

(104) Qui$_i$ croyais$_j$-tu [$_{AgroP}$ t$_j$ [$_{VP}$ *qui*$_i$ [$_{VP}$ t$_j$ [$_{CP}$ *qui*$_i$ [$_{IP}$ *qui*$_i$ [$_{VP}$ *qui*$_i$ aimer Anne]]]]]]

In LF, feature movement motivated by Case checking takes place from a copy of *qui* and a legitimate LF output results.

   (103b) can be ruled out similarly to (95b). If the embedded-clause subject remains in its base-generated position within the embedded VP, the construction is ruled out by the EPP because the embedded SpecIP remains empty at SS. If, on the other hand, the embedded subject moves to the embedded SpecIP and remains there at SS, the construction is ruled out by Greed. Finally, if the embedded subject undergoes overt object shift by moving to the matrix SpecAgro$_O$P in order to ensure that the embedded SpecIP is filled without violating Greed, the construction is ruled out by the ban on A-movement crossing CP boundaries, derivable from the economy principles (see section 2.2.1), on a par with constructions of the type in (105), discussed in section 3.4. (See section 3.4 for evidence that the infinitival complement of *croire* is a CP.)

(105) *Pierre$_i$ était cru   [$_{CP}$ t$_i$ aimer   Anne]
       Pierre was believed   to-love Anne

   Under the current analysis the contrast between (106a) and (106b) with respect to participle agreement can also be accounted for. As observed by Ruwet (1982), Kayne (1989), and Branigan (1991, 1992), participle agreement with *wh*-movement is possible with subjects of small clauses, but not with subjects of infinitivals.

(106) a. *la fille qu'il   a   dite   savoir   le français
         the girl that he has said-FEM-SING to-know the French
     b. la fille qu'il   a   dite   malade
         the girl that he has said-FEM-SING sick

Recall that the reason why the embedded subject in (106a) cannot move through the matrix SpecAgro$_O$P on its way to SpecCP is that this would involve A-movement crossing a CP boundary. The embedded-clause subject in (106a) then can only be checked through LF feature movement out of the copy in the matrix VP-adjoined position, that is, through LF adjunction to Agro$_O$. Turning now to (106b), notice that the complement of *croire* in (106b) is a small clause. It is often assumed that small clauses lack any functional projections (see Stowell 1981, 1983). Several authors have argued that small clauses do contain some kind of I; that is, they are IPs (see note 49). However, there seems to be general consensus that small clauses do not contain a CP projection. Given this, nothing prevents the embedded-clause subject from moving through the matrix SpecAgr$_O$P on its way to SpecCP in (106b). (We are dealing here with *wh*-movement via SpecAgr$_O$P, discussed in section 4.4.1.6.) Unlike in (106a), in (106b) such movement does not violate the ban on A-movement out of CPs. Given that the operator can move through SpecAgr$_O$P in (106b) but not in (106a), we can account for the contrast between (106a) and (106b) with respect to participle agreement simply by assuming that participle agreement is a reflex of Spec-head agreement with Agr$_O$. Participle agreement is not possible when an NP undergoes Case checking by Agr$_O$ through LF feature adjunction. This is in line with Chomsky's (1995) observation that morphological agreement is more likely to be a reflex of the Spec-head relation than the feature-head relation. Since the operator in (106b) can be Case-checked under Spec-head agreement with Agr$_O$, it can trigger participle agreement. Given that the operator in (106a) must be Case-checked through LF feature adjunction, participle agreement is not possible in (106a). We can then have a uniform account of the impossibility of participle agreement in (106a) and simple transitive constructions such as (107). Since French is not an overt object shift language, like the embedded-clause subject in (106a), the direct object NP in (107) is Case-checked through LF feature adjunction to Agr$_O$, which does not license participle agreement.

(107) *Il a   dite   une histoire
      he has said-FEM-SING a   story

Now consider (108).

(108) l'histoire qu'il   a   dite
      the story that he has said-FEM-SING

Recall that, as argued in Bošković, in press a, direct object elements undergoing overt Ā-movement to a position higher than Agr$_O$ must pass through SpecAgr$_O$P overtly (if possible) even in languages that otherwise do not have overt object shift (a similar conclusion is reached in Branigan 1992). The movement is licensed by the economy principles, possibly the Minimize Chain Links Principle (see note 50). Given this, the possibility of participle agreement in (108) can readily be accounted for.

The impossibility of participle agreement in (109), a problem for Kayne's (1989) analysis of participle agreement, which allows adjunction to Agr_OP to trigger participle agreement, also receives a straightforward account.

(109) *la langue   que Jean a   dite   que la fille sait
      the language that Jean has said-FEM-SING that the girl knows

The Case-checking $SpecAgr_OP$ for the direct object NP in (109) is located in the most embedded clause. The NP is not allowed to move through the higher $SpecAgr_OP$ since this move would at least violate locality restrictions on A-movement, and possibly several other constraints. The NP can adjoin to the matrix Agr_OP. However, under the current analysis this does not suffice to license participle agreement. It is well known, however, that participle agreement with *wh*-movement in (108) is not obligatory.

(110) l'histoire qu'il   a   dit
      the story that he has said

This can be accounted for by assuming either that Spec-head agreement with Agr_O is only optionally phonologically realized as participle agreement or that undergoing Spec-head agreement in the Spec-head configuration is optional, in which case the direct object could undergo Spec-head agreement with Agr_O in (108) in LF.[64] If we take the latter option, we need to assume that only overt Spec-head agreement with Agr_O results in participle agreement. This analysis implies that Spec-head agreement is an operation rather than merely a configuration, so that it does not necessarily take place once the relevant configuration is established. For relevant discussion, see section 4.5.

Let us return now to the saving effect of Ā-movement on French *croire*-class infinitivals with lexical subjects. Postal (1993) argues that heavy NP shift from the infinitival subject position can rescue English *wager*-class infinitivals, but not French propositional infinitivals.

(111) a. You alleged [t_i to be crazy] [the man you met last year in New Orleans]$_i$
      b. *Tu   croyais [t_i aimer Anne] [l'homme que tu   as
          You believed   to-love Anne the man that you have
          rencontré l'année dernière à la Nouvelle Orléans]$_i$
          met   the year last   in the New Orleans
          'You believed to love Anne the man that you met last year in New Orleans'

However, Postal (1974) observes that heavy NP shift is also disallowed from the subject position of English *want*-class infinitivals, and he argues that constructions such as (112a) exhibit a garden path effect. Since *want* allows PRO to occur in the subject position of its infinitival complement, (112a) is parsed as involving a control structure (i.e., as containing PRO controlled by the matrix subject in the subject position of the infinitival). Strong evidence for Postal's analysis is provided by the fact that when the possibility of a garden path is removed, as in Postal's (112b), where the infinitival subject clearly cannot corefer with the matrix subject, heavy NP shift is allowed from the subject position of *want*-class infinitivals.

(112) a. *I want [to leave now] all of those men who are tracking mud on my carpet
   b. I only want [to become doctors] those students who have a genuine interest in alleviating human suffering

Note now that (111b) can be analyzed as involving the same kind of garden path effect as (112a). In fact, as with *want*-class infinitivals, when the possibility of a garden path is removed, a fully acceptable sentence results.

(113) Pierre croit   être   doctoresses   les femmes qu'il   a
      Pierre believes to-be doctors (FEM) the women that he has
      rencontrées l'année dernière à la   Nouvelle Orléans
      met   the year last   in the New Orleans
      'Pierre believes to be doctors the women he met last year in New Orleans'

In light of (113), I conclude that French does not differ from English with respect to the saving effect of heavy NP shift on movement from the subject position of relevant infinitivals. The saving effect can readily be accounted for under the feature movement analysis. The NPs undergoing heavy NP shift in (111a) and (113) can be Case-checked through LF feature movement to the matrix Agr_O+V complex. (Depending on the landing site of heavy NP shift, LF feature movement would take place either out of a copy or out of the shifted NP itself.)

In summary, I have shown in this section that adopting Greed and the Move F theory sheds a new light on the contrast between A- and Ā-movement from the subject position of *wager*-class and French propositional infinitivals with respect to Case theory. Greed and the Move F theory enable us to account for the contrast in question without appealing to Case checking in the Agr_OP-adjoined position as an option available only for *wh*-phrases. A number of properties of French participle agreement have also been accounted for.

4.5   Constraints Affecting A-Movement and A-Positions

In the previous sections I have examined the operation of three constraints that have important ramifications for A-positions and movement into A-positions: Greed; the requirement that the strong N feature of I be checked, which I will refer to as the "EPP"; and the requirement that Case features of traditional Case assigners be checked, for which I will adopt Howard Lasnik's term "Inverse Case Filter." The data I have examined so far indicate that the constraints in question are all needed to account for the full range of facts pertaining to A-positions and movement to A-positions. No further reduction seems to be possible here. I will briefly demonstrate this using the data discussed in the previous sections. I will then show that the application of the constraints in question results in considerable redundancy. Following the standard research strategy that constraints should not overlap in their effects, I will attempt to eliminate the redundancy. Some amount of redundancy will remain, and I will suggest that it is necessary on empirical grounds.

4.5.1   Greed, the EPP, and the Inverse Case Filter
In this section I will show that Greed, the EPP, and the Inverse Case Filter are all needed to account for syntactic properties of A-movement and A-positions. To illustrate this, I will use only the constructions whose ungrammaticality can be accounted for only if one of the constraints in question is invoked. For the time being I will ignore the constructions that are redundantly ruled out by the constraints in question. Since most of the data given below have already been discussed at length in the previous sections, in most cases I will simply give the relevant constructions and refer the reader to the sections where the constructions were originally discussed. I will first discuss Greed.

In section 4.3.2 I argued that Greed is needed to rule out A-movement from Case-checking to non-Case-checking positions, illustrated in (114).

(114) a. *John has BELIEVED/conjectured $Peter_i$ to seem t_i is ill
      b. *the belief $Peter_i$ to seem t_i is ill
      c. *[$Peter_i$ to seem t_i is ill]$_j$ is widely believed t_j

In addition, in section 4.4.1.1 I argued that Greed is crucially involved in the account of the following data concerning the position of the floating quantifier:

(115) a. *The diplomats tried all to like Yeltsin
      b. ?The protesters tried all to be/get arrested

Finally, in section 4.4.2 I presented an analysis of (116) on which the derivation in question cannot be ruled out unless Greed is adopted. (Recall that overt object shift, which I assume takes place in classical ECM constructions, is ruled out in (116) by the Minimize Chain Links Principle.)

(116) a. SS *John wagered [$_{IP}$ the students$_i$ to [$_{VP}$ t$_i$ know French]]
      b. LF *John$_j$ FF(the students)$_i$+FF(wager)$_k$+Agr$_O$ [$_{V_{ag}P}$ t$_j$ t$_k$
             [$_{VP}$ t$_j$ t$_k$ [$_{IP}$ t$_i$ to [$_{VP}$ t$_i$ know French]]]]

Let us now turn to the EPP. Consider again (114a–c). As discussed above, movement of *Peter* violates Greed; but why are the sentences still ungrammatical if *Peter* remains in situ?

(117) a. *John has BELIEVED/conjectured [$_{IP}$ to seem Peter is ill]
      b. *the belief [$_{IP}$ to seem Peter is ill]
      c. *[$_{IP}$ To seem Peter is ill]$_i$ is widely believed t$_i$

(117a–c) can be straightforwardly ruled out by appealing to the EPP. As far as I can see, no other condition of the grammar has the same effect.

Another construction that is ruled out only by the EPP is (118), on the derivation on which the matrix SpecIP is empty at SS and the direct object NP *Mary* undergoes LF feature movement to the matrix I to check its own Case feature and I's. (This is so only if the LF feature movement of *Mary* is not ruled out by locality constraints on movement.)

(118) *Was told Mary that Peter would leave

As discussed in section 4.4.1.1, the EPP and Greed together are also needed to account for the data in (115). (Recall that these data cannot be accounted for by appealing to either Greed or the EPP alone.)

Let us turn now to the Inverse Case Filter. In section 4.4.2 I presented an analysis on which phrases undergoing *wh*-movement from a Caseless position can be Case-checked through LF feature movement as long as there is a Case-checking position between the final landing site of the *wh*-phrase and the position from which its *wh*-movement originates. Given this, the Inverse Case Filter is needed to account for (119a). Since I of the infinitival complement in (119a), specified as [+tense], bears a null Case feature, (119a) is ruled out because the Case feature of the infinitival I remains unchecked. Given that the [−tense] infinitival I in (119b) does not have a null Case feature, the problem does not arise in (119b).

(119) a. *Who$_i$ did you [$_{AgroP}$ Agr$_O$ [$_{VP}$ *who$_i$* [$_{VP}$ demand [$_{IP}$ *who$_i$* to *who$_i$*
         kiss Mary]]]]

     b. Who$_i$ did you [$_{AgroP}$ Agr$_O$ [$_{VP}$ *who$_i$* [$_{VP}$ wager [$_{IP}$ *who$_i$* to have
         who$_i$ kissed Mary]]]]]

Another possible motivation for the Inverse Case Filter concerns movement from a nonmatching to a matching Case-checking position:

(120) *He$_i$ strikes t$_i$ that Mary is clever

He in (120) is located in a Case-checking position prior to movement to the matrix SpecIP. However, this Case-checking position does not match the Case *he* is marked for. Since the particular Case *he* is marked for cannot be checked prior to movement to SpecIP, its movement to SpecIP is in a sense motivated by Case checking and thus should be in accordance with Greed. Although it is possible to rule out (120) by adopting some additional assumptions concerning how Greed operates, it seems preferable to adopt Greed in its simplest form and rule out (120) by appealing to the Inverse Case Filter, in particular, because the Case feature of *strike* remains unchecked. (However, see Chomsky 1995 for another way of ruling out (120).)

   In light of these data, I conclude that Greed, the EPP, and the Inverse Case Filter are all independently motivated and cannot be dispensed with. Given that all three constraints are needed in the grammar, a conceptual problem arises, namely, that the constraints in question overlap in their effects to a considerable extent. Consider (121)–(122).

(121) a. *John$_i$ is likely [$_{IP}$ t$_i$ [$_{VP}$ t$_i$ sleeps often]]
     b. *Peter believes John$_i$ to seem [$_{IP}$ t$_i$ [$_{VP}$ t$_i$ sleeps often]]

(122) a. *Is likely [$_{IP}$ John$_i$ [$_{VP}$ t$_i$ sleeps often]]
     b. *Peter believes [$_{IP}$ to seem [$_{IP}$ John$_i$ [$_{VP}$ t$_i$ sleeps often]]]

(121a–b) are ruled out by both Greed and the Inverse Case Filter. Movement of *John* to its final SS position in both (121a) and (121b) is an instance of A-movement from a Case-checking position and thus violates Greed. In addition, both constructions violate the Inverse Case Filter. (121a) has one NP (*John*) and two Case checkers (the matrix I and the embedded I), and (121b) has two NPs (*Peter* and *John*) and three Case checkers (the matrix I, the lower embedded-clause I, and *believe*). As a result, in both (121a) and (121b) the Case feature of one of the Case checkers must remain unchecked.

(122a) and (122b) are ruled out by both the Inverse Case Filter and the EPP. (We are considering here the derivation in which the SpecIP of the matrix clause in (122a) and the embedded clause in (122b) is completely empty.) The Inverse Case Filter is violated in (122a–b) for the same reason it is violated in (121a–b). The EPP is violated because the matrix SpecIP in (122a) and the higher embedded SpecIP in (122b) remain empty at SS. Greed, the EPP, and the Inverse Case Filter thus overlap in their effects. The locus of the overlap is the Inverse Case Filter. Whereas Greed and the EPP do not appear to be redundant with respect to each other, the Inverse Case Filter overlaps in its effects with both Greed and the EPP. Elimination of redundancies has often driven research in generative grammar and yielded desirable results. Pursuing the trend, I will consider whether the redundancy between the Inverse Case Filter and Greed/the EPP can be eliminated. I will first examine the overlap between Greed and the Inverse Case Filter. (121a), repeated as (123), illustrates the overlap.

(123) *John$_i$ is likely [$_{IP}$ t$_i$ [$_{VP}$ t$_i$ sleeps often]]

(123) is actually merely an illustration of a whole class of examples that is redundantly ruled out by both Greed and the Inverse Case Filter. All constructions involving movement from a Case-checking to a Case-checking position violate both Greed and the Inverse Case Filter. Since, as argued above, both Greed and the Inverse Case Filter are needed for independent reasons, the redundancy cannot be eliminated by eliminating one of the constraints altogether. There is, however, a way of eliminating the redundancy between Greed and the Inverse Case Filter from the system while still keeping both constraints. Suppose that Case checking is actually an operation, rather than merely a configuration. In other words, it is "something you do," not "something you are."[65] Being an operation— given the standard assumption that all operations (i.e., instances of Affect α) are in principle optional—Case checking would not necessarily have to take place once the relevant configuration is established. In other words, the presence of an NP in a Case-checking configuration would not necessarily trigger Case checking. In more traditional terms, this amounts to claiming that Case assignment is in principle optional. Note that the operational view of Case checking is conceptually superior to the configurational view. The configurational view encodes obligatoriness of Case

checking. In traditional terms, under this view Case assignment is obligatory, which almost completely overlaps with both the Case Filter and the Inverse Case Filter (see Lasnik 1985 for some relevant discussion). Now consider (123) under the operational view of Case checking. Under this view *John* in (123) does not have to undergo Case checking when it is located in the embedded SpecIP. (It can still satisfy the EPP.) However, if *John* does not undergo Case checking in the embedded SpecIP, its movement to the higher SpecIP can still be driven by Case checking, in accordance with Greed. (123) is then not excluded by Greed. In fact, Greed is satisfied in (123) in the same way it is satisfied in *John$_i$ is likely* [$_{IP}$ t_i to [$_{VP}$ t_i *sleep often*]]. However, on the derivation in question (123) is still ruled out by the Inverse Case Filter because the nominative Case feature of the embedded I remains unchecked if *John* is Case-checked in the matrix SpecIP. Under this analysis movement from Case-checking to Case-checking positions is in fact never ruled out by Greed. This is desirable, since such movement inevitably violates the Inverse Case Filter.[66] However, it is easy to verify that Greed still rules out A-movement from Case-checking to non-Case-checking positions (see (114a–c)), which cannot be ruled out by the Inverse Case Filter. The relevance of Greed for (115a–b) and (116) also remains unaffected. The redundancy between Greed and the Inverse Case Filter is thus eliminated without any undesirable side effects. All that was needed to eliminate the redundancy was to adopt the operational view of Case checking, which, as noted above, is conceptually preferable to the configurational view.

Let us now turn to the overlap between the Inverse Case Filter and the EPP, illustrated by (122a), repeated here as (124).

(124) *Is likely [$_{IP}$ John$_i$ [$_{VP}$ t_i sleeps often]]

(124) is ruled out by the EPP because the matrix SpecIP remains empty at SS. In addition, the construction violates the Inverse Case Filter because the nominative Case of the higher I remains unchecked if *John* is Case-checked in the embedded SpecIP.[67] As always, the redundancy displayed by (124) raises a potential problem. In dealing with the problem, I will take a different route from the one I took above with respect to the overlap between the Inverse Case Filter and Greed. Instead of trying to eliminate the redundancy, I will try to justify it on empirical grounds. Specifically, I will suggest that it may be empirically necessary; that is, it is inherent to the system.

Although there is a general trend in generative grammar to eliminate redundancy from the grammar, in some cases redundancy is embraced, in particular, when dealing with degrees of ungrammaticality. In the current framework degrees of ungrammaticality are generally dealt with in terms of either different types or number of constraints that are violated in a particular derivation. An excellent example of one such approach is provided by Epstein (1990), who accounts for different degrees of ungrammaticality of several constructions in terms of the number of constraints they violate. Epstein characterizes the relevant notion of degree of ungrammaticality as follows (p. 318):

(125) *Grammaticality metric*
If a sentence S has a derivation D incurring violations $V_i–V_n$ at Levels L1–L4, and another sentence S′ ... has a derivation D′ incurring exactly the same violations at exactly the same levels, plus at least one other additional violation, then S′ has a greater degree of ungrammaticality than does S (where "has a derivation" should be read as "has a best possible derivation").

Bearing (125) in mind, consider the following constructions:

(126) a. **Is likely John sleeps often
     b. *John$_i$ is likely t$_i$ sleeps often

As discussed above, (126a) violates the Inverse Case Filter and the EPP. (126b), on the other hand, violates only the Inverse Case Filter. As indicated by the judgments given in (126), the speakers I consulted find (126a) to be worse than (126b). The difference in the degree of ungrammaticality between (126a) and (126b) can readily be accounted for if (126b) violates the Inverse Case Filter and (126a) violates the EPP as well as the Inverse Case Filter. Given this and (125), (126a) is in fact predicted to be worse than (126b) since it incurs the same violation as (126b) does plus one other. The overlap between the Inverse Case Filter and the EPP, illustrated by (126a), may therefore be justified—an instance of nonvacuous redundancy. The argument given here is not complete, however. To complete it, we need another minimal pair involving the same predicates that consists of one construction that violates only the EPP and one construction that violates the EPP as well as the Inverse Case Filter. I have not been able to construct such examples. The conclusion reached here thus remains tentative.

To summarize, I have shown that the redundancy between the Inverse Case Filter and Greed can be eliminated if Case checking is considered to be an operation rather than merely a configuration. As for the redundancy between the Inverse Case Filter and the EPP, I have suggested that it is empirically necessary, that is, an instance of nonvacuous redundancy.

4.5.2 The Inverse Case Filter and the Case Filter

Before concluding this chapter, I will briefly examine another example of redundancy that also involves the Inverse Case Filter. The redundancy concerns the relation between the Inverse Case Filter and the requirement that all NPs be Case-checked, which I will refer to as the "Case Filter," following the traditional terminology. As shown above, the Inverse Case Filter is motivated independently of all other constraints relevant to A-positions. The same clearly holds for the traditional Case Filter. In the system without c-selection, which I have argued for, the Case Filter is needed to account for the ungrammaticality of (127a–d).

(127) a. *John remarked it
      b. *that Peter likes Mary, which John remarked
      c. *John inquired the time
      d. *John's/the proof something

Given that, as argued above, the facts concerning A-movement favor Greed over Enlightened Self-Interest, the requirement that Case features of NPs be checked is also needed to provide an appropriate driving force for A-movement, which makes its effects felt throughout the system. Apparently both the Inverse Case Filter and the Case Filter are needed. However, as the ungrammaticality of (128) shows, requiring that both NPs (i.e., traditional Case assignees) and traditional Case assigners be Case-checked is superfluous.

(128) *John destroyed he

(128) is ruled out by both the Inverse Case Filter and the Case Filter because the Case features of both the verb and the direct object NP remain unchecked. This situation arises quite generally in constructions involving the same number of traditional Case assigners and Case assignees and a Case mismatch. It is not clear whether we are dealing here with a true vacuous redundancy or with a nonvacuous redundancy of the kind discussed above. Recall that in some cases violating an additional constraint increases ungrammaticality. We clearly do not want to eliminate this kind of nonvacuous redundancy from the system since it seems to be real. Unfortunately, it is not possible to determine conclusively

whether (128) involves nonvacuous redundancy or not. To do that, we need a minimal pair involving a construction that violates only one of the constraints under consideration and another construction that violates both of them without any additional violations. The closest minimal-pair partner for (128) that violates the Case Filter but not the Inverse Case Filter seems to be *It was destroyed he. However, this construction involves another violation in addition to the Case Filter, since the LF affix it cannot be attached to an appropriate element.[68] Another candidate, *John remarked it, which violates only the Case Filter, does not seem to be similar enough to (128) to draw any definite conclusions. The same problem may arise when comparing (128) with nominals such as *John's destruction he. These nominals may also involve additional violations (see Grimshaw 1990). It is thus not clear whether the redundancy between the Inverse Case Filter and the Case Filter, illustrated by (128), is an instance of a true vacuous redundancy or not. However, the very fact that the issue under consideration cannot be settled conclusively should raise a red flag.

Note that there is a sense in which even constructions such as (129) involve an overlap between the Case Filter and the Inverse Case Filter.

(129) John [$_{VP}$ kissed Mary]

Suppose that Mary does not undergo LF feature movement to the matrix Agr + V complex. The construction is then ruled out by the Case Filter because the Case feature of Mary remains unchecked. However, in addition to the Case Filter, (129) violates the Inverse Case Filter, because the Case feature of the verb remains unchecked. Similar examples can easily be constructed with other traditional Case assigners. What we need to do now is determine whether the way of deriving (129) discussed here involves vacuous or nonvacuous redundancy. To do this, we need to determine how bad (129) is on the derivation discussed above. However, this is impossible to determine. The problem is that there is a good derivation for (129) in which Mary undergoes LF Case checking. Since our judgments reflect only the best possible derivations, the good derivation covers up the effects of the derivation in which Mary is not Case-checked. (It is a fact that every good sentence has an infinite number of ungrammatical derivations that are not reflected by our judgments.)[69] I conclude, therefore, that it is not possible to determine conclusively whether the redundancy between the Case Filter and the Inverse Case Filter discussed with respect to (128) and (129) is vacuous or nonvacuous—a warning sign that something might have been missed.

It should be emphasized here that the Inverse Case Filter has been crucially involved in all the redundancies discussed above. This could be taken as a sign that the Inverse Case Filter should be dispensed with, which would be the most straightforward way of eliminating the redundancies in question. However, dispensing with the filter would require a new account of the grammaticality of (119b) that would not make it necessary to appeal to the filter to account for the ungrammaticality of (119a).

4.6 Conclusion

In this chapter I have examined the relevance of infinitival complementation for existential constructions. I have argued that *be* is a partitive Case assigner and that Greed holds. In order to reconcile these conclusions with the expletive replacement/adjunction analysis, I have adopted Chomsky's and Lasnik's proposal that *there* is an LF affix and I have proposed that to overcome its morphological inadequacy, *there* undergoes affix hopping in LF. As a result of affix hopping, *there* and its associate end up adjoined at LF without violating Greed. I have argued that on empirical grounds the affix-hopping analysis is superior to both Chomsky's (1993) and Lasnik's (1995a) category-raising analyses and Chomsky's (1995) and Lasnik's (1995b) feature movement analyses of existential constructions. In addition to handling a number of properties of existential constructions, some of which have not previously been accounted for, the analysis presented in this chapter has important theoretical consequences for the economy principles and the question of what drives the operation Move α. Thus, the analysis provides support for Chomsky's (1993) claim that α can move only to satisfy a formal requirement on α. Movement is not allowed to take place merely to satisfy a requirement on the target. To the extent that it is successful, this analysis also provides evidence for the existence of lowering operations in LF, which is in accordance with Chomsky 1995, where lowering is ruled out in overt but not covert syntax. I have also argued for overt object shift in classical ECM constructions. I have argued that object shift takes place overtly in ECM constructions in spite of Procrastinate because it is necessary for convergence. In addition, I have proposed a new analysis of the grammaticality of *wh*-extraction from the subject position of *wager*-class infinitivals and French propositional infinitivals based on the Move F theory. Finally, I have examined several apparent redundancies involving constraints affecting A-positions and A-movement and suggested a way of eliminating some of them.

Chapter 5
Participle Movement

5.1 Introduction

So far I have discussed only infinitival nonfinite complements. In this chapter I turn to participial complements, concentrating on participial complementation in Serbo-Croatian.[1]

The syntax of Serbo-Croatian participles has attracted a great deal of attention in the literature. To account for the surface position of these participles, a number of theoretically anomalous claims have been made. For example, it is standardly assumed that when they precede auxiliaries, Serbo-Croatian participles are located under C^0 (see Progovac 1996, Wilder and Ćavar 1994a,b, Percus 1993, Roberts 1994, Rivero 1991, 1994b, Tomić 1996, among others), although crosslinguistically, the option of undergoing movement to C^0 in finite clauses is restricted to finite verbs.[2]

(1) [$_{CP}$ Istukao$_i$ *je* t$_i$ Petra]
      beaten is Peter
  '(He) beat Peter'

Furthermore, constructions in which the participle precedes the auxiliary have been argued by a number of authors, most notably by Rivero (1991, 1994b) and Roberts (1992, 1994), to involve long head movement (i.e., head movement skipping another lexically filled X^0 position, occupied by the auxiliary). Long head movement is theoretically a rather anomalous operation. Considerable energy has been expended in the literature in attempting to fit it into the theory. The goal of this chapter is to re-examine P-movement in Serbo-Croatian. The claims that P moves to C in Serbo-Croatian and that (1) involves long head movement will be subjected to close scrutiny. On the basis of previously unnoticed data, I will argue that Serbo-Croatian participles neither move to C nor undergo long head movement. I will present an analysis of P-movement in Serbo-Croatian that does not involve any theoretically anomalous mechanisms, and that extends rather straightforwardly to P-movement in Standard Dutch and Polish. I will also examine the relevance of P-movement for a number of phenomena and theoretical mechanisms, including second position cliticization, economy of derivation, excorporation, and the direction of adjunction operations.

5.2 Participle Movement in Serbo-Croatian

In this section I will provide evidence that participles in Serbo-Croatian can move out of VP even when they linearly follow the auxiliary, thereby confirming the conclusion concerning the surface position of Serbo-Croatian participles reached in chapter 4. In particular, I will argue that Serbo-Croatian participles undergo head movement to a position below T^0. I will then show that participle preposing in front of the auxiliary patterns in all relevant respects as participle movement whose landing site is linearly preceded by the auxiliary.[3]

Given the standard assumption that participles are base-generated adjacent to direct object NPs, (2)–(3) show that Serbo-Croatian participles can move across VP adverbs. (Only traces of P-movement are indicated in the examples below.)

(2) a. Jovan *je* potpuno   zaboravio Petra
       Jovan is completely forgotten Peter
       'Jovan completely forgot Peter'

   b. Jovan *je* zaboravio$_i$ potpuno t$_i$ Petra

(3) a. Jovan *je* juče   istukao Petra
       Jovan is yesterday beaten Peter
       'Jovan beat Peter yesterday'

   b. Jovan *je* istukao$_i$ juče t$_i$ Petra

However, Serbo-Croatian participles cannot move across sentential adverbs.[4]

(4) a. Jovan *je* nesumnjivo istukao Petra
       Jovan is undoubtedly beaten Peter
       'Jovan undoubtedly beat Peter'

   b. *Jovan *je* istukao$_i$ nesumnjivo t$_i$ Petra

c. Jovan *je* vjerovatno zaspao
   Jovan is probably fallen-asleep
   'Jovan probably fell asleep'
d. *Jovan *je* zaspao$_i$ vjerovatno t$_i$

The facts concerning the interpretation of adverbs such as *mudro* 'wisely' confirm the conclusion drawn by examining (2)–(4). Jackendoff (1972) shows that adverbs such as *mudro* are ambiguous between manner and subject-oriented adverb readings. On the former reading *mudro* is a VP adverb. On the latter reading it is a sentential adverb. The fact that, unlike in (5a), in (5b) *mudro* can have only the manner reading indicates that Serbo-Croatian participles can move across VP adverbs, but not across sentential adverbs.

(5) a. Jovan *je* mudro prodao svoju kuću
       Jovan is wisely sold   his   house
       'It was wise of Jovan to sell his house'
       'Jovan sold his house in a wise manner'
    b. Jovan *je* prodao$_i$ mudro t$_i$ svoju kuću
       'Jovan sold his house in a wise manner'
       '*It was wise of Jovan to sell his house'

The same point can be made with respect to *pravilno* 'correctly'. In (6a) *pravilno* can have either the manner or the subject-oriented adverb reading. In (6b), on the other hand, it can have only the manner reading.

(6) a. Jovan *je* pravilno odgovorio Mariji
       Jovan is correctly answered   Maria
       'Jovan did the right thing in answering Maria'
       'Jovan gave Maria a correct answer'
    b. Jovan *je* odgovorio$_i$ pravilno t$_i$ Mariji
       'Jovan gave Maria a correct answer'
       '*Jovan did the right thing in answering Maria'

Given these data, I conclude that Serbo-Croatian participles that follow auxiliaries can move across VP adverbs, but not across sentential adverbs.

The group of adverbs that have to precede Serbo-Croatian participles is roughly the same group of adverbs that are allowed to either precede or follow modals and tensed auxiliaries in English declarative clauses. Watanabe (1993) proposes that the adverbs in question are located between Agr$_S$ and Tense (T) in English, which I will assume to be the Tense

Phrase (TP)-adjoined position, with modals and finite auxiliaries having the option of either staying under T (7b) or moving to Agr$_S$ (7a).

(7) a. [$_{Agr_SP}$ John can$_i$ [$_{TP}$ undoubtedly [$_{TP}$ t$_i$ play the guitar]]]
     b. [$_{Agr_SP}$ John [$_{TP}$ undoubtedly [$_{TP}$ can play the guitar]]]

We can implement this technically as follows: Assume that English modals and auxiliaries can have either strong or weak Agr features. Given Chomsky's (1993) assumption that strong features are illegitimate PF objects, if modals and auxiliaries are taken from the lexicon with strong Agr features, they must move to Agr$_S$ in the overt syntax, so that the features can be checked before entering PF. If these features are weak, modals and auxiliaries do not have to move to Agr$_S$ before LF. (Since Serbo-Croatian auxiliaries only optionally move across sentential adverbs (see (4)–(6) and (8)), I will also assume that their Agr features can be either strong or weak. As shown in section 5.2.2, Serbo-Croatian auxiliaries can actually stay in their base-generated position at SS.)

Given that sentential adverbs in Serbo-Croatian are located in the same structural position as in English (i.e., adjoined to TP), it is expected that Serbo-Croatian participles cannot move across the adverbs in question. Since participles are not specified as [+tense], it seems plausible that the final landing site of P-movement following the auxiliary is lower than T. I conclude, therefore, that adverb placement facts provide evidence that Serbo-Croatian participles following auxiliaries can move out of VP. However, their landing site must be below TP, the attachment site of sentential adverbs.

Note now that participles exhibit the same behavior in constructions in which they precede auxiliaries, which are standardly analyzed as involving P-to-C movement. Thus, (8a,c), where P-movement lands in a position higher than the sentential adverb *nesumnjivo* 'undoubtedly', are ungrammatical.

(8) a. *Istukao$_i$ *je* nesumnjivo t$_i$ Petra
         beaten   is undoubtedly   Peter
         'He undoubtedly beat Peter'
     b. cf. Istukao$_i$ *je* t$_i$ Petra
     c. *Zaspao$_i$ *je* vjerovatno t$_i$ Jovan
         fallen-asleep is probably   Jovan
         'Jovan probably fell asleep'
     d. cf. Zaspao *je* Jovan

The ungrammaticality of (8a,c) can be accounted for on a par with that of (4b,d) if P-preposing in (8a,c) lands below TP, the adjunction site of sentential adverbs. In other words, regardless of whether P-movement lands in front of or following the auxiliary, its landing site is below TP, hence lower than C.[5]

Recall that the adverb *pravilno* 'correctly' is ambiguous between the manner and subject-oriented adverb readings. On the manner reading it is a VP adverb, and on the subject-oriented adverb reading it is a sentential adverb. Now consider (9).

(9) a. Jovan *je* pravilno odgovorio Mariji
      Jovan is correctly answered   Maria
      'Jovan did the right thing in answering Maria'
      'Jovan gave Maria a correct answer'
   b. Odgovorio$_i$ *je* pravilno t$_i$ Mariji
      answered   is correctly   Maria
      'He gave Maria a correct answer'
      '*He did the right thing in answering Maria'
   c. Jovan *je* mudro prodao svoju kuću
      Jovan is wisely sold   his   house
      'It was wise of Jovan to sell his house'
      'Jovan sold his house in a wise manner'
   d. Prodao$_i$ *je* mudro t$_i$ svoju kuću
      sold   is wisely   his   house
      'He sold his house in a wise manner'
      '*It was wise of him to sell his house'

As noted above, (9a), where the adverb can be adjoined to either VP or TP, is ambiguous. However, the ambiguity is resolved in (9b), where the adverb can have only the manner reading. The same holds for *mudro* 'wisely', which can also have either the manner or the subject-oriented adverb reading. Whereas (9c) is ambiguous, in (9d) the adverb can have only the manner reading. P-preposing to a position in front of the auxiliary apparently eliminates the option of the adverbs in question being located in the TP-adjoined position. This indicates that the landing site of the preposing is below TP, contrary to standard assumptions.

To summarize, I have argued so far that adverb placement data provide evidence against the standard assumption that participles move to C in Serbo-Croatian. They also provide evidence against the standard assumption that Serbo-Croatian clitics are located in a structurally fixed position.

As illustrated in (10), Serbo-Croatian clitics cluster together in the second position of the sentence immediately dominating them (see Browne 1974). Splitting the clitic cluster or locating it in any other position in (10a–d) would lead to ungrammaticality.

(10) a. Mi *smo mu je* predstavili juče
          we are him her introduced yesterday
          'We introduced her to him yesterday'

   b. Zašto *smo mu je* predstavili juče
          why   are him her introduced yesterday
          'Why did we introduce her to him yesterday'

   c. Ona tvrdi   da   *smo mu je* mi predstavili juče
          she claims that are him her we introduced yesterday
          'She claims that we introduced her to him yesterday'

   d. Predstavili *smo mu je* mi juče
          introduced are him her we yesterday
          'We introduced her to him yesterday'

It is standardly assumed in the recent literature that the second position of Serbo-Croatian clitics is structurally fixed; that is, it always corresponds to the same structural position.[6] Under this assumption the clitics in (11a) and (11b) are also located in the same structural position.

(11) a. Jovan *je* nesumnjivo istukao Petra
          Jovan is undoubtedly beaten Peter
          'Jovan undoubtedly beat Peter'

   b. Istukao$_i$ *je* t$_i$ Petra
          beaten   is   Peter
          'He beat Peter'

   c. cf. *Istukao$_i$ *je* nesumnjivo   t$_i$ Petra
                beaten   is undoubtedly   Peter
          'He undoubtedly beat Peter'

The clitic in (11a) must be located in a position that is higher than the adjunction site of the sentential adverb *nesumnjivo*. Given that participles cannot move to a head position higher than *nesumnjivo* (see (11c) and (4b)), the clitic in (11b) must be located in a position that is lower than the adjunction site of *nesumnjivo*. Notice also that the same judgments hold with clitic clusters.

(12) a. Vi *ste mu je* nesumnjivo predstavili juče
          you are him her undoubtedly introduced yesterday
          'You undoubtedly introduced her to him yesterday'

b. Predstavili$_i$ *ste mu je* t$_i$ juče
   introduced are him her yesterday
c. *Predstavili$_i$ *ste mu je* nesumnjivo t$_i$ juče
   introduced are him her undoubtedly yesterday

The same point can be made with respect to *pravilno* 'correctly' and *mudro* 'wisely', which are ambiguous between the TP, subject-oriented adverb reading and the VP, manner reading. The fact that (9a,c) are ambiguous indicates that the adverbs in (9a,c) can be adjoined to TP. The clitic then must be located higher than TP in (9a,c). On the other hand, the non-ambiguity of (9b,d), where the adverbs can have only the manner reading, indicates that the material preceding the adverb, which includes the clitic, is located below TP. As (13a–b) show, the same judgments again hold with clitic clusters.

(13) a. Mi *smo mu je* mudro predstavili juče
        we are him her wisely introduced yesterday
        'We introduced her to him in a wise manner yesterday'
        'It was wise of us to introduce her to him yesterday'
    b. Predstavili$_i$ *smo mu je* mudro t$_i$ juče
        introduced are him her wisely yesterday
        'We introduced her to him in a wise manner yesterday'
        '*It was wise of us to introduce her to him yesterday'

The data considered so far lead me to conclude that in Serbo-Croatian there is no fixed structural position for clitics and that participles do not move to C, contrary to what is generally assumed in the recent literature. (For more evidence that there is no fixed structural position for clitics in Serbo-Croatian, see Bošković 1995b.) The latter conclusion is not only empirically but also theoretically well motivated. If participles can move to C in Serbo-Croatian, a question immediately arises about what motivates the movement. I see no plausible driving force for it. Given Greed, which requires that all movement be motivated by feature checking of the moved element, P-to-C movement in Serbo-Croatian must be motivated by feature checking of the participle. Note now that crosslinguistically, nonfinite main verbs do not move to C in finite clauses. In fact, in languages in which V-to-C movement clearly takes place in finite clauses, only finite main verbs move to C. This indicates that the feature [+finite], which participles do not have, drives the movement in question. P-to-C movement thus seems to lack feature motivation. In other words, no morphological property of the participle, or for that matter the C node in general, seems to require that P move to C. Motivating P-to-C movement thus appears to be a problem for the P-to-C analysis.

To provide a principled motivation for P-movement under the P-to-C analysis, it has often been argued (see Rivero 1991, 1994a, and Wilder and Ćavar 1994a, among others) that P-movement in Serbo-Croatian is a last resort operation driven by the need to provide a host for clitics; that is, it takes place when a clitic is found in sentence-initial position to provide a host for the clitic. The last resort analysis is inconsistent with Greed. There is also empirical evidence against the last resort analysis. In particular, there is evidence that providing a host for a clitic is neither a sufficient nor a necessary condition for P-movement in Serbo-Croatian. The facts concerning the question particle *li* indicate that providing a host for a clitic does not suffice to drive P-movement in Serbo-Croatian even when the clitic would otherwise remain stranded in sentence-initial position. (See in this respect Lasnik 1995d, where it is also argued that the need to provide a host for a phonologically "weak" element cannot by itself drive syntactic movement.)

The question particle *li* is a second position clitic and therefore cannot appear sentence initially. There is a general consensus, which I find no reason to doubt, that this particle is located under C^0. Given this, the position of *li* can serve as a probe for determining the location of verbal elements. Consider (14a–b), where main verbs are adjoined to *li*.

(14) a. [$_C$ Ljubi$_i$ *li*] t$_i$ nju
         kisses Q   her
         'Does he kiss her'
     b. *[$_C$ Poljubio$_i$ *li*] *je* t$_i$ nju
         kissed   Q   is   her
         'Did he kiss her'

(14a), involving a finite main verb serving as a host for the second position clitic *li*, shows that finite verbs can move to C in Serbo-Croatian. On the other hand, the ungrammaticality of (14b), with a participial main verb, noted by Rivero (1993), shows that participles cannot move to C in Serbo-Croatian. Note that, as (15) shows, the ungrammaticality of the construction cannot be attributed to some cooccurrence restrictions on the clitics *li* and *je*.

(15) Da *li je* poljubio nju
     that Q is kissed her
     'Did he kiss her'

The ungrammaticality of (14b) thus provides further evidence against the standard P-to-C movement analysis of P-preposing in Serbo-Croatian. (14b) also shows that providing a host for a clitic does not suffice to drive head movement of verbal elements. If this were the case, we would expect (14b) to be grammatical, just as (14a) is.

The data in (14) indicate that the need to provide a host for a clitic is not a sufficient condition for P-movement. There is also evidence that it is not a necessary condition. Rivero (1994a) and Embick and Izvorski (1995) note that in Bulgarian P-movement is possible even when the auxiliary is not a clitic. The same holds for Serbo-Croatian. Consider the following examples with the traditional pluperfect (16a) and future II tense (16b), involving nonclitic auxiliaries. (Note that future II is used only in certain subordinate clauses.)

(16) a. Istukao$_i$ bejaše t$_i$ Petra
        beaten was   Peter
        'He had beaten Peter'
   b. Kad istukao$_i$ bude t$_i$ Petra, pozovi me
        when beaten   be   Peter call   me
        'When he beats Peter, call me'

In contrast to the auxiliary in (1), the auxiliaries in (16) are not clitics. Nonetheless, the participle is allowed to move across the auxiliaries.[7]

In light of the data in (14)–(16), I conclude that the need to provide a host for a clitic is neither a sufficient nor a necessary condition for P-movement in Serbo-Croatian. Notice also that P-movement in (16) is not obligatory. (17a–b), with the participle following the auxiliary, are also grammatical.

(17) a. Bejaše istukao Petra
   b. Kad bude istukao Petra, pozovi me

The optionality of P-preposing in (16)–(17) provides strong evidence against the last resort analysis of P-movement. Given all of these arguments, I conclude that P-preposing in Serbo-Croatian is not a last resort operation driven by the need to provide a host for clitics. Since, as discussed above, it is not possible to motivate P-to-C movement by a morphological deficiency of the participle, or the C node, under the P-to-C movement analysis it does not seem to be possible to provide a principled motivation for P-preposing. We thus have another, this time conceptual, argument against the P-to-C movement analysis, in addition to the more empirical arguments given above concerning adverb placement and the question particle *li*.

As shown by Embick and Izvorski (1995), who discuss the corresponding data in Bulgarian, certain data concerning nonclitic auxiliaries provide more evidence against the standard assumption that Serbo-Croatian P-movement lands in C. Consider the following constructions:

(18) a. *Zaspali$_i$ Marko i   Petar bejahu t$_i$
          fallen-asleep Marko and Peter were
          'Marko and Peter had fallen asleep'
     b. cf. Zaspali$_i$ bejahu t$_i$
     c. ?*Kad zaspali$_i$ Marko i   Petar budu t$_i$, pozovi me
          when fallen-asleep Marko and Peter be   call   me
     d. Kad zaspali$_i$ budu t$_i$, pozovi me

As noted above, pluperfect and future II auxiliaries are not second position clitics; that is, they can in principle be preceded by either more than one constituent or none at all. Given that the ungrammaticality of (18a,c) cannot be attributed to the second position effect (for an analysis of the second position effect that takes into account the data considered here, see Bošković 1995b, where I attribute this effect to PF requirements on clitics), it does not seem to be possible to account for the ungrammaticality of (18a,c) under the P-to-C movement analysis of P-preposing. Note that, as English *Has John t left* indicates, subjects do not interfere with movement of verbal elements to C^0. Given this, following Embick and Izvorski's observation concerning Bulgarian, I take the ungrammaticality of (18a,c) to indicate that the landing site of P-preposing in Serbo-Croatian is below the SS position of subjects, which clearly cannot be C. Like the data concerning sentential adverbs and the question particle *li*, as well as the more theoretical issues concerning the driving force behind P-preposing, the data concerning subject placement in pluperfect and future II constructions indicate that the landing site of P-movement in Serbo-Croatian is below C. Therefore, I conclude that, contrary to what is generally assumed in recent work on the subject, there is nothing exceptional about Serbo-Croatian participles and the C system. In fact, Serbo-Croatian seems to be rather well behaved in that it allows finite verbs (see (14a)) but not participles to move to C. (Additional evidence against the P-to-C analysis is provided in the following section.)

5.2.1 Long Head Movement or Adjunction?
The question to be asked now is, where exactly is the participle located in constructions such as (19)?

(19) Istukao$_i$ *je* t$_i$ Petra
     beaten is   Peter
     'He beat Peter'

Assuming that both the participle and the auxiliary are X^0s, there are two possibilities: (a) the participle is located under an X^0 node above the auxiliary (i.e., it undergoes long head movement), or (b) the participle is adjoined to the auxiliary. Both analyses have been proposed in the literature. Rivero (1991, 1994a) and Roberts (1992, 1994) propose that the participle skips the X^0 position where the auxiliary is located and moves to C^0. Progovac (1996) and Wilder and Ćavar (1994a,b), on the other hand, propose that the participle adjoins to the auxiliary, which is located under C^0.[8] Given the above discussion, the specific analyses cannot be right since they all place the participle under C^0. However, even if we assume that the final landing site of the participle is below C^0, we still have the two possibilities noted above: long head movement and adjunction. Consider first the long head movement analysis. It is clear that even if long head movement is allowed, head movement cannot be left without any locality constraints. Let us therefore assume, following Roberts (1992), that to the extent that long head movement is possible, it must obey Relativized Minimality (see Rizzi 1990a). Roberts argues that the A/Ā distinction applies not only to XPs but also to X^0s. Following the logic of Relativized Minimality, he then suggests that Ā- but not A-heads block head movement to Ā-head positions. Given the standard assumption in the relevant literature that participles and auxiliaries are A-heads, in order for a participle to move across an auxiliary it must move to an Ā-head position, or Relativized Minimality will be violated. Given the discussion in the previous section, the long head movement analysis thus requires an Ā-head position located between T and the auxiliary. The problem is that there are no plausible candidates for this position. C^0 apparently cannot serve as the landing site for P-movement. It will become clear below that the same holds for Neg^0, another Ā-head. C^0 and Neg^0 exhaust the standard inventory of Ā-heads. Rather than positing an Ā-functional head for which we have no independent evidence, let us see how far the adjunction analysis can take us. Notice first that, given Chomsky's (1993) proposal that all movement must have morphological motivation, P-to-Aux adjunction must be driven by feature checking; that is, there must be a feature shared by the participle and the auxiliary that is checked by the adjunction. Following Wilder and Ćavar (1994b), I will refer to this feature as

"[+aux]." In sections 5.3 and 5.4 I will show that P-to-Aux adjunction is not restricted to Serbo-Croatian.

There is one obvious problem that arises on the adjunction analysis. If the participle adjoins to the auxiliary and the auxiliary can move above sentential adverbs, why can't the auxiliary pied-pipe the participle in constructions such as (20a), giving (20b) or (20c)?

(20) a. Jovan je_i nesumnjivo t_i istukao Petra
         Jovan is   undoubtedly   beaten Peter
         'Jovan undoubtedly beat Peter'

     b. *Jovan [je + istukao$_j$]$_i$ nesumnjivo t_i t_j Petra

     c. *[Istukao$_j$ + je]$_i$ nesumnjivo t_i t_j Petra

I suggest that the answer lies in the process of excorporation, discussed by Roberts (1991). I propose that after the participle adjoins to the auxiliary, the auxiliary excorporates and moves to a higher X^0 position. It is clear that excorporation must be obligatory in (20b–c); otherwise, (20b–c) would still be ruled in. Watanabe's (1993) theory of excorporation ensures this.

Watanabe argues that, given the configuration in (21), where all features of Z are checked and Y has a feature to check by adjunction to X, Y must excorporate and adjoin alone to X. Since Z has no features to be checked, the principles of economy of derivation (carry as little material as possible) prevent Z from undergoing head movement together with Y. The derivation in which Y pied-pipes Z is blocked by the more economical derivation in which Y moves alone. Head movement to X obviously carries less material in the latter derivation.[9]

(21)   * ⌐‾‾‾‾⌐
       X   [Y + Z], where X, Y, and Z are heads.
          ⌊____⌋
       +F +F

Watanabe gives several arguments for the economy account of excorporation. A strong piece of evidence for this account is provided by certain facts concerning Italian causative constructions discussed by Guasti (1991). Consider (22a–b).

(22) a. I   professori non fanno$_i$ più [$_{VP}$ t_i + commentare$_j$
         the professors NEG make   not   comment
         tutti [$_{VP}$ t_j lo stesso libro a Lia]]
         all   the same book to Lia
         'The professors do not all make Lia comment on the same book'

b. *I professori non [fanno + commentare$_i$]$_j$ più [$_{VP}$ t$_j$ tutti [$_{VP}$ t$_i$ lo stesso libro a Lia]]

Essentially following Guasti (1991), Watanabe argues that the embedded verb in (22a) is adjoined to the matrix V^0 node. The fact that the quantifier *tutti*, associated with the matrix subject, follows the embedded verb indicates that the embedded verb has moved into the matrix clause. Notice, however, that matrix negation intervenes between the matrix and the embedded verb. Watanabe argues that after the embedded verb adjoins to the matrix verb, since all the features of the embedded verb are checked, the economy principles prevent the embedded verb from moving along with the higher verb, which moves for feature checking. (22b), involving pied-piping of the embedded verb, is thus ruled out. (See also Roberts 1991 for instances of V-excorporation out of Dutch verbal clusters that can be interpreted as providing evidence for Watanabe's economy account of excorporation. Roberts's examples are discussed in section 5.3. For more evidence for Watanabe's economy account of excorporation, see section 5.2.2.)

Given the above discussion, let us reconsider (20a–c), the relevant derivations for which are given in (23).

(23) a.   Jovan *je$_i$* nesumnjivo   t$_i$+ istukao$_j$ t$_j$ Petra
          Jovan is   undoubtedly   beaten   Peter

     b. I   Jovan nesumnjivo *je*+istukao$_j$ t$_j$ Petra
        II *Jovan [*je*+istukao$_j$]$_i$ nesumnjivo t$_i$ t$_j$ Petra

     c. I   Nesumnjivo istukao$_j$+*je* t$_j$ Petra
        II *[Istukao$_j$+*je*]$_i$ nesumnjivo t$_i$ t$_j$ Petra

Recall that, as shown in the previous section, the auxiliary can move across sentential adverbs. Given this, the question arose under the P-to-Aux adjunction analysis why the auxiliary cannot pied-pipe the participle when moving across sentential adverbs. It seems safe to assume that after P-to-Aux adjunction, all features of the participle are checked. Given Watanabe's theory of excorporation, *je*, which I assume moves to check its Agr features in (23) (recall that *je* can actually move either overtly or covertly), is not allowed to pied-pipe the participle. (23b–c) are thus ruled out in the same way as Italian (22b).

There is actually another derivation not considered by Watanabe that has to be ruled out in the constructions under consideration. Consider, for example, (23b). Suppose that Aux moves to Agr$_S$ and then the participle moves to adjoin to the Aux+Agr$_S$ complex.

(24) a. I   Jovan je_i nesumnjivo t_i istukao Petra
         Jovan is undoubtedly   beaten Peter
     b. II *Jovan je_i + istukao$_j$ nesumnjivo t_i t_j Petra

Since under the definition of checking domain in Chomsky 1993 the participle is in the checking domain of the auxiliary after adjunction, its [+aux] feature can be checked. The derivation in (24) is, however, ruled out via economy of derivation. To account for Superiority Condition effects, Chomsky (MIT lectures 1989, 1990; see also Bošković, in press a, and Kitahara 1993b) argues that every feature must be checked in the most economical way (i.e., through the shortest movement possible). Thus, ?*$What_i$ *did John tell who that he should buy* t_i, where *what* checks the [+wh] feature located under C^0, is ruled out because a more economical derivation is available in which *who* moves to SpecCP (*Who$_i$ did John tell* t_i *that he should buy what*). In the latter derivation fewer nodes are crossed to check the [+wh] feature. Now, given that all features must be checked in the most economical way, the derivation in (24) is ruled out because a more economical derivation is available in which the participle checks the [+aux] feature by adjoining to the auxiliary before the auxiliary undergoes movement. Since in this derivation fewer nodes are crossed to check the [+aux] feature, its availability blocks (24) via economy of derivation.

To summarize, under the analysis pursued so far, in (25a) the participle adjoins to the auxiliary, which is located in its base-generated position.[10] In (25b), on the other hand, after the participle adjoins to the auxiliary, which, like its English counterpart, can optionally move to Agr$_S$ at SS, the auxiliary excorporates and moves to Agr$_S$. (Its final landing site could actually be even higher than Agr$_S$.)

(25) a. [$_{AuxP}$ Poljubio$_i$ *je* [$_{VP}$ t_i Mariju]]
             kissed   is   Maria
         'He kissed Maria'
     b. U gradu je_i vjerovatno poljubio$_j$+t_i t_j Mariju
         in city   is   probably   kissed   Maria
         'In the city he probably kissed Maria'

5.2.2 Past Perfect and Participle Movement

Certain facts concerning the past perfect tense provide strong evidence that Serbo-Croatian participles indeed adjoin to Aux at SS. They also show that the adjunction is obligatory.

The past perfect tense is formed by using the present tense form of *biti* 'to be', the participle of *biti*, and the participle of the main verb.

(26) Vas dvoje *ste* bili čekali Marijinu prijateljicu
you two   are been waited Maria's   friend
'You two had been waiting for Maria's friend'

(27a) shows that lexical material can intervene between the auxiliary (I will refer only to the finite auxiliary as "Aux") and the two participles. However, no lexical material can intervene between the participles when they are preceded by the auxiliary (27b–c).[11]

(27) a.   Vas dvoje *ste* Marijinu prijateljicu$_i$ bili   čekali t$_i$
you two   are Maria's   friend   been waited
b.   *Vas dvoje *ste* bili Marijinu prijateljicu$_i$ čekali t$_i$
c.   *Marijinu prijateljicu$_i$ *ste* bili vas dvoje čekali t$_i$

It is tempting to take (27b–c) as evidence that the participles are adjoined at SS. Notice, however, that although no lexical material can intervene between the participles when they follow the auxiliary, the auxiliary itself can intervene between the participles. In fact, not only can the auxiliary follow the first participle and precede the second participle, it can also follow the second participle.[12]

(28) a.   Bili$_i$ *ste* t$_i$ čekali Marijinu prijateljicu
been are   waited Maria's   friend
'You had been waiting for Maria's friend'
b.   Čekali$_i$*ste* bili   t$_i$ Marijinu prijateljicu
waited are been   Maria's   friend
'You had been waiting for Maria's friend'

I will show now that these facts can readily be accounted for under the adjunction+excorporation analysis. Notice first that the second participle in (28b) cannot adjoin to the auxiliary, skipping the first participle, since this would violate the Head Movement Constraint even under Roberts's relaxed version of it. Being verbal elements, both participles should be considered A-heads. The derivation under consideration would then involve A-head movement crossing an A-head in violation of Relativized Minimality applied to head movement. Notice, however, that if P-to-Aux movement is driven by feature checking, we would expect both participles to undergo feature checking via adjunction to the auxiliary.[13] Let us assume that the [+aux] feature of Serbo-Croatian participles is strong and therefore has to be eliminated overtly. I assume that the direction of P-to-Aux adjunction is free; that is, it can proceed either to the left or to the right. To the extent that it is successful, the analysis presented below will thus provide evidence against Kayne's (1994) claim that rightward adjunction is not allowed. However, the analysis is consistent with Chomsky 1994, where rightward adjunction is allowed in the case of head movement, but not in the case of XP-movement.

Bearing all this in mind, consider the following derivation for (28b):

(29) a. [$_{AuxP}$ *ste* [$_{VP}$ bili [$_{VP}$ čekali Marijinu prijateljicu]]]
          are   been   waited Maria's friend

    b. [$_{AuxP}$ [$_{Aux}$[$_{Aux}$ *ste*] bili$_i$] [$_{VP}$ t$_i$ [$_{VP}$ čekali Marijinu prijateljicu]]]

    c. [$_{AuxP}$[$_{Aux}$ Čekali$_j$ [$_{Aux}$[$_{Aux}$ *ste*] bili$_i$]] [$_{VP}$ t$_i$ [$_{VP}$ t$_j$ Marijinu prijateljicu]]]

Bili first adjoins to the right of the auxiliary to check its [+aux] feature. Given the mechanism of equidistance, *čekali* can now skip the trace of *bili* and left-adjoin to the auxiliary, giving (29c). Chomsky (1993) defines the domain of a nontrivial, two-member chain CH (α_i, α_j) as the set of nodes that are contained in the least full-category maximal projection dominating α_i and that do not themselves contain any α. (All notions are irreflexive unless otherwise indicated.) The minimal domain of the chain CH (α_i, α_j) is, then, the smallest subset K of the domain of the chain CH, such that for any member of the minimal domain some member of K reflexively dominates it. Given these definitions, t$_i$ and the landing site of *čekali*, a position adjoined to *ste*, belong to the same minimal domain, namely, the domain of the chain (*bili*$_i$, t$_i$), and are therefore equidistant from the base-generated position of *čekali*. As a result, direct adjunction of *čekali* to *ste* in (29c), which skips the trace of *bili*, does not lead to a violation of the Minimize Chain Links Principle.[14]

Now consider (28a). In this construction first *bili* left-adjoins to *ste*, after which *čekali* can right-adjoin to *ste* without violating the Minimize Chain Links Principle, the landing site of *čekali* and the trace of *bili* being equidistant from the base-generated position of *čekali*.

(30) a. [$_{AuxP}$ *ste* [$_{VP}$ bili [$_{VP}$ čekali Marijinu prijateljicu]]]
          are   been   waited Maria's friend

    b. [$_{AuxP}$[$_{Aux}$ bili$_i$ [$_{Aux}$ *ste*]] [$_{VP}$ t$_i$ [$_{VP}$ čekali Marijinu prijateljicu]]]

    c. [$_{AuxP}$[$_{Aux}$[$_{Aux}$ Bili$_i$ [$_{Aux}$ *ste*]] čekali$_j$] [$_{VP}$ t$_i$ [$_{VP}$ t$_j$ Marijinu prijateljicu]]]

The derivations in (29) and (30) are of some theoretical importance, since they show that equidistance is relevant to head movement as well as XP-movement. All the constructions where equidistance provides an escape hatch from the Minimize Chain Links Principle in Chomsky 1993 involve XP-movement. Now we have evidence that equidistance also applies to X^0-movement, which is the null hypothesis.[15]

Under the analysis pursued here not only the first but also the second participle is adjoined to the auxiliary in (28a–b). The fact that, in spite of the possibility of scrambling in Serbo-Croatian, no XPs can intervene between the auxiliary and the second participle in (31a–b) provides strong evidence that the second participle is indeed adjoined to the auxiliary. It also shows that P-to-Aux adjunction is obligatory.

(31) a. *Bili *ste* Marijinu prijateljicu$_i$ čekali t$_i$
     been are Maria's friend waited
  b. *Čekali *ste* Marijinu prijateljicu$_i$ bili t$_i$
     waited are Maria's friend been

Returning now to (27), recall that Serbo-Croatian auxiliaries can optionally move to Agr$_S$ at SS. Given this, the grammaticality of (27a) comes as no surprise. After the participles adjoin to the auxiliary, the auxiliary excorporates to check its Agr features.

As for (27b–c), the fact that no lexical material can intervene between the participles is expected as well, since the participles are adjoined to the same node. It is easy to verify that (32) is also straightforwardly accounted for under my analysis, given auxiliary excorporation. Moreover, (32) provides further evidence that the direction of P-to-Aux adjunction is free.

(32) Vas dvoje *ste* čekali bili Marijinu prijateljicu
    you two are waited been Maria's friend
    'you two had been waiting for Maria's friend'

It is worth mentioning in this context that the data under consideration provide more evidence that there is no structurally fixed second position for clitics in Serbo-Croatian. Given the above discussion, the clitic in (27a) and the clitic in (28a–b) must be located in different structural positions. Whereas in (28a–b) the clitic is located under Aux^0, in (27a) the clitic must be located in a position higher than Aux^0.

Now consider the contrast between (33a) and (33b).

(33) a. *Čekali bili *ste* Marijinu prijateljicu
    waited been are Maria's friend

b. **Bili čekali *ste* Marijinu prijateljicu
   been waited are Maria's friend

Both (33a) and (33b) are ruled out because the second position requirement on Serbo-Croatian clitics, discussed in section 5.2.3 and Bošković
1995b, is violated. However, (33b) is clearly worse than (33a).[16] The
contrast can readily be accounted for under the current analysis. Recall
that *bili* must adjoin to the auxiliary before *čekali* does, or the Minimize
Chain Links Principle will be violated. (The adjunction of *bili* to the
auxiliary makes the landing site of *čekali* and the base-generated position
of *bili* equidistant from the base-generated position of *čekali*.) It seems
plausible that some version of the A-over-A Principle bans adjunction to
the lower segment of a segmented category.[17] Given that such adjunction
is not allowed, after *bili* adjoins to the left of the auxiliary in (34a), the
second participle must adjoin to the higher segment of the segmented Aux
node, giving (34b) but not (34c). The contrast between (33a) and (33b) is
thus accounted for.[18]

(34) a.   [$_{Aux}$ bili$_i$ [$_{Aux}$ *ste*]] t$_i$ čekali Marijinu prijateljicu
            been   are   waited Maria's friend
     b.   *[$_{Aux}$ Čekali$_j$ [$_{Aux}$ bili$_i$ [$_{Aux}$ *ste*]]] t$_i$ t$_j$ Marijinu prijateljicu
     c.   **[$_{Aux}$ Bili$_i$ [$_{Aux}$ čekali$_j$ [$_{Aux}$ *ste*]]] t$_i$ t$_j$ Marijinu prijateljicu

In summary, I have shown so far that some rather complex previously
unnoticed data concerning double participle constructions can readily be
accounted for under the P-to-Aux adjunction analysis. On the other hand,
I see no principled way of accounting for the data under the long head
movement analysis of P-preposing. In light of this, I conclude that the
adjunction analysis, instantiated as P-to-Aux adjunction, is to be preferred to the long head movement analysis on empirical grounds.

   Note also that under my analysis P-movement in front of the auxiliary
and P-movement following the auxiliary are given a uniform account. P-
movement always lands in the same position. Furthermore, the movement
is obligatory. The same result clearly cannot be achieved under alternative
analyses of P-movement; hence, the analysis presented here seems to be
preferable on conceptual grounds as well. Also, given that P-movement
always takes place to the same position, and is obligatory, it seems natural to analyze it in terms of feature checking.

   However, María-Luisa Rivero (personal communication) suggests that
constructions such as (35), containing a conjunction intervening between
the participles, are problematic for the P-to-Aux adjunction analysis.

(35) ?Kupio i   pročitao *je* sve knjige
     bought and read   is all books
     'He bought and read all books'

(35) seems problematic if the preposed participles are located under the same X^0 node and if *i* must project a phrase, in which case the construction would contain an XP inside an X^0. However, under these assumptions (35) is problematic not only for the P-to-Aux adjunction analysis, but also for every recent analysis of Serbo-Croatian P-movement in the literature, all of which treat this phenomenon as an instance of head movement. Since there is considerable evidence that P-movement indeed involves head movement (see Rivero 1991 for conclusive evidence to this effect), one of the assumptions that make (35) problematic under the head movement analysis of P-preposing must be wrong: either *i* is just a head, or the construction does not involve head coordination. Kayne (1994) in fact argues that heads can never be coordinated. (His argument is based on the impossibility of coordinating clitics; see section 3.2.) Given Kayne's claim, (35) cannot involve head coordination and Rivero's problem disappears. Essentially following Kayne's analysis of "superficial" examples of head coordination in English and French, (35) could be analyzed as involving phrasal coordination (possibly AuxP coordination) with a right-node-raised direct object NP and the auxiliary clitic in the first conjunct deleted under identity with the clitic in the second conjunct (see (36a)). It is easy to verify that the grammaticality of (36b–c) is also expected under this analysis. (The analysis also goes through under the base generation analysis of right node raising, argued for in Bošković 1996a, Kayne 1994, and Wexler and Culicover 1980.)[19]

(36) a. ?[$_{AuxP}$ Kupio e$_i$ e$_j$] i [$_{AuxP}$ pročitao *je*$_i$ e$_j$] sve knjige$_j$
           bought   and   read   is   all books
         'He bought and read all books'
    b. [$_{AuxP}$ Kupio *je*$_i$ e$_j$] i [$_{AuxP}$ pročitao e$_i$ e$_j$] sve knjige$_j$
           bought is   and   read   all books
    c. [$_{AuxP}$ Kupio *je* e$_j$] i [$_{AuxP}$ pročitao *je* e$_j$] sve knjige$_j$
           bought is   and   read   is   all books

Before I conclude this section, a note is in order concerning VP-preposing constructions such as (37), which at first sight seem problematic, since *čekali* appears not to have undergone SS adjunction to the auxiliary. I assume that before the relevant movements take place, (37) has the structure shown in (38).[20]

(37) Čekali Marijinu prijateljicu niste
     waited Maria's friend   not+are
     'Waiting for Maria's friend you were not'

(38) [$_{\Sigma P}$ ni [$_{AuxP}$ *ste* [$_{VP}$ čekali Marijinu prijateljicu]]]

Suppose that *čekali* first adjoins to *ste*, which then excorporates to adjoin
to Neg, or Σ in Laka's (1990) terminology (see (39a–b)). (Note that auxiliaries incorporated with Neg are not clitics.) Assuming that Lasnik and
Saito's (1984) γ-marking takes place derivationally, as proposed by
Chomsky and Lasnik (1993), both traces are marked [$+\gamma$], thus satisfying
the traditional ECP/the Minimize Chain Links Principle. After the head
movements take place, AuxP is preposed and the result is (39c). (The
construction is good without AuxP-preposing as well. Thus, *Niste čekali
Marijinu prijateljicu* is also well formed.)

(39) a. [$_{\Sigma P}$ ni [$_{AuxP}$ ste+čekali$_j$ [$_{VP}$ t$_j$ Marijinu prijateljicu]]]
        not   is waited   Maria's friend
     b. [$_{\Sigma P}$ ni+ste$_i$ [$_{AuxP}$ t$_i$+čekali$_j$ [$_{VP}$ t$_j$ Marijinu prijateljicu]]]
     c. [$_{AuxP}$ t$_i$+čekali$_j$ [$_{VP}$ t$_j$ Marijinu prijateljicu]]$_k$ [$_{\Sigma P}$ ni+ste$_i$ t$_k$]

Under my analysis (37) thus involves remnant AuxP-preposing. A similar
process is also found in German (see Den Besten and Webelhuth 1987
and Huang 1993).[21]

The analysis can readily be extended to (40), which also involves a
nonclitic form of the auxiliary.

(40) Čekali Marijinu prijateljicu jesmo
     waited Maria's friend   ARE
     'We did wait for Maria's friend'

Essentially following Wilder and Ćavar (1994a), I assume that the nonclitic auxiliary *jesmo* must move overtly to Laka's (1990) Σ^0, the position
under which *not* and the emphatic *do* are generated in English. (Note the
translation in (40).) Given this, (40) can be accounted for in the same way
as (37). *Čekali* first adjoins to *jesmo*, which then excorporates to adjoin
to Σ^0 (see (41a–b)). After the *jesmo*-to-Σ^0 movement, remnant AuxP-
preposing takes place and (41c) is derived.

(41) a. [$_{\Sigma P}$[$_{AuxP}$ jesmo+čekali$_j$ [$_{VP}$ t$_j$ Marijinu prijateljicu]]]
           ARE   waited   Maria's friend
     b. [$_{\Sigma P}$ jesmo$_i$ [$_{AuxP}$ t$_i$+čekali$_j$ [$_{VP}$ t$_j$ Marijinu prijateljicu]]]
     c. [$_{AuxP}$ t$_i$+čekali$_j$ [$_{VP}$ t$_j$ Marijinu prijateljicu]]$_k$ [$_{\Sigma P}$ jesmo$_i$ t$_k$]

Note incidentally that (42) provides more evidence for Watanabe's (1993) economy analysis of excorporation.

(42) a. [$_{\Sigma P}$[$_{AuxP}$ čekali$_j$+jesmo [$_{VP}$ t$_j$ Marijinu prijateljicu]]]
         waited ARE   Maria's friend
     b. *[$_{\Sigma P}$[čekali$_j$+jesmo]$_i$ [$_{AuxP}$ t$_i$ t$_j$ Marijinu prijateljicu]]
         'We did wait for Maria's friend'

As noted above, the nonclitic auxiliary *jesmo* must adjoin to Laka's Σ^0. Under the economy account of excorporation, (42) is then straightforwardly ruled out because *jesmo* unnecessarily pied-pipes the participle, whose features are all checked after adjunction to the auxiliary, when moving to Σ^0. In fact, (42) is ruled out for the same reason as (22b) and (23b–c).

5.2.3 Linear Ordering of Participles and Clitics
There is still one question concerning P-movement in Serbo-Croatian that has to be addressed: when can participles linearly precede auxiliary clitics? As illustrated in (43), a participle can precede an auxiliary clitic when no lexical material precedes the participle within its own clause. A participle cannot linearly precede an auxiliary clitic when it is itself preceded by lexical material within its clause.

(43) a. Otišao *je* juče
         left   is yesterday
         'He left yesterday'
     b. *Mislim da   otišao *je* juče
         think   that left   is yesterday
     c. cf. Mislim da   *je* otišao juče
             think   that is left   yesterday
         'I think that he left yesterday'
     d. *Jovan otišao *je* juče
         Jovan left   is yesterday
     e. cf. Jovan *je* otišao juče
             Jovan is left   yesterday
         'Jovan left yesterday'
     f. *Zašto otišao *je* juče
         why   left   is yesterday
     g. cf. Zašto *je* otišao juče
             why   is left   yesterday
         'Why did he leave yesterday'

(43a–g) illustrate the second position effect. Note that the blocking effect of the complementizer on participle movement in (43b) is generally taken as evidence for P-to-C movement in Serbo-Croatian (see Rivero 1991 and Wilder and Ćavar 1994a, among others). However, this conclusion is clearly unwarranted. Given the line of reasoning used to arrive at the conclusion, (43d) leads us to conclude that the participle moves to subject position. (43f), on the other hand, provides evidence for P-to-SpecCP movement. Clearly these are undesirable results. Rather, the constructions in (43) simply indicate that Serbo-Croatian clitics must be located in the second position of their clause regardless of the syntactic status of the preceding elements.[22] (44), where nothing precedes the clitic, also illustrates the second position effect.

(44) *Je otišao (Jovan) juče
       is left   Jovan yesterday

Recently several attempts have been made to formulate a purely structural account of the second position effect in Serbo-Croatian (see Progovac 1996, Rivero 1994b, Roberts 1994, Wilder and Ćavar 1994b, among others). All the accounts crucially depend on locating the clitic cluster in a structurally fixed position and high in the tree, so that there is enough space for only one element to precede the clitic cluster. However, as argued above, both assumptions are untenable.[23] In fact, given that there is no structurally fixed position for clitic clusters, which can be located rather low in the tree, and given the variety of elements that can help satisfy the second position requirement (subject XPs, topic XPs, wh-XPs, verbal heads, complementizers), it is difficult to imagine a principled, purely structural account of the second position effect. (Freeze (1992) argues against purely structural accounts of the second position effect for Mayo, and Anderson (1993) argues against structural accounts in general.) What we need here is a constraint on linear ordering that does not pay attention to either the structural position of the relevant elements or their syntactic status (whether they are X^0s or XPs); this need suggests that we are dealing with a PF rather than a syntactic requirement. This in fact has been the traditional intuition, the purely structural approach being a fairly recent invention. That the traditional approach is on the right track is confirmed by the fact that the second position effect disappears when the auxiliary verb is not a clitic. Thus, (45a–b), involving nonclitic auxiliaries, are grammatical.[24]

(45) a. On tvrdi   da   istukao bejaše Petrovog prijatelja
        he claims that beaten was   Peter's   friend
        'He claims that he had beaten Peter's friend'
     b. Kad istukao bude Petrovog prijatelja, pozovi me
        when beaten be   Peter's   friend   call   me
        'When he beats Peter's friend, call me'

The contrast between (45a–b) and (43b,f) confirms that structural approaches to the second position effect are on the wrong track, since no
difference between these examples is expected under any of the structural
approaches proposed in the literature. The facts under consideration
provide strong evidence that clitichood of the auxiliary is responsible for
the second position effect, as was traditionally felt to be the case.[25] Since
the phenomenon of second position cliticization falls outside the domain
of this book, I will not discuss it further here, apart from observing that
the phenomenon is more amenable to phonological/PF accounts than
syntactic/structural accounts. However, see Bošković 1995b, where I offer
a PF account of the second position effect based on lexical properties of
clitics.

To summarize, I have examined participle movement in Serbo-Croatian,
a phenomenon that has attracted a great deal of attention in the literature,
and I have argued against the standard P-to-C analysis of Serbo-Croatian
participle preposing. The data I examined also indicate that Serbo-
Croatian participles do not undergo long head movement, skipping
another lexically filled X^0 position. The facts concerning participle movement in Serbo-Croatian thus do not provide support for the existence of
long head movement, contrary to what has been previously argued in the
literature. I have shown that Serbo-Croatian participles must adjoin to
Aux at SS. I have also provided evidence for the existence of excorporation—in particular, Watanabe's (1993) economy account of excorporation, which restricts excorporation to certain well-defined configurations.
In addition, I have provided evidence that rightward adjunction is an
available option for head movement, contrary to what is argued in Kayne
1994, but in accordance with Chomsky 1994. I have also shown that the
mechanism of equidistance is relevant to head movement. Finally, I have
shown that the facts concerning participle movement considered above
provide evidence that there is no fixed structural position for clitics in
Serbo-Croatian. These facts thus provide empirical evidence against
purely structural accounts of the second position effect.

P-to-Aux adjunction, argued for above, may not be restricted to Serbo-Croatian. Thus, Borer (1995) shows that participles and auxiliaries are adjoined at SS in Hebrew. The Italian data discussed by Belletti (1990) suggest that in Italian, participles also obligatorily adjoin to Aux at SS.[26] This opens up the possibility that participles universally adjoin to Aux. In languages in which participles do not adjoin to Aux at SS, the adjunction would take place in LF. Exactly when the adjunction takes place would depend on the strength of the [+aux] feature, which drives the adjunction.

The actual state of affairs may be slightly more complicated, however. Recall that the Serbo-Croatian data discussed in the previous sections provide evidence that in constructions involving one auxiliary and one or more participles, such as (46), the participle adjoins to the auxiliary.

(46) John has kissed Mary

However, there is evidence that in somewhat more complicated constructions, not attested in Serbo-Croatian, in which the auxiliary is preceded by another verbal element, the participle adjoins to the verbal element in question. I will argue in section 5.3 that the facts concerning verbal clusters in Standard Dutch indicate that in constructions such as (47) the participle adjoins to the modal verb.

(47) John could have kissed Mary

I will also argue that the auxiliary undergoes feature checking via adjunction to the higher modal verb. On the other hand, the participle and the auxiliary themselves do not seem to be involved in feature checking. In other words, the participle does not undergo adjunction to the auxiliary. The conclusion that I will reach on the basis of the Dutch data is that the participle must adjoin to the highest verbal head within its clause (see, however, note 37). In constructions such as (46), discussed above with respect to Serbo-Croatian, the highest head happens to be the auxiliary. On the other hand, in constructions such as (47), which I will discuss directly below with respect to Dutch, the highest head is the modal.[27]

5.3 Participle Movement in Standard Dutch

I will begin by examining (48).[28]

(48) Ik denk dat Jan het boek moet hebben gelezen 1-2-3
     I think that Jan the book must have   read
     'I think that Jan must have read the book'

Following Zwart (1993a), I assume that Dutch is a V-initial or, more generally, head-initial language. According to Zwart, direct objects in Dutch are generated following verbs and then undergo movement to the left of the verb. On the VO analysis (48) has the following structure if we disregard the possibility that some of the verbal elements have undergone head movement:

(49) Ik denk dat Jan het boek$_i$ [$_{VP}$ moet [$_{VP}$ hebben [$_{VP}$ gelezen t$_i$]]]
      I think that Jan the book   must   have   read

Let us now examine whether any V-movement must take place in (49). Since I will claim below that the participle at some point must adjoin to the modal, I will focus on the question of whether *gelezen* must be adjoined to *moet* in (49). Note first that *gelezen* cannot adjoin to *moet* unless *hebben* first adjoins to *moet*; if it does, the Minimize Chain Links Principle will be violated. (The adjunction of *hebben* to *moet* makes the base position of *hebben* and the landing site of *gelezen* equidistant from the base position of *gelezen*.) Given this, both verbal elements following the modal must adjoin to the modal in the derivation under consideration. Notice now that lexical material can intervene between *moet* and *hebben*, indicating that *moet* is not adjoined to the verbs following it at SS.[29]

(50) dat Jan het boek moet uit hebben gelezen 1-2-3
      that Jan the book must out have   read
      'that Jan must have finished reading the book'

(50) does not rule out the possibility that the auxiliary and the participle adjoin to the modal, after which the modal excorporates to move to a higher functional head. (51), however, does rule out this possibility.

(51) dat Jan het boek moet hebben uit gelezen 1-2-3

Suppose that the participle must adjoin overtly to the modal, in which case the auxiliary would also have to adjoin to the modal. If this were the case, even if the modal has the option of excorporating and moving to a higher functional head, we would not expect to find any lexical material intervening between the auxiliary and the participle, since the two would be adjoined to the same node. (I assume here that all the features of the auxiliary would be checked after adjunction to the modal, so that (51) cannot be analyzed as involving modal+auxiliary excorporation.) The grammaticality of (51) thus indicates that the participle does not have to adjoin to the modal in the overt syntax.

Having examined a construction in which the participle need not adjoin overtly to the modal, I will turn now to the constructions in which it must. The data in question will thus show that movement of the participle to the modal is optional—a state of affairs that can be accounted for if the feature driving the movement can be either strong or weak. In (51) the relevant feature must be weak, since the participle apparently does not undergo overt adjunction to the modal. In (52), on the other hand, the adjunction must be overt.[30]

(52) dat Jan het boek gelezen moet hebben 3-1-2

It seems plausible to analyze (52) as involving P-to-Mod adjunction. There is also independent evidence for the adjunction. Recall that in order for *gelezen* to adjoin to *moet*, *hebben* must also adjoin to *moet*; otherwise, the Minimize Chain Links Principle will be violated. (The base-generated position of *hebben* and the landing site of *gelezen* will not be equidistant from the base-generated position of *gelezen*.) Let us also assume that, as in similar constructions in Serbo-Croatian, the direction of adjunction is free; that is, it can take place either to the left or to the right.[31] Given this, in (52) *hebben* must first right-adjoin to *moet*, after which *gelezen* left-adjoins to it. Since all the verbal elements are located under the same node, in contrast to what happens in (48) (cf. (50)–(51)), we do not expect it to be possible to break up the verbal cluster in (52). The expectation is borne out.

(53) a. *dat Jan het boek gelezen uit moet hebben 3-1-2
     b. *dat Jan het boek gelezen moet uit hebben 3-1-2

The data in (52)–(53) are thus readily accounted for under the adjunction-to-the-modal analysis. The grammaticality of (54) is also expected.[32]

(54) ??dat Jan het boek gelezen hebben moet 3-2-1

In (54) *hebben* first left-adjoins to *moet*, after which *gelezen* can adjoin to the modal without violating the Minimize Chain Links Principle. As in the case of (52), under the current analysis we predict that, in contrast to (48), (54) does not allow material to be inserted between the verbal elements since they are located under the same node. The prediction is again borne out.

(55) a. *dat Jan het boek gelezen hebben uit moet 3-2-1
     b. *dat Jan het boek gelezen uit hebben moet 3-2-1

The analysis makes another prediction. Recall that if both participles precede the verbal head they are adjoined to in Serbo-Croatian, second-first participle order is preferable to the first-second participle order in Serbo-Croatian double participle constructions (see (33)). The explanation I gave for this in section 5.2.2 is that the first-second participle order involves adjunction to the lower segment of a segmented category, which is disallowed. Given the account of the Serbo-Croatian contrast in (33), we expect that switching the order of the participle and the auxiliary in (54) will lead to ungrammaticality. As (56) shows, the expectation is borne out.

(56) *dat Jan het boek hebben gelezen moet 2-3-1

In (56) *hebben* must adjoin to the modal before *gelezen* does; otherwise, the Minimize Chain Links Principle will be violated. However, given that *hebben* is already adjoined to *moet* at the point at which *gelezen* adjoins to *moet*, to derive (56), *gelezen* must adjoin to the lower segment of the segmented category headed by the modal, violating the A-over-A Principle (see also note 17). The contrast between (54) and (56) is thus accounted for.[33]

(57) a.   ... [$_{VP}$ moet [$_{VP}$ hebben [$_{VP}$ gelezen ...]]]
     b.   ... [$_{VP}$[$_V$ hebben$_i$ [$_V$ moet]] [$_{VP}$ t$_i$ [$_{VP}$ gelezen ...]]]
     c. *... [$_{VP}$[$_V$ hebben$_i$ [$_V$ gelezen$_j$ [$_V$ moet]]] [$_{VP}$ t$_i$ ... [$_{VP}$ t$_j$ ...]]]

The last grammatical order of the verbal cluster under consideration is shown in (58).

(58) dat Jan het boek moet gelezen hebben 1-3-2

Under the analysis presented here, (58) can be derived if *hebben* and *gelezen* first adjoin to the modal, and the modal then excorporates to move to a higher functional head. The analysis makes a straightforward prediction: that lexical material could intervene between the modal and the verbal elements following it, but not between the verbal elements that follow the modal, since they are adjoined to the same node. The prediction is borne out.

(59) a.   dat Jan het boek moet uit gelezen hebben 1-3-2
     b. *dat Jan het boek moet gelezen uit hebben 1-3-2

It should be pointed out here that the data concerning V-raising in Dutch provide a rather straightforward piece of evidence for Watanabe's (1993) economy account of excorporation, as observed by Roberts (1991) in a somewhat different system. We have seen that the second and third verbs in modal+auxiliary+participle clusters have the option of adjoining to the modal in the overt syntax. However, although *hebben* and *gelezen* may adjoin to *moet* in the overt syntax, they cannot move to C together with *moet* in V2 clauses.

(60) a. *[$_{CP}$ Gisteren gelezen moet hebben [$_{IP}$ Jan het boek]]
            yesterday read   must have   Jan the book
        'Yesterday, Jan must have read the book'
    b. *[$_{CP}$ Gisteren gelezen hebben moet [$_{IP}$ Jan het boek]]
    c. *[$_{CP}$ Gisteren moet hebben gelezen [$_{IP}$ Jan het boek]]
    d. *[$_{CP}$ Gisteren gelezen moet [$_{IP}$ Jan het boek hebben]]
    e. *[$_{CP}$ Gisteren moet gelezen [$_{IP}$ Jan het boek hebben]]
    f.   cf. [$_{CP}$ Gisteren moet [$_{IP}$ Jan het boek gelezen hebben]]

The ungrammaticality of (60a–e) provides more evidence for the economy account of excorporation. Since all features of the auxiliary and the participle are checked after adjunction to *moet*, the economy principles prevent *moet* from pied-piping the auxiliary and the participle when undergoing movement to C.

There is one more order of the verbal elements considered here that remains to be discussed. This order also raises a potential problem. Consider (61).

(61) *dat Jan het boek hebben moet gelezen 2-1-3

There are two ways of deriving (61) that need to be considered. Given that, as discussed above, P-movement is not obligatory in Dutch, (61) can be derived by adjoining *hebben* to the left of *moet*, leaving *gelezen* in situ. This derivation can be ruled out by assuming that the feature of the auxiliary that drives adjunction to the modal is weak, whereas the corresponding feature of the participle can be either strong or weak. Aux-to-Mod adjunction in (61) would then violate Procrastinate. Note, however, that the auxiliary would still be able to undergo overt adjunction to the modal in spite of Procrastinate when this is necessary to prevent the derivation from crashing. Given that, as argued in chapter 4, as well as Bošković 1995a and Chomsky 1994, violations of the Minimize Chain Links Principle lead to a crashed derivation, the auxiliary would undergo overt adjunction to the modal only when the participle does (i.e., when the participle is taken from the lexicon with a strong feature that drives adjunction to the modal), in order to ensure that the participle can reach the modal without violating the Minimize Chain Links Principle, which would cause the derivation to crash. Overt Aux-to-Mod adjunction in, for example, (52)–(55), where P-to-Mod adjunction takes place overtly, is thus "licensed" by the Minimize Chain Links Principle. The derivation in which the participle remains in situ in (61) is, however, ruled out by Procrastinate.

However, (61) can also be derived by adjoining *gelezen* to the modal overtly, as a result of which Aux-to-Mod adjunction would not violate Procrastinate. More precisely, if the direction of adjunction is free in the case of both Aux- and P-adjunction, (61) can be derived by first adjoining *hebben* to the left of the modal and then adjoining *gelezen* to the right of the modal. Why is this derivation disallowed? Since Aux- and P-adjunctions create overlapping paths in the derivation in question, the derivation could be ruled out by appealing to Pesetsky's (1982b) ban on crossing dependencies, which would also rule out (56). However, the status of the ban on crossing dependencies is not clear in the current theory.

Another way of ruling out the derivation under consideration would be to posit a condition such as (62).

(62) Target X from right to left.

The condition in (62) requires that, with multiple direction adjunction to the same element, rightward adjunction precedes leftward adjunction, as a result of which *gelezen* would have to adjoin to *moet* before *hebben* does in the derivation under consideration. The derivation is then readily ruled out via the Minimize Chain Links Principle, since *gelezen* crosses *hebben*, which does not belong to the same minimal domain as the target site of *gelezen*, on its way to *moet*. Recall, however, that the 2-1-3 order of adjoined verbal elements is allowed in Serbo-Croatian, as illustrated by (28a), discussed in section 5.2.2 and repeated here as (63). (Recall that *bili* must move before *čekali*.)

(63) Bili$_i$ *ste* čekali$_j$ t$_i$ t$_j$ Marijinu prijateljicu 2-1-3
      been are waited   Maria's friend
      'You had been waiting for Maria's friend'

Apparently the 2-1-3 order of overtly adjoined verbal elements is, in principle, possible. We thus need a "shallow" way of ruling out the overt P-movement derivation of (61) that will leave room for crosslinguistic variation. The ban on crossing dependencies is not expected to be subject to crosslinguistic variation. The same may hold for (62), though here the situation may be somewhat less clear.[34] I will leave open the ungrammaticality of (61) and merely note two additional ways of ruling out the overt P-movement derivation that are more susceptible to crosslinguistic variation since they crucially depend on lexical properties of relevant elements. Neither of them seems fully satisfactory to me, however. The derivation under consideration could be ruled out if the participle with a strong feature that drives adjunction to the modal has an additional lexical requirement forcing it to merge in the sense of Halle and Marantz (1993), Bobaljik (1994), and Lasnik (1995d) with an element to the left of the V node under which *moet* is generated, a prerequisite for merger being PF adjacency, as discussed in the works cited. Alternatively, we could rule out the derivation in question by assuming that whereas the direction of Aux-adjunction is free (i.e., it can take place either to the left or to the right), P-adjunction must take place to the left in Dutch. It is easy to verify that requiring that P-adjunction always take place to the left has no undesirable side effects for the data discussed above. (Recall that Chomsky (1994), who accepts Kayne's (1994) claim that XP-adjunction must take place to the left, assumes that the direction of head adjunction is free.)

In conclusion, the Dutch data considered above appear to indicate that, given a modal+auxiliary+participle sequence of verbal elements, the auxiliary and the participle must adjoin to the modal, the highest verbal head in the sequence, at some point in the derivation. Interestingly, when another element is added to the verbal cluster, the initial verbal element again seems to be the locus of adjunction. This is illustrated in (64). The ungrammaticality of (64b–d) indicates that all the verbal elements in (64a) are adjoined to the same node. This is shown in (64e).

(64) a. dat Jan het boek gelezen moet kunnen hebben 4-1-2-3
          that Jan the book read   must can   have
          'that Jan must have been able to read the book'
      b. *dat Jan het boek gelezen uit moet kunnen hebben
      c. *dat Jan het boek gelezen moet uit kunnen hebben
      d. *dat Jan het boek gelezen moet kunnen uit hebben
      e. dat Jan het boek [$_{VP}$ gelezen$_k$+moet+kunnen$_i$+hebben$_j$ [$_{VP}$ t$_i$
          [$_{VP}$ t$_j$ [$_{VP}$ t$_k$]]]]

Note that, given the structure in (64e), adjunction of *gelezen* to *moet* does not result in a Minimize Chain Links Principle violation. *Gelezen* is allowed to skip t$_j$ since its landing site and t$_j$ belong to the same minimal domain, namely, that of the chain ($hebben_j$, t_j), and are therefore equidistant from the base-generated position of *gelezen*. *Gelezen* is also allowed to skip t_i since its landing site and t_i both belong to the minimal domain of the chain ($kunnen_i$, t_i).

Recall now that in Serbo-Croatian auxiliary+participle+participle constructions the participles must adjoin to the auxiliary. The general conclusion that the Dutch and Serbo-Croatian data considered here point to is that, given a sequence of verbal elements (modals, auxiliaries, and participles), all verbal elements must adjoin to the highest element in the sequence at some point in the derivation.[35]

5.4 Participle Movement in Polish

Interesting confirmation of the conclusion reached at the end of section 5.3 is provided by Polish. As argued convincingly by Borsley and Rivero (1994), in constructions such as (65) the participle is adjoined to the auxiliary. (According to Borsley and Rivero, the adjunction is optional.)

(65) [$_{\text{AuxP}}$ Chciał$_i$-eś [$_{\text{VP}}$ t_i tę   książkę]]
      liked   AUX   this book
      'You liked this book'

Significantly, when another auxiliary is added right above the perfective auxiliary, the participle adjoins to the higher auxiliary.[36]

(66) Chciał$_i$ by-ś t_i tę   książkę
      liked   would AUX   this book
      'You would like this book'

The fact that no lexical material can intervene between the participle and the conditional auxiliary provides evidence that these two elements are adjoined.

(67) *Chciał tę   książkę by-ś
      liked this book   would AUX
      'You would like this book'

Note also that in order for the participle to adjoin to the conditional auxiliary without violating the Minimize Chain Links Principle, the perfective auxiliary must also adjoin to the conditional auxiliary. This makes the landing site of *chciał* and the base position of *ś* equidistant from the base position of *chciał*.

(68) Chciał$_i$+by+ś$_j$ t$_j$ t$_i$ tę książkę

That the adjunction indeed takes place is confirmed by the fact that no XPs can intervene between the auxiliaries.

(69) *Chciał by tę książkę-ś

Note that adding a higher verbal head above the perfective auxiliary excludes the possibility of P-to-*(e)ś* adjunction (cf. (65)).

(70) *By   chciał-eś tę   książkę
       would like AUX   this book
       'You would like this book'

Apparently, if overt P-movement is to take place in the constructions under consideration, the participle must adjoin to the conditional rather than the perfective auxiliary. The Polish data considered here thus confirm that, given a sequence of one or more modals/auxiliaries followed by a participle, the participle adjoins to the highest head in the sequence. If there is more than one modal/auxiliary in the sequence, it also must adjoin to the highest head. A kind of restructuring process thus seems to be at work here.[37] The null hypothesis is that the restructuring process, which I argued above takes place in Serbo-Croatian, Polish, and Dutch, is universal and that languages differ only with respect to the level at which the restructuring takes place.

5.5 Conclusion

In this chapter I have provided evidence for V-clustering in auxiliary/ modal+participle constructions. More specifically, I have argued that in multiple-V constructions involving participles and auxiliaries/modals all verbal elements end up adjoined to the highest verbal head in the sequence at some level of representation. In addition to providing evidence for V-clustering, the analysis presented here provides evidence that rightward adjunction is an available option at least for head movement, contrary to what is argued in Kayne 1994. I have shown that a considerable amount of crosslinguistic data can be accounted for in a principled way if the direction of head adjunction is in principle free. I have also provided evidence for the existence of excorporation, in particular, Watanabe's (1993) economy account of excorporation, which allows—in fact, forces— excorporation only in certain well-defined configurations. In addition, I have shown that equidistance is applicable to X^0-movement as well as XP-movement. Finally, I have provided evidence that Serbo-Croatian participles do not undergo long head movement, skipping another lexically filled X^0 position, as previously claimed in the literature, and that there is no fixed structural position for clitic clusters in Serbo-Croatian, which militates against purely structural accounts of the second position effect.

Notes

Chapter 1

1. In the split-I framework of Pollock (1989) and Chomsky (1991), adopted in this book, *John* in (1) is Case-marked under Spec-head agreement with the complex Agr$_S$ + Tense head, created by adjunction of Tense to Agr$_S$.

2. Since under standard minimalist assumptions in some cases NPs do not move to a Case position before LF, nouns are assumed to be taken from the lexicon with Case features, whose appropriateness to their structural position is later checked.

Chapter 2

1. This chapter is a revised and considerably expanded version of Bošković 1996b. The earliest version of the chapter is Bošković 1992.

2. Chomsky (1981) achieves the same result by assuming that *appear* but not *illegal* is lexically specified as triggering CP-deletion. See section 2.2.4.1 for arguments against this account.

3. Since Tense is assumed to be adjoined to Agr$_S$ at SS in English, when the distinction between Agr$_S$ and Tense is not crucial I will refer to the Agr$_S$+Tense complex as I and its maximal projection as IP. (It is actually not quite clear whether Agr$_S$P is present in infinitives.)

4. Terzi (1992) shows convincingly that the subject position of the embedded clause in the following Greek example can be filled by PRO. For relevant discussion, see also Watanabe 1993.

(i) O Yiannis theli PRO na   fai
     Yiannis wants   SUBJ.PART eats
     'Yiannis wants to eat'

5. (i) is an example of an infinitival complement headed by a lexical complementizer from Italian (however, see Kayne 1991 for an alternative analysis and Watanabe 1993 for criticism of the analysis).

(i) Gianni decise di   PRO vincere
     Gianni decided COMPL   to-win
     'Gianni decided to win'

6. The Last Resort Condition "requires that movement is permitted only to satisfy some condition" (Chomsky and Lasnik 1993, 523). The tacit assumption here is that NP raising is driven by the need to check the Case features of the NP undergoing movement, in accordance with Chomsky's (1993) Greed, which requires that α move only to satisfy a requirement on α (see chapter 4).

Note that prior to NP-movement PRO in (4b) is located in a Case-checking position that does not match the Case PRO is marked for. Still, PRO is not allowed to move to a position in which null Case can be checked. The same point can be made with respect to *he* in (i), due to Howard Lasnik (personal communication).

(i) *He$_i$ seems to t$_i$ that Mary is ill

Apparently, an NP located in a Case-checking position is not allowed to undergo movement to another Case-checking position even if its Case feature does not match the Case feature of the position the NP is already located in. To maintain the Last Resort Condition account of (4b) and (i), we need to assume that regardless of whether the Case features of the Case checker and Case checkee match, when an NP is found in a Case-checking position a Case-checking relation is established, thus preventing the NP from moving into another Case-checking position. This view is apparently adopted by Chomsky and Lasnik (1993). There is, however, an alternative way of ruling out movement from Case-checking to Case-checking position that readily extends to (i) and (4b). Suppose that such movement is in principle allowed. As Martin (1992a) shows, constructions involving such movement can still be ruled out if Case features of traditional Case assigners must be "discharged" or, in minimalist terms, checked. On this view, if *he* undergoes Case checking in the matrix SpecIP in (i), the construction is ruled out because the Case feature of *to* remains unchecked. In this chapter, following Chomsky and Lasnik (1993), I will refer to all instances of movement from Case-checking to Case-checking position as "Last Resort Condition violations" without committing myself to one of the two possible analyses of the ungrammaticality of such movement (Greed or the requirement that Case features of traditional Case assigners be discharged). I will delay the discussion of exactly how such movement should be ruled out until chapter 4.

7. Attempts were made before Chomsky and Lasnik 1993 to account for the distribution of PRO via Case theory. It has often been suggested that the distribution of PRO can be captured if it is assumed that PRO does not tolerate Case. The proposal is empirically seriously flawed, however, as Chomsky and Lasnik demonstrate.

8. As noted in chapter 1, I do not discuss gerunds in this book. For some relevant discussion of gerunds, see Martin 1992b, where it is argued, contra Stowell (1982), that gerunds are specified as [+tense].

9. As noted by Pesetsky (1992), who essentially follows Enç (1991), when either an overt (ia) or an implicit (ib) adverb of quantification is present, eventive predicates can be embedded under *believe*.

(i) a. John believed Mary to always sing the anthem
    b. John believed Mary to sing the anthem

In such constructions, the adverb of quantification binds the temporal argument of the eventive predicate—hence the obligatoriness of the habitual reading in (i). (The grammaticality of (5a) on the nonhabitual reading shows that an implicit adverb of quantification does not have to be present when an eventive predicate is embedded under a control predicate.)

As for constructions such as *John believed Peter to have brought the beer* and *John believes Peter to be bringing the beer right now*, Martin (1992b) argues that *have* and *be*, which can be taken to be specified as [+tense], serve as binders of the temporal argument of the embedded-clause main verb.

It is worth noting in this context that, on the basis of the obligatoriness of the habitual reading in constructions such as *Mary sings the anthem*, which contrasts in the relevant respect with *Mary sang the anthem*, Enç (1991) argues that English has no "present tense." As a result, the temporal argument of *sing* can be bound only by an implicit adverb of quantification (or some kind of habitual/generic operator)—hence the obligatoriness of the habitual reading. (This implies that finite I can check nominative Case regardless of its Tense specification.) Some other languages apparently differ from English in the relevant respect. Thus, in French *Marie chante l'hymne* can either have the habitual reading or mean that Marie is singing the anthem right now, which indicates that French has "present tense"; that is, the I of the construction is specified as [+tense] and therefore can bind the temporal argument of *chanter*.

10. Notice also the ungrammaticality of (i).

(i) *John met someone but I don't know who$_i$ Peter said [$_{CP}$ t$_i$ [$_{C'}$ C e]]

If the null C in (i) can undergo agreement with the trace in its Spec, we would expect that, in contrast to what we find in (6f), IP-ellipsis can be licensed in (i). The fact that (i) is ungrammatical provides evidence against the accounts of the C-trace effect that are crucially based on the assumption that, in contrast to *that*, the null complementizer undergoes Spec-head agreement with the trace in its Spec (see Lasnik and Saito 1992 and Rizzi 1990a, among others).

11. As illustrated by *I don't believe they will win the World Cup, but John believes they are likely to*, VP-ellipsis is possible with some traditional raising predicates such as *likely*, a possibility that seems unexpected given the standard assumption that their complement contains no PRO. However, Lasnik and Saito (1992) and Martin (1992b), provide convincing evidence that *likely* is ambiguous between a control and a raising predicate, which accounts for the fact that it allows VP-ellipsis. Martin notes that, as expected, when we rule out the control option by using expletive *there*, which cannot control PRO, VP-ellipsis becomes unacceptable (e.g., *John doesn't believe there is likely to be any Asian team in the final game, but I believe there is likely to*). Martin shows that some other traditional raising predicates, such as *seem*, which allow VP-ellipsis, also allow the control option (see section 3.4). According to Martin, the infinitival complement of the predicates in question can be specified either as [+tense], which results in a control structure, or [−tense], which results in a raising structure.

12. Note that the clean semantic division between the verbs that allow PRO in the subject position of their infinitival complement and those that do not is

unexpected under the standard CP-deletion/binding-theoretic account of the phenomena under consideration, on which whether or not a verb allows PRO in its infinitival complement depends on arbitrary lexical properties (i.e., whether or not the verb is lexically specified as a CP deleter). As shown in the text, the relevant facts can be accommodated in a more principled way under the Case-theoretic account of the distribution of PRO.

13. As shown by Motapanyane (1994), an example of the impossibility of A-movement out of CPs is provided by Romanian subjunctive complements, which can be introduced by the complementizer *ca* (ia). However, when A-movement takes place out of a subjunctive complement, the complementizer cannot be present (ib–c). ((ia–c) are from Rivero 1989.)

(i) a. Trebuia ca studenţii să plece
         must-3SG that students-the SUBJ.PART leave
         'It must have been that the students left'
    b. Studenţii trebuiau să plece
         students-the must-3PL SUBJ.PART leave
         'The students must have left'
    c. *Studenţii trebuiau ca să plece
         students-the must-3PL that SUBJ.PART leave

This can be accounted for if A-movement is not allowed to take place out of CPs (see section 2.3.2.1 for arguments that *ca*-less complements are IPs). Note that there is no *that*-trace effect in Romanian, so that (ic) cannot be ruled out on a par with *Who do you think that left*. (Watanabe (1993) proposes an alternative account of (ib–c) crucially based on his two-layered theory of Case checking. However, I show in note 21 that this theory of Case checking cannot be maintained.)

For more examples of the impossibility of A-movement out of CPs, see (for Serbo-Croatian and French) sections 2.2.4.2 and 3.4 and (for Japanese) Murasugi and Saito 1994 and Saito 1994.

The impossibility of A-movement out of CPs may actually be a consequence of the economy principles. Manzini's (1994) Locality, an economy constraint that requires every movement to be as short as possible, in fact forces *studenţii* in (ic) to pass through the embedded SpecCP. (In Manzini's system, movement must proceed through the domain of each head.) The Improper Movement Constraint then prevents *studenţii* from undergoing A-movement. Saito (1994) proposes a similar analysis of the ban on A-movement out of CPs that is also based on the interaction of the Minimize Chain Links Principle and the Improper Movement Constraint. Notice also that if, as argued by Saito (1992) and Takahashi (1994), the Improper Movement Constraint can be deduced from the economy principles, the impossibility of A-movement out of CPs actually follows from those principles.

14. As *John was persuaded to leave* illustrates, object control passives, where a controller is present, are acceptable. This suggests that the failure of control is indeed responsible for the ungrammaticality of (13).

15. That (12a) can be ruled out by the Last Resort Condition was also noticed independently by Howard Lasnik (personal communication).

16. Evidence for the presence of the null C is provided by the ungrammaticality of (i).

(i) *I wanted very much [$_{CP}$ C [$_{IP}$ him to leave]]

Given that a null complementizer must be present in (i), under standard assumptions the construction is ruled out by the ECP because the null complementizer is not properly governed (see section 2.2.4.1 for relevant discussion and possible treatments of this phenomenon within the minimalist system).

It is possible that the null C receives Case features from the higher verb, given the ungrammaticality of the passive (ii).

(ii) *It was wanted [$_{CP}$ C [$_{IP}$ him to leave]]

This can be implemented as follows: In Bošković 1995a I suggest that Agr has N and V Case features, which are matched against the Case features of V or Tense adjoined to Agr and the NP in SpecAgrP. (On this view Case features are treated like φ features.) Suppose that, like Agr, the null C in constructions such as (14a) and (ii) also has N and V Case features. Its N Case feature could be checked against the NP in the infinitival subject position (see the discussion directly below in the text). In (14a) its V Case feature would be checked by adjunction to the higher verb, which is specified as [+accusative]. Since the higher verb is passivized and therefore not specified as [+accusative] in (ii), the V Case feature of the null C remains unchecked in (ii).

17. Under this analysis we need to assume that the *for-to* I checks accusative rather than null Case.

18. Two *Natural Language & Linguistic Theory* reviewers argue that *expect* raises a problem for the analysis developed here. Like *want*, *expect* allows PRO (e.g., *I expected to leave*), lexical subjects (e.g., *I expected (for) John to leave*), and VP-ellipsis (e.g., *They didn't expect John to win, but they expected Mary to*). However, unlike *want* and like *believe*, *expect* allows passive raising (e.g., *John is expected to leave*). Bresnan (1972) provides convincing evidence that *expect* is three-ways ambiguous. On its intentional reading, which describes the subject's desire, it belongs to the *want*-class. *I expect for John to go there* illustrates this reading. On its predictive reading, which describes beliefs, *expect* belongs to the *believe*-class. *There are expected to be soldiers in the town* illustrates this reading. As expected, ellipsis is not allowed on this reading (e.g., **John doesn't believe there are any soldiers in the town, but there are expected to*). Finally, on its compulsive reading, *expect* belongs to the *persuade*-class and takes an animate NP complement in addition to the infinitival complement. This reading is illustrated by *You are expected to remove the tables after the dinner*. It is easy to verify that, given the three-way ambiguity of *expect*, the potentially problematic behavior noted above can readily be accounted for.

19. Stowell does not discuss (21c). Note that I use here the traditional terms "ECP" and "government" for ease of exposition. As noted above, the status of government is dubious. In the current framework Stowell's proper government requirement on null heads can readily be reformulated as a condition on identification of null heads. (It is well known that null elements do not occur freely in

the structure.) C-command would probably have to be involved in the proper statement of the condition. Thus, a null C would have to be c-commanded by the higher verb.

An alternative, proposed by Pesetsky (1992), is to treat the null complementizer as an affix that must undergo affixation to a verbal head, which could be a result of a more general requirement that all null morphemes be affixes. The requirement could provide a single uniform way of licensing null heads. On Pesetsky's analysis (see also Ormazabal 1995), affixation takes place through head movement of C to V, which may be blocked in (21b–c) because the affixed C does not c-command its trace after the embedded clause undergoes movement. An alternative is to assume that C-V affixation takes place through the process of merger (see Halle and Marantz 1993, Bobaljik 1994, Lasnik 1995d)) under PF adjacency. In (21b–c) merger would be blocked because the null C and the matrix V are not adjacent at PF, and the constructions would be ruled out because of the presence of a stranded affix. The affixation analysis is appealing. Unfortunately, it cannot account for the full range of relevant facts. Thus, it is well known that null complementizers that enter into a Spec-head relation with an operator (or its trace) are for some reason exempt from the traditional head government requirement. (Here I consider binding of a variable to be a prerequisite for operator status.)

(i) a. $[_{CP}$ What$_i$ C $[_{IP}$ John likes t$_i$]] is apples
   b. Who$_i$ do you believe sincerely $[_{CP}$ t$_i$ C $[_{IP}$ t$_i$ is crazy]]

I see no principled way of accounting for the contrast between (i) and (21b–c) under the affixation analysis. ((24a) is also potentially problematic for the C-to-V movement analysis. For other problems that arise on this analysis, see section 2.4.) The contrast seems to be more amenable to an analysis whereby the head government requirement on null heads is reformulated as a condition on identification of null elements. Here, for ease of exposition, I will continue to use the traditional term "ECP". (For an ECP analysis of (ib), see Snyder and Rothstein 1992.)

20. Stowell (1982) suggests that the embedded clause in (22b) is specified as [−tense]. If this were the case, since C is not required in [−tense] clauses under Stowell's analysis, the ECP would not be violated in (22b). I believe, however, that the infinitival I in (22b) is specified as [+tense], though it is somewhat difficult to see this owing to the stativity of the matrix predicate. It is clear, however, that whether the act of buying a car has happened or will yet happen is left unspecified in (22b); this fact can be accounted for if we assume that the infinitival complement of *desirable* contains [+tense, −finite] I, associated with irrealis interpretation. Certain facts concerning the interpretation of the infinitival in question provide evidence for this assumption. It is well known that, as *John tried to have won* illustrates, perfective *have* is incompatible with irrealis infinitivals, specified as [+tense, −finite], plausibly because of a Tense clash between perfective *have* and irrealis Tense. Given this, the ungrammaticality of *To have bought a car was desirable at that time* indicates that the infinitival complement of *desirable* also contains irrealis Tense or, more precisely, [+tense, −finite] I. Note also that eventive predicates are allowed in the infinitival complement of *desirable* (e.g., *To win was desirable at that time*). Recall now that eventive predicates are allowed only in

clauses that are specified as [+tense] (see (5)). Given this, the possibility of eventive predicates in the infinitival complement of *desirable* also indicates that, like the infinitival complement of *try* and unlike the infinitival complement of *believe*, the infinitival embedded under *desirable* is specified as [+tense].

21. The data under consideration also provide evidence against Watanabe's (1993) two-layered theory of Case checking. Watanabe argues that Case checking under Spec-head agreement with Agr creates a feature that forces Agr to raise to a functional head above it. Under this proposal, Case-checking SpecIPs must be dominated by a CP. However, the data considered in this section, as well as those discussed in section 2.3, provide evidence that the SpecIP position in which null Case and nominative Case are checked does not have to be dominated by a CP. (Nominative Case-checking SpecIPs are discussed in section 2.3.)

22. Given Chomsky's (1993) claim that all movement is driven by morphological considerations, scrambling would have to involve some kind of feature checking. The precise nature of the feature in question, however, is not clear. Saito (1989) suggests that it is some kind of focus feature. For a discussion of scrambling and economy, see Fukui 1993, where it is argued that scrambling operations are costless in languages that allow them; that is, they are exempt from the Last Resort Condition.

23. It is tempting to interpret the data in (i) as providing more evidence against the binding-theoretic account of the distribution of PRO.

(i) a. *What the terrorists believe is [$_{CP}$ they will hijack an airplane]
     b. *They believed and we claimed [$_{CP}$ Peter would visit the hospital]
     c. *It was believed at that time [$_{CP}$ John would fail Mary]

(ii) a. *What the terrorists believed was [PRO to have hijacked an airplane]
     b. *They suspected and we believed [PRO to have visited the hospital]
     c. *They believed at that time [PRO to have failed Mary]

As noted above, under the standard analysis (ia–c) are ruled out by the ECP because the null C heading the embedded clauses is not properly governed. The ungrammaticality of the constructions thus provides evidence that the embedded clauses in (i) are barriers to government, and the same should then hold for the embedded clauses in (ii). Given that the embedded clauses in (ii) are barriers to government, PRO is ungoverned in (iia–c), as required under the binding-theoretic account. Notice also that, as (22) and (23a–b) show, PRO can in principle appear in the relevant configurations so that nothing seems to go wrong with respect to control in (ii). The data considered in this note can be taken to indicate that regardless of whether or not PRO is governed, it cannot appear in the subject position of the infinitival complement of *believe*. This is expected under the Case-theoretic account of the distribution of PRO, which rests on the requirement that PRO be Case-checked by [+tense, −finite] I, but not under the binding-theoretic account, on which PRO can in principle appear in the subject position of the infinitival complement of *believe* as long as PRO is ungoverned. However, it may still be possible to account for (ii) under the binding-theoretic account by assuming that the relevant clauses in (ii) undergo LF reconstruction to a position governed by *believe* (see section 4.4.1.4) and that the binding conditions, which determine the distribution of PRO, are checked at LF after reconstruction, whereas the head government requirement on null heads holds at a level prior to reconstruction.

24. Since Law 1991 and the earliest version of this chapter, Bošković 1992, were written, several works have appeared where principles similar to (31) have been proposed. (See Chomsky 1995, Doherty, in press, Grimshaw 1994, Radford 1994, Safir 1993, and Speas 1994, among others. On grounds similar to mine, Doherty and Grimshaw also apparently independently argue that the MSP forces IP status on zero finite complements.)

"Lexical structure" in (31) refers to structure involving projections of heads bearing categorial features. *Satisfaction of lexical requirements* refers to the satisfaction of l-/s-selectional requirements and checking of features specified in lexical entries. If a projection is needed for feature checking, or to satisfy l-/s-selectional requirements, its presence is unaffected by the MSP. For example, Agr_OP must be present in *John likes Mary*; otherwise, the Case features of *Mary* and the Agr_O features of the verb would not be checked. Note also that I assume that, as argued in Kitagawa 1986, Webelhuth 1992, and Bošković 1995a, complementizer *that* is nominal in nature. As a result, since the MSP is not relevant to elements bearing categorial features, complementizer *that* is also unaffected by the MSP.

In section 2.3.3 I return to the issue of how the relevant economy principle should be formulated and show that the effects of (31) follow from derivational constraints, in particular, the ban on superfluous steps in a derivation.

25. Assuming that, in contrast to Op-relative elements, *wh*-relative elements have a [+wh] feature that has to be checked under Spec-head agreement with an appropriate functional head, *wh*-relatives such as *the man who she loves* would be CPs in spite of the MSP (see note 32 for evidence for different categorial status of Op-and *wh*-relatives).

Note also that (32a) involves null operator adjunction to an adjunct. Such adjunction is allowed even in Chomsky's (1986a) system, which otherwise severely restricts the possibilities for adjunction (see Chomsky's analysis of parasitic gaps).

26. Law (1991) makes the same point.

27. In Bošković 1994b I adopted a slightly revised version of the condition, which was considered by Saito (University of Connecticut lectures 1993) but not ultimately adopted in Saito and Murasugi 1993. (The basic idea behind the condition remains the same.)

28. I show in Bošković 1994b that (38) has considerable motivation. Thus, a constraint like (38) may be needed to prevent the Minimize Chain Links Principle, which requires that each chain link be as short as possible, from forcing a phrase in an adjoined position to keep adjoining to the same node. I show as well that (38) also enables us to dispense with D-Structure and the θ-Criterion, in accordance with Chomsky's (1993) Minimalist Program. In particular, I show that (38) enables us to rule out ungrammatical instances of movement into θ-positions, while still allowing movement into θ-positions to take place in certain well-defined configurations, in which I argue the movement indeed does take place (see also

chapter 3). Note that (38) also rules out adjunction of X to its own XP and substitution of X to SpecXP, which raised a problem in Chomsky 1994 (where it was called "self-attachment").

29. A reviewer for *Natural Language & Linguistic Theory* raises a question concerning what drives the movement of the null operator in (39). There are several factors that could be responsible for this movement. The operator is clearly required in its raised position to establish construal with the relative head. As the reviewer notes, this cannot drive the movement, given Chomsky's (1993) claim that movement cannot be driven merely by a search for interpretability. However, I assume that, like other NPs in English, null operators are free to undergo topicalization. (The exact driving force behind topicalization remains to be determined.) If Op in (39) does not topicalize, the constructions are ruled out for semantic reasons, because Op cannot be construed with the relative clause head. This problem does not arise if Op undergoes topicalization. As for (33), where Op is arguably located in a position in which it can be construed with the relative clause head prior to movement, I adopt Rizzi's (1990a) proposal that null operators are anaphoric and that anaphoric elements are incompatible with agreement processes. Given this, the null operator in relative clauses cannot remain in an agreeing position such as SpecIP, or, to be more precise, SpecAgr$_S$P. It is then forced to topicalize. As noted above, topicalization is not allowed in this context. Howard Lasnik (personal communication) suggests an alternative motivation for Op-movement in (33), which can also be extended to (39). Chomsky (1993) argues that question operators can be interpreted in A-positions. As a result, they remain in situ at LF. (The assumption here is that there is no LF *wh*-movement, so that any *wh*-phrase that is in situ at SS remains in situ at LF. See section 3.3 for evidence to this effect.) If, in contrast to question operators, relative operators can be interpreted only in Ā- but not in A-positions—that is, they must establish an Op-variable relation—relative operators would be forced either to move to SpecCP or undergo topicalization. As Howard Lasnik points out, the fact that, unlike overt question operators, overt relative operators cannot remain in situ provides some evidence for different modes of interpretation for the two operator types.

30. Andrew Radford (personal communication) points out that short zero subject relatives can also be found in Shakespeare's works (i). As expected, null subjects are also found there (ii). (I am grateful to Andrew Radford for these examples.)

(i) a. There is a lord will hear you play tonight (*Taming of the Shrew*)
    b. Thou hast hawks will soar above the morning lark (*Taming of the Shrew*)
    c. You are the man must stead us all (*Taming of the Shrew*)
    d. Youth's a stuff will not endure (*Twelfth Night*)

(ii) a. Hast any more of this (*The Tempest*)
     b. What didst not like (*Othello*)
     c. Wast ever in court, shepherd (*As You Like It*)
     d. Lives, sir (*Othello*)

Short zero-subject relatives also seem to be possible in Black English and some dialects in the southwestern United States. Pesetsky (1982a) argues that the availability of such constructions in Black English should be accounted for on a par with their availability in null-subject languages. Unfortunately, I do not have the relevant data that could determine whether the same holds for southwestern dialects.

Andrew Radford (personal communication) offers an interesting alternative to the above analysis of the possibility of short zero-subject relatives in null-subject languages. He suggests that in null-subject languages the null operator can remain in situ in SpecIP, in which case it is licensed by virtue of being a null subject rather than a null operator. In other words, it is licensed as pro. As Radford points out, a desirable side effect of this analysis is that it can readily be extended to account for the possibility of short zero-subject relatives in English infinitivals. Since, in contrast to pro, PRO is allowed in English, the subject can remain in SpecIP in *I'm looking for somebody [PRO to fix my car]*, where it is licensed as a (*wh-*)PRO rather than as a null operator. (Notice, however, that short zero-subject infinitival relatives sound quite bad in a number of contexts in English. Consider, for example, **I showed [the man to fix the car] to John.*)

31. I am grateful to Daiko Takahashi for bringing these data to my attention.

32. As expected, a resumptive pronoun is allowed in *the book* [CP *which I was wondering whether I would get it in the mail*] (cf. note 25).

Note that my analysis of the data discussed in this section is crucially based on the distinction between specifiers and adjuncts. As a result, to the extent that it is successful, it provides evidence that the distinction is still needed, contrary to what is argued in Kayne 1994.

33. I assume that adjunction to heads—for example, V-to-I adjunction—does not suffice to satisfy the proper government requirement on null heads.

34. There may actually be a contrast with respect to the possibility of extraposition between presupposed and nonpresupposed relatives.

(i) a.   *A doctor was available Op$_i$ John spoke to t$_i$
    b.   ??No doctor was available Op$_i$ John spoke to t$_i$

(ib), involving a nonpresupposed relative, seems to be better than (ia), involving a presupposed relative. If the contrast (which as far as I know has not previously been noted in the literature) is real, it can be accounted for as follows under the IP analysis: Given the grammaticality of (ib), nothing should go wrong with respect to the ECP in (ia). As noted above, null heads that are in a Spec-head relation with an operator are exempt from the ECP. Given that a null operator is adjoined to the relative clause in (ia–b), the grammaticality of (ib) may indicate that being in a checking relation with an operator in fact exempts null heads from the ECP. (I am assuming here Chomsky's (1993) definition of checking domain.)

Let us now examine the ungrammaticality of (ia) more closely. In his discussion of factive clausal complements, Hegarty (1992) argues that the event position of a presupposed clausal complement must be θ-bound by the complementizer of the complement in order for the complement to be properly interpreted. Essentially following Hegarty's theory of presupposition, suppose that the event position of presupposed relatives must be θ-bound either by the relative clause complementizer or by the determiner head of the relative. θ-binding by the complementizer/

determiner (within the discourse frame) makes the event position referentially transparent, thus yielding the presupposition that the event in question actually occurred. (ia) is then ruled out because the event position of the relative clause remains unbound. D does not c-command the event position after extraposition, and C is not present in the relative clause under the IP analysis. On the other hand, since the relative clause in (ib) is not presupposed, its event position does not have to be θ-bound by either D or C. As a result, the relative can be freely extraposed. I assume that the event position of the relative is existentially quantified out, yielding the correct interpretation. If real, the surprising contrast in (i) thus receives an account under the IP analysis.

35. For evidence for the IP analysis, also see Bowers 1987, Hegarty 1990, 1991, Law 1990, Li 1990, and Webelhuth 1992, among others.

   Note that, given the discussion in section 2.3.1, (21b–c) are still ruled out by the ECP even under the IP analysis, because the phonologically null head of the embedded clause—namely, I—is not properly governed. Since the head of the infinitival IP in (22a–b) is the lexical particle *to*, the ECP is not violated in those examples. (This analysis can be extended to (23)–(25).) The question now is how the head of root declarative clauses is licensed. This question is independent of the IP analysis, since it arises even if all finite clauses are CPs. Banfield's (1973) discourse-based category Expression might serve as an appropriate licenser for root I. However, it is worth mentioning in this context that Rizzi (1990b) observes that the theory of licensing cannot require that every element be licensed by something else. There must be an independently licensed position from which the chain of licensing can start; otherwise, no syntactic structure would be possible at all. Rizzi argues on independent grounds that the independently licensed position from which the chain of licensing starts is root I. The theory of event position binding proposed by Hegarty (1992), according to which root but not embedded I is "strong" enough to bind the event position, points to the same conclusion. For an alternative IP analysis of (21b–c) under which the problem noted here with respect to root clauses does not arise, see Webelhuth 1992.

36. One weak argument for an obligatory CP in complement clauses is that C specifies the illocutionary force of a clause (i.e., whether a clause is interrogative, declarative, etc.). As pointed out by Andrew Radford (personal communication), we could get around this under the IP analysis by assuming that declarative is the default interpretation of clauses, a rather natural assumption.

37. Some speakers accept embedded topicalization without *that* in some contexts. Howard Lasnik (personal communication) suggests that in the contexts in question these speakers analyze the superficial embedded clause involving topicalization as a matrix clause, and the superficial matrix clause as an adsentential (see Bresnan 1969 for discussion of adsententials).

38. Motapanyane (1994) shows that in Romanian, adjunction to CP is also allowed when the CP is not an argument, but disallowed when it is an argument.

39. Since we are dealing here with selection for the contents present below the C^0 node rather than just CP, I assume that the presence of the complementizer in question is a result of l-selection. Unfortunately, no comprehensive classification

of ASL verbs with respect to the possibility of long *wh*-extraction, which is crucially needed to further investigate the issue, can be found in the literature.

40. However, *ca să* sequences have a somewhat degraded status.

41. I am grateful to Arhonto Terzi for bringing these facts to my attention.

42. Interestingly, although overt subject NPs are allowed in subjunctive complements (see (53)), they are not allowed to precede *să* in bare IP subjunctives (ia). However, they can precede *să* in subjunctive CPs (ib).

(i) a. *Vreau Ion să   vină   mîine
        I-want Ion PRT comes tomorrow
    b. Vreau ca Ion să vină mîine
        I-want that Ion PRT comes tomorrow

Barbosa (1994) argues that preverbal lexical subjects in pro-drop languages with rich agreement are actually adjuncts, the phonologically null pronominal pro being the "real" subject in relevant constructions. Given Barbosa's proposal, the lexical subject in (ia–b) is adjoined to IP. As a result, (ia) is ruled out on a par with (54a) by the ban on adjunction to arguments. The ban is not violated in (ib), where the subjunctive IP, to which the subject is adjoined, is not an argument.

43. I also gave two arguments for the IP analysis based on factive complementation and one argument based on *wh*-extraction from extraposed clauses. Since I do not discuss factive complements here, I will not repeat the factive complementation arguments. As for the extraction argument, it was framed in the *Barriers* system (Chomsky 1986a) and does not readily translate to the current framework.

44. I assume that all contraction takes place at the same level, which is the null hypothesis. Bresnan (1971) argues that (56a–b) involve procliticization. However, see Kaisse 1983, Selkirk 1972, and Wood 1979, among others, for convincing arguments that (56a–b) involve encliticization.

I confine myself here to discussing contraction with *is* and *has*, since contraction with other forms of the verbs in question (and with modals) is very restricted. (I examine only fully contracted vowelless forms of the auxiliaries.) Thus, *have* fails to contract with the higher verb in *Which students did he say've given up syntax*. However, this does not tell us anything about possible blocking effects of *wh*-trace on contraction since, as noted by Kaisse (1983), *have* quite generally fails to undergo contraction if the host of contraction is not a pronoun. (This includes *wh*-words.) Thus, contraction is also impossible in *Larry and Moe've given up syntax* and *John may've gone there*.

45. Bobaljik (1994) also argues that *wh*-traces are invisible at PF (i.e., do not block PF processes that require PF adjacency).

46. Lasnik (in preparation) also argues, on the basis of contraction in pseudo-gapping constructions, that base-generated null heads block PF contraction.

47. Some recent accounts of *wanna*-contraction, such as those of Snyder and Rothstein (1992) and Kitahara (1993a), which attempt to extend Jaeggli's account to (56a–b), are also problematic in that they appeal to Case theory to rule out a PF representation.

48. Travis (1991) and Zwart (1991, 1993b) argue that subject-initial verb-second (V2) clauses in Germanic V2 languages are IPs. This may also be a consequence of the MSP. The MSP may also be responsible for the IP status of gerunds (see Munn 1991 and references therein for arguments that gerunds are IPs). Andrew Radford (personal communication) notes that the MSP may force NP status and rule out the DP option for (seemingly) unquantified nominals (e.g., *People buy soaps*). I leave detailed exploration of ramifications of the MSP for future research.

49. Under Chomsky's approach the notion of logical equivalence is relevant to choosing an optimal derivation. (This is where effect on LF output comes into play.) I put aside the (very serious and complex) issue of whether this is the right approach (see Chomsky 1995 and references therein). How this issue should be resolved depends on, among other things, whether quantifier raising exists and how it should be treated in the minimalist framework, a very murky question.

50. In Bošković 1996b I argue that certain facts concerning the interpretation of PRO also provide evidence that the infinitival complement of *try*-class verbs must be an IP. Following the governed-anaphora account of the interpretation of PRO (see Bouchard 1984, Hornstein and Lightfoot 1987, Franks and Hornstein 1992, Koster 1984, Munn 1991, and Sportiche 1983), I argue that the obligatoriness of control with *try*-class verbs, as well as the nonobligatoriness of control in constructions such as (i), can be accounted for if, in contrast to the infinitival complement in (i), the infinitival complement of *try* must be an IP.

(i) John asked [$_{CP}$ how$_i$ [$_{IP}$ PRO to behave oneself t$_i$]]

I essentially repeat the arguments of the authors arguing for the governed-anaphora approach to the interpretation of PRO and show that this approach to the interpretation of PRO fits in nicely with the Case-theoretic approach to the distribution of PRO, giving a comprehensive theory of syntactic and interpretive properties of PRO. Since, as is well known (see Bošković 1996b and references cited therein), the interpretation of PRO has always been a sore point for the binding-theoretic account of the distribution of PRO, the fact that the Case-theoretic account can be complemented with a theory that accounts for the interpretation of PRO provides one more argument that the Case-theoretic account is superior to the binding-theoretic account.

51. Gerunds probably raise the most serious problem for Pesetsky's position (see Stowell 1982 and Munn 1991, among others, for arguments that gerunds are IPs).

52. Ormazabal proposes that, in order to be interpreted properly, irrealis complements must be IPs and propositional complements must be CPs. However, he does not give a principled semantic explanation for the correlation between categorial status and semantic types that he attempts to establish, and as a result his analysis remains rather stipulative.

53. It should be pointed out that Pesetsky 1992 contains an excellent discussion of the semantics of the complementizer *for*. However, the view of (post-)LF syntax that Pesetsky adopts goes against the spirit of the Minimalist Program.

54. As Pesetsky notes, there are exceptions to Myers's generalization, namely, the morphemes -*er* and -*able*.

55. Chomsky's analysis must be revised under the DP hypothesis. The revision is straightforward, given Lasnik's (1995a) arguments that inherent Case can be assigned under Spec-head agreement as long as the element that θ-marks the relevant NP is located under the head that undergoes Spec-head agreement with the NP in question. Thus, Lasnik argues that partitive Case is assigned inherently in the LF representation of (ia), after the indefinite NP moves to SpecAgr$_O$P and *arrive*, a partitive Case licenser, moves to Agr$_O$. (I ignore further movement of *arrive*.) Lasnik assumes that the indefinite NP is in a θ-licensing configuration with *arrive* after LF object shift. (See section 3.2 for evidence to this effect. Here I ignore expletive replacement, which is discussed in chapter 4.)

(i) a. SS There have arrived three men
    b. LF There have [$_{Agr_O P}$ three men$_i$ Agr$_O$+arrived$_j$ [$_{VP}$ t$_j$ t$_i$]]

According to Lasnik, the element that satisfies the θ-licensing requirement on inherent Case marking does not actually have to bear any Case feature as long as it is adjoined to the element that assigns inherent Case. Thus, Lasnik argues that in existential constructions involving the verb *be*, such as *There has been a fireman available*, the indefinite NP is assigned inherent Case by *be* after moving to SpecAgr$_O$P at LF (see (ii)). Since *be* is a light verb, the lower predicate *available* adjoins to *be*. Given that *available* θ-marks the indefinite NP, the merged predicate located under Agr$_O$ satisfies the θ-licensing requirement on inherent Case marking.

(ii) There has [$_{Agr_O P}$ a fireman$_i$ Agr$_O$+been$_j$+available$_k$ [$_{VP}$ t$_j$ t$_i$ t$_k$]]

Suppose now that (66b) has the following structure, with the noun *destruction* undergoing head movement to Agr, located under D:

(iii) [$_{DP}$ Rome's$_i$ Agr+destruction$_j$ [$_{NP}$ t$_j$ t$_i$]]

Since, like *arrive* and *available* in (i)–(ii), *destruction* in (iii) is in a θ-licensing relation with the relevant NP, the NP can be assigned inherent genitive Case. (Note that *destruction* actually does not have to bear any Case features; that is, genitive Case could be assigned by Agr in D or some kind of possessive morpheme. The D+N complex would still satisfy all the requirements for inherent Case licensing, just like the Agr$_O$+*be*+*available* complex does in (ii).)

56. Concerning (67d), Pesetsky (1992) notes that *it* is generally not very good when following *of* in nominals even when it is θ-marked by the relevant noun, as illustrated by *my destruction of it*. However, (67d) is much worse than *my destruction of it*, which indicates that it violates an additional constraint.

57. *Sign* is used as an example of a nondeverbal noun by Safir (1985).

58. Pesetsky makes some speculative remarks concerning nondeverbal nouns that are crucially based on his speculation that for some reason nonderived nouns cannot take clausal complements. However, see Safir 1985 for convincing arguments to the contrary.

It is worth mentioning here that Kayne (1984) argues that (64b) is ruled out by the ECP, the offending element being the trace left by the movement of *John*. On the other hand, Chomsky (1986b) suggests that (64b) is ruled out for semantic reasons on a par with *algebra's knowledge*, because the possessive NP is not "affected" by the head noun. For yet another account of (64b), see Higginbotham 1983.

Note that (64c) may also be ruled out because it contains a PP in a subject position. It is well known that, as (i) shows, PPs cannot occur in unambiguous subject positions. (See Bresnan 1991 for convincing arguments that PPs that appear to occur in subject positions (e,g., *John considered under the bed to be a good place to hide*) are actually nominals with elliptied heads ([$_{NP}$ *place* [$_{PP}$ *under the bed*]]).)

(i) a. *I believe to John to be given a book
    b. *I believe into the room to have walked a soldier

59. (74) is ambiguous. It can mean either that John simply shuffled the times of the meetings with Susan or that John again arranged the meetings with Susan, the former reading being more salient.

60. Notice also that passivization improves (69d). This is not expected under the C-affixation analysis, which predicts (69d) and (i) to be equally unacceptable.

(i) ??The problem was rediscovered to be unsolvable

61. Ormazabal argues that C-incorporation makes A-movement out of CPs possible. However, in chapter 3 I show that A-movement is not allowed to take place out of a CP headed by a null complementizer even when the complementizer would undergo C-to-V incorporation on Ormazabal's analysis.

Pesetsky and Ormazabal argue that C-incorporation also takes place out of zero finite declarative complements. However, as mentioned in note 19, the contrast between (ia) and (ib) raises a problem for the C-affixation analysis.

(i) a. *You believe sincerely John is a liar
    b. Who$_i$ do you believe sincerely t$_i$ is crazy

Under Pesetsky's analysis, the data in (i) must be interpreted as indicating that, in contrast to the null C in (ia), the null C in (ib) is not an affix. Since on Pesetsky's analysis the null C heading the infinitival complement of *believe* is lexically specified as [+affix], I see no principled way of accounting for the contrast between (ia) and (ib). The facts concerning zero null-operator relatives, discussed in section 2.3.1, are also problematic. Note that whether or not a relative head is deverbal has no bearing on the obligatoriness of *that* in relative clauses, contrary to what is expected under the C-affixation analysis. Thus, both (iia) and (iib) are acceptable and both (iic) and (iid) are not.

(ii) a. The person John criticized stood up
     b. The rumor John spread angered Bill
     c. *The person stood up John criticized
     d. *The rumor angered Bill John spread

The data in (i)–(ii) indicate that licensing of null heads cannot be reduced to Myers's generalization and the requirement that null heads undergo affixation through head movement. (For more empirical evidence against the C-affixation analysis of zero finite declarative complements, see Doherty, in press.) It seems safe to assume that whatever accounts for the facts in (i)–(ii) should also account for licensing of null heads in general; if this is correct, then the C-affixation analysis would be superfluous.

Chapter 3

1. I will not discuss infinitival complements of English modal verbs and Romance restructuring infinitivals. These are discussed at length in Bošković 1994b, where I argue that root restructuring constructions such as the Spanish examples in (i) have the structure in (ii), involving movement into a θ-position. (There I also provide empirical evidence based on Hankamer and Sag's (1976) deep/surface anaphora distinction that root restructuring verbs assign a primary rather than a secondary θ-role to their subject, so that we are dealing here with movement into a "real" θ-position.)

(i) a. Juan lo quiere ver
       Juan it wants to-see
       'Juan wants to see it'
    b. Yo lo puedo comer
       I   it can   to-eat
       'I can eat it'

(ii) a. Juan$_i$ lo$_j$ quiere$_k$ [$_{VP}$ t$_i$ t$_k$ [$_{VP}$ t$_i$ ver t$_j$]]
     b. Yo$_i$ lo$_j$ puedo$_k$ [$_{VP}$ t$_i$ t$_k$ [$_{VP}$ t$_i$ comer t$_j$]]

Finally, I extend the movement-into-a-θ-position analysis of Romance root restructuring infinitivals to English modal constructions involving root readings of modals.

2. As shown in Pesetsky 1992 and discussed below, the actual descriptive generalization is somewhat more complicated.

One might argue that constructions such as *John proved Peter to be crazy* are counterexamples to Pesetsky's agentive hypothesis, since they appear to involve an agentive verb exceptionally Case-marking a lexical NP. It seems to me, however, that *prove* should not be considered an agentive verb. Notice, for example, the grammaticality of *That he has run away/His running away does not prove John to be guilty/that John is guilty*, where the matrix subject clearly cannot be an agent. Such constructions are ungrammatical with real agentive verbs (e.g., **That he has run away/His running away wagered that John is guilty*). (I consider the ungrammaticality of such constructions to be a necessary but not a sufficient prerequisite for true agentivity.) In fact, even in *John proved himself to be guilty*, John does not seem to be a real agent with respect to proving, as indicated by the possibility of continuing the sentence with *by not being at home when the crime occurred*. In light of this, it seems more appropriate to view *prove* as some kind of causative rather than as an agentive verb. (In this respect, see Pesetsky 1992. The same point can be made with respect to some other verbs, for example, *show* and *reveal*.) However, in certain contexts it is possible to force agentivity on the subject of *prove*.

Significantly, when *prove* is unambiguously interpreted as an agentive verb, ECM becomes degraded, which confirms Pesetsky's agentive hypothesis.

(i) a. ?*For your homework, prove the Case Filter to hold at LF
    b.   cf. For your homework, prove that the Case Filter holds at LF

Pesetsky (1992) makes the same point with respect to psychological verbs. He shows that for a number of psychological verbs (he examines *assume, remember, understand, feel,* and *imagine*), which normally allow ECM, ECM becomes degraded when agentivity is forced on them.

3. I tentatively assume that the V Case feature can be located under either lower V or V_{ag}.

4. See below for discussion of simple transitive constructions.

5. Given that inherent Case marking takes place under θ-role assignment (see Chomsky 1986b), Pesetsky's observation could be interpreted as indicating that agentive verbs can assign Case inherently, but not structurally, which would also rule out (5a–b). However, under this analysis we would still have to account for the curious correlation between agentivity and inherent Case marking. In fact, the very existence of the correlation indicates that we are dealing here with something more systematic than idiosyncratic lexical properties of particular verbs, such as the specification that a particular verb assigns a particular inherent Case.

6. The following constructions from Pesetsky 1992 are of interest here:

(i) a. Mary declared Bill to be dead
    b. Bill was declared to be dead

According to Pesetsky, (ib) is ambiguous between a simple description of a speech act and a "description of a formal declaration which is important in some system of rules" (p. 139). (ia), on the other hand, has only the latter reading, which, according to Pesetsky, involves a θ-relation between the infinitival subject and the matrix verb.

7. Note that *estimate* cannot be analyzed as an object control verb, an analysis that would be consistent with the facts discussed above, for two reasons. First, since the infinitival complement of *estimate*, which is interpreted as a Proposition, is specified as [−tense], PRO cannot appear in its subject position, since it would not be Case-checked. Second, as Postal's (1974) *I estimate there to be two million people in that valley* shows, constructions containing an expletive following *estimate* are grammatical. (See below for an account of this type of construction, which indicates that *estimate* only optionally θ-marks the embedded-clause subject. I show that a way of passing the traditional Case Filter is available to expletive *there* that is not available to lexical NPs; this property of *there* explains the grammaticality of the construction.)

8. That Agr_OP can intervene between VP shells was first proposed by Koizumi (1993). However, the execution of the idea is quite different here. In fact, under my analysis split VPs are allowed only in a subset of the configurations in which they are present under Koizumi's analysis.

9. See note 55, chapter 2. I assume here that, in contrast to the semantically vacuous Agr_O, semantically contentful elements such as V_{ag}, which is itself a θ-role assigner, are opaque to θ-role assignment of other elements. As a result, V adjoined to V_{ag} cannot θ-mark the NP in the $SpecV_{ag}P$. In this respect, see Saito and Hoshi 1994, where it is also argued that a head X can assign its θ-roles after adjunction to a head Y when the head Y is semantically empty.

10. Note that object insertion into $SpecAgr_OP$ in *$John_i$ [$_{Agr_OP}$ $Mary$ [$_{VP}$ t_i $likes$]], where the main verb remains in situ, is ruled out by the Minimize Chain Links Principle since the NP in $SpecAgr_OP$ blocks subject movement to SpecIP. The thematic hierarchy may also be violated in this construction since the experiencer θ-role is assigned before the theme. (See note 11 for the role of the thematic hierarchy in the current analysis.)

11. I assume here that the agent θ-role and the theme θ-role cannot be combined; that is, the combination would be uninterpretable.

Note that if the second or third way of analyzing (17) considered here is adopted, we must either dispense with the thematic hierarchy or make some additional assumptions to preserve it. (For ease of exposition, I will refer here to the θ-role assigned by V_{ag} in (17) as "agent" and the θ-role assigned by the main verb as "actor.") To preserve the thematic hierarchy, we need to assume that the actor θ-role is freely ranked with respect to the theme. Alternatively, the agent and the actor roles could be considered as one θ-role for the purposes of the thematic hierarchy, so that only the higher SpecVP in (17) is relevant for the hierarchy. (Only in this position does *John* bear both the agent and the actor θ-roles.)

12. In Chomsky's system the ambiguous status of nonbranching elements with respect to the X^0/XP distinction is a natural consequence of the Inclusiveness Condition, which allows the computational system only to rearrange elements taken from the lexicon but not to add additional elements such as bar levels, and the contextual definition of maximal and minimal projections, which takes maximal and minimal projections to be relational rather than inherent properties of categories (see Muysken 1982).

13. Note that, as the ungrammaticality of (5a) shows, elements such as *Peter* must have a more complex internal structure than pronouns; that is, they cannot be analyzed as X^0s. See in this respect Longobardi 1994, where it is argued that pronouns are bare nonbranching Ds, whereas proper names involve Ds taking NP complements.

14. Note that *him* must be unstressed for the constructions to be acceptable.

15. Although he notes that the relevant judgments are not clear, Postal (1974) suggests that idiom chunks can also be exceptionally Case-marked by *wager*-class verbs. Interestingly, the example that Postal gives, *I estimate tabs to have been kept on over 800 leftists*, involves an idiom chunk that may be analyzable as an X^0. On the other hand, my informants detect little or no contrast between *John alleged little progress to have been made on that project* and *John alleged little headway to have been made on that project*, the latter involving an unambiguously phrasal idiom chunk. However, the data examined by Keyser and Roeper (1992) indicate

that some superficially complex idiom chunks may be able to undergo incorporation, at least in some contexts (see Keyser and Roeper 1992, 93 fn. 6). Given this interfering factor and the unclarity of relevant judgments, I will ignore idiom chunks in the discussion of ambiguous XP/X^0 elements.

16. As noted by Postal (1974), heavy NP shift also has an ameliorating effect on ECM with *wager*-class verbs.

(i) You wagered [t_i to be t_i crazy] [all the men you met at that party]$_i$

In this chapter I will adopt Ura's (1993b) analysis of (24), which can readily be extended to (i), given that the landing site of heavy NP shift can be at least as high as the Agr$_O$P-adjoined position. (Under preminimalist assumptions, heavy NP shift was considered to be a VP-internal operation; see Postal 1993 and references therein. However, none of the standard arguments for the VP-internal status of heavy NP shift carries over to the minimalist system in a way that would prevent extending Ura's analysis of (24), discussed immediately below, to (i). The saving effect of heavy NP shift will be discussed in more detail in section 4.4.2.)

Postal observes that right node raising also saves constructions such as (5a–b), as shown by *John wagered to be smart, and Ted alleged to be crazy, all the men you met at that party*. However, I argue in Bošković 1996a that such constructions actually involve across-the-board heavy NP shift and thus reduce to (i). One piece of evidence for this claim is that the right-dislocated NP in this kind of construction must be heavy (e.g., **John wagered to be smart, and Ted alleged to be crazy, Bill*), which is a requirement for heavy NP shift (e.g., **Mary kissed yesterday Bill*) but not right node raising (e.g., *Mary kissed, and Peter hit, Bill*). See Bošković 1996a for more relevant discussion. (Following Wexler and Culicover (1980) and Kayne (1994), I argue in Bošković 1996a that true right-node-raising constructions do not involve rightward movement at all.)

17. According to Ura, actual Case checking takes place in LF after V adjoins to Agr$_O$. Overt adjunction to Agr$_O$P thus counts as Ā-movement, which suffices to render intervening A-Specs irrelevant. Ura suggests that the Agr$_O$P-adjoined position is reanalyzed as an A-position in LF after V adjoins to Agr$_O$ and Case-checks the element, actually a copy of the *wh*-phrase, adjoined to Agr$_O$P. The mechanism of reanalysis can be dispensed with under the alternative Move F analysis of (24) proposed in section 4.4.2.

18. There is considerable redundancy between the Last Resort Condition and the requirement that Case features of traditional Case assigners be checked, which will be eliminated in section 4.5. Until then I will continue to use the term "Last Resort Condition violations" for constructions involving movement from Case-checking position to Case-checking position that is not licensed by the Minimize Chain Links Principle.

19. A question arises about what happens with the Case feature of *croire* and *constater*. One possibility is that *croire* and *constater* only optionally bear Case features; that is, they can be taken from the lexicon without Case features. Alternatively, the Case features of the matrix verbs in (29a–b) could be checked by the infinitival complements. Under this analysis French infinitivals would at least have

the option of bearing Case features, an option that has been proposed in the literature (see Rochette 1988 and references therein).

20. Thanks are due to Michèle Bacholle and Viviane Déprez for discussion of possible interpretations of some of the French examples in (30). ((30a) is taken from Déprez 1989.) Note that since the nonhabitual reading is usually not very salient, some contextualization is generally necessary. (We seem to be dealing here with some poorly understood contextual conditions.) Note also that when the matrix verb is in the past tense, a sort of a counterfactual implication is present (see, for example, (30b)). The implication is not enforced. Thus, *Anna croyait arriver en retard hier* can also be continued as follows: *et elle est arrivée en retard* 'and she did arrive late'. No counterfactual implication is present when the matrix verb is in the present tense (30a,c,d). English *believe* behaves in a similar way. Thus, in *John believed Mary to be intelligent* there seems to be an implication that Mary was not intelligent. The implication is not enforced since the sentence can be continued with *and she was intelligent*. As in French, such an implication is not present when the matrix verb is in the present tense. Even the English finite counterpart of (30b), *Anne$_i$ believed that she$_i$ arrived late yesterday* (the same holds for French), seems to have an implication that Anne did not arrive late, which can be canceled by continuing the sentence with *and she did arrive late*. Given that the facts concerning counterfactuality mentioned in this note are present in both French and English and in both finite and nonfinite clauses, they clearly do not interfere with the point made here.

21. Portuguese, Spanish, and Italian behave like French in the relevant respects. They allow PRO in propositional infinitivals. As expected, they also allow eventive predicates.

(i) a. A Ana julgou   chegar   atrasada ontem   ma afinal   chegou
       the Ana believed to-arrive late   yesterday but actually she-arrived
       a   horas (Portuguese)
       on time

   b. Anna creía   llegar   tarde ayer   aunque en verdad estaba
      Anna believed to-arrive late   yesterday though in fact   she-was
      bien de tiempo (Spanish)
      right on time

   c. Anna credeva di arrivare in ritardo ieri   mentre era   in realtà
      Anna believed to arrive   late   yesterday though she-was actually
      in orario (Italian)
      on time

Note in this context that, as discussed by Pesetsky (1992), English also has one verb, *claim*, that allows PRO in its infinitival complement although its infinitival complement is purely propositional (e.g., *John claimed to know French*). This can be accounted for if the infinitival complement of *claim* is specified as [+tense]. Constructions such as ?**John claimed to arrive late yesterday*, however, do not seem to be much better than **John believed Peter to arrive late yesterday*. *Claim* thus remains problematic.

22. Passive raising is marginally possible from the infinitival complement of verbs that can take small clause complements. (For most speakers this is possible only when the infinitival verb is *être* 'to be'.) Rizzi (1980) proposes that in these cases an analogic process makes syntactic possibilities of small clause complements, discussed below, available with infinitivals. Kayne (1984) adopts this analysis.

23. On this analysis the grammaticality of (i) indicates that the complement of *sembler* in (i) has no Tense node.

(i) a. Pierre$_i$ semble [t$_i$ aimer   Marie]
       Pierre seems   to-love Marie
    b. Il$_i$ semble [t$_i$ y   avoir   quelqu'un dans le   jardin]
       it seems   there to-have someone   in   the garden
       'There seems to be someone in the garden'

Rochette (1988) suggests that (ia-b) are examples of "effective" use of *sembler*. Effective verbs offer supplemental information to the action or state of the embedded verb concerning the subject's relation—causal, potential, or other—to the state or action (see Long 1974 and Rochette 1988). Some other effective verbs in French are modals, aspectuals, verbs of movement, and causatives. Rochette argues that the relationship between effective verbs and their complements requires a degree of closeness that cannot be achieved if the complement has Tense. As a result, according to Rochette, the complement of effective verbs must be syntactically realized as VP. Given this, the Last Resort Condition is not violated in (ia-b). (*Il* could be inserted directly into the matrix SpecIP.)

It should be pointed out, however, that Martin (1994) provides evidence that English *seem* may function as a control verb in certain contexts. The same may hold for French *sembler*. The control option, on which Tense must be present in the infinitival complement to Case-check PRO, is enforced when the infinitival complement contains an eventive predicate. The presence of Tense in the embedded clause in (ii) is necessary to prevent the temporal argument of the embedded predicate from remaining unbound. The Tense also licenses PRO.

(ii) Pierre a   semblé arriver   à l'heure hier
     Pierre has seemed to-arrive at the time yesterday
     'Pierre seemed to arrive on time yesterday'

Note that expletive *il* is excluded when the embedded predicate is eventive.

(iii) *Il$_i$ a   semblé t$_i$ arriver   quelqu'un à l'heure hier
       it has seemed   to-arrive someone   at the time yesterday

The infinitival in (iii) must be at least an IP, given that Tense must be present in the embedded clause to bind the temporal argument of the embedded predicate. To avoid violating the EPP, the expletive then must be inserted into the embedded SpecIP. Since the embedded SpecIP is a Case-checking position, movement of *il* to the matrix SpecIP violates the Last Resort Condition.

24. Under Déprez's analysis, Aux-to-C movement must take place in the constructions under consideration in order for the trace in the subject position of the infinitival clause to be licensed with respect to the ECP. (Note that Déprez's analysis is theoretically untenable in the minimalist system.)

25. In Bošković 1996b I suggest that the presence of a complementizer in (38a–b) is a result of l-selection. Note, however, that, unlike in English, finite complements of *believe*-type verbs in French must be introduced by an overt complementizer. This indicates that they also must be CPs. The uniform CP status of French propositional complements can be accounted for if, in contrast to English propositional I, French propositional I has a feature that must be checked through adjunction to C. (I leave the precise nature of this feature for future research.) Since C in French propositional complements is then needed for feature checking, its presence is not affected by the Minimal Structure Principle.

26. The grammaticality of *Peter believed Mary to have bought strawberries* and *Peter was believed to have bought strawberries* then provides evidence that the infinitival complement of *believe* is an IP, as is standardly assumed, and contra Pesetsky (1992) and Ormazabal (1995). Ormazabal argues that C-incorporation, which in his and Pesetsky's analysis takes place in *John believes Peter to be crazy*, makes A-movement out of CPs possible. Since (31a–b) are headed by a null C, which in Ormazabal's system incorporates into the higher V, if this is indeed the case then C-to-V incorporation should also make A-movement out of embedded CPs possible in (31a–b), so that there should be no contrast between (31a–b) and the corresponding constructions with *believe* under Ormazabal's analysis.

27. I assume that the infinitival I in (38a–d) is lexically filled by the infinitival inflection *er*, which merges with the verb at PF in the sense of Bobaljik (1994), Halle and Marantz (1993), and Lasnik (1995d).

Chapter 4

1. Chomsky proposes that the associate adjoins to rather than replaces the expletive to account for the fact that, as discussed at length in section 4.3.3.1 below, the associate of the expletive is interpreted in its SS position rather than in the SpecIP position occupied by the expletive. Note, for example, that *someone* in (1a) must have narrow scope with respect to *likely*, in contrast to *someone* in (1b). The adjunction analysis clearly does not solve the problem concerning the interpretation of the associate, since the associate adjoined to the expletive located in SpecIP still c-commands all elements dominated by the IP. (Note that Chomsky accepts the segment theory of adjunction, according to which XP adjoined to YP c-commands everything that YP does.) In fact, if this were not the case, LF adjunction of the associate to the expletive would be ruled out in Chomsky's (1991) system because the trace left by the movement of the associate is not antecedent-governed. The facts concerning the interpretation of the associate in *there* constructions thus remain a serious problem for the expletive replacement/adjunction analysis that must be solved before the analysis can be accepted. One of the main goals of this chapter is to reconcile the facts concerning the interpretation of the associate with the expletive replacement/adjunction analysis in a principled way.

2. After this chapter (which is based on Bošković 1994d) was originally written, two other works appeared that discuss expletive replacement in a slightly different system in which features are allowed to undergo movement, namely, Chomsky 1995 and Lasnik 1995b. I discuss these works separately in section 4.3.5.

3. Following Belletti (1988) and Lasnik (1992), Lasnik (1995a) assumes that partitive Case assignment is optional. Thus, in *John is in the garden* partitive Case is not assigned. There may actually be some selectional dependency between *there* and *be* (see Lasnik 1995a). It is possible that only *be* that selects *there* assigns partitive Case.

4. Recall that only lexical elements that can be analyzed as X^0s and are therefore able to undergo Case checking by incorporating into the higher verb can be exceptionally Case-marked by *wager* and *allege*. ECM via object shift with *wager* and *allege* is ruled out by the Minimize Chain Links Principle.

5. Lasnik (1992) provides another argument that *be* Case-licenses the associate of *there*. Consider (ia–c).

(i) a. I want there to be someone in the garden at 6 o'clock
   b. *I want there someone in the garden at 6 o'clock
   c. cf. I want someone in the garden at 6 o'clock

Lasnik observes that if indefinite NPs in existential constructions are Case-marked after adjunction to the expletive, there seems to be no way of accounting for the contrast between (ia) and (ib), since the position in which *there* is found in (ib) is accessible to Case marking (cf. (ic)). On the other hand, if the only source of Case assignment for the indefinite NP is the verb *be*, the contrast is straightforwardly accounted for. (In Lasnik's (1992) system this implies that *there* also needs Case; otherwise, the Case taken by the small clause subject in (ic) would be available for *someone* in (ib).) In (ia) the indefinite NP is Case-marked by *be*. (ib), on the other hand, is ruled out because the indefinite NP remains Caseless owing to the absence of *be*, which otherwise does not have to be present in the constructions in question (cf. (ic)).

6. Some verbs can take either an infinitival or a finite complement without much difference in meaning.

(i) a. Mary is hoping [that she will graduate on time]
   b. Mary is hoping [PRO to graduate on time]
   c. Mary showed [that the task was very demanding]
   d. Mary showed [the task to be very demanding]

It seems safe to assume that we are dealing here with arbitrary selection for lexical contents below the X^0 level, that is, with l-selection. Pesetsky (1992) in fact himself argues that whether a verb can take a finite, an infinitival, or both a finite and an infinitival clausal complement is determined by l-selection.

7. As noted above, in Bošković 1994b I suggested that *remark* also belongs to this class. Notice, however, that **Mary has been remarked to like Peter* is worse than (10), which indicates that, like *announce*, *remark* may not be able to take an infinitival complement because of its l-selectional restrictions. If this is indeed the case, *remark* does not belong to the BELIEVE-class. (One of my informants, however, accepts *Mary has been remarked to like Peter*. For this speaker *remark* does belong to the BELIEVE-class.)

8. Note that, given the predicate-internal subject hypothesis, **I have conjectured* [$_{IP}$[*that John likes Mary*]$_i$ *to be* t_i *surprising*] is also ruled out by Greed. However,

there may be additional violations in this construction. According to Kuno (1973), processing and prosodic reasons also contribute to its unacceptability.

9. The point made with respect to BELIEVE-class verbs could also be made with respect to the ditransitive verb *tell*. *Tell* can take either a propositional complement (*John told Mary that Bill was crazy*) or an irrealis complement (*John told Mary to leave*). Given this, the ungrammaticality of **Peter told Jane John$_i$ to seem t$_i$ is ill* and **Peter told Jane Mary$_i$ to seem to t$_i$ that John is in the garden* on the propositional reading of *tell* could also be used to show that A-movement to SpecIP cannot be driven merely by an inadequacy of I.

10. Note that if traditional Case assigners must check a Case feature, we need to assume that clauses can bear a Case feature, otherwise, the Case feature of the matrix I will remain unchecked in (i).

(i) a. That John likes Mary is likely
    b. To park there is illegal

However, since clauses may appear in Caseless positions (e.g., *the proof that John is guilty* and *an attempt to escape*), it must be the case that they can also be taken from the lexicon in a Caseless form. This is exactly the conclusion reached in Bošković 1995a, where I argue that clauses have both Cased and Caseless forms. Chomsky (1986b) also argues that clauses can be assigned Case.

Stowell (1981) proposes an alternative account of (ia–b) on which clauses are banned from appearing in Case-marked positions because they cannot be assigned Case. On this account "subject" clauses in (ia–b) are forced to move away from SpecIP, nominative Case being assigned to their traces. However, Stowell's account is theoretically untenable in the minimalist framework. For one thing, it is not possible to ensure that traces of moved elements but not moved elements themselves are accessible to Case marking under the checking theory of Case, on which elements are taken from the lexicon either with or without Case features; they do not acquire them during the derivation. Furthermore, as shown in Bošković 1995a, Delahunty 1983, Plann 1986, and Safir 1985, among others, Stowell's account is also empirically seriously flawed. Bošković 1995a and Delahunty 1983 are particularly damaging for Stowell's account since they provide evidence that "subject clauses" are indeed subjects; that is, they are located in SpecIP at SS.

11. Note that **the belief there to be a man in the house* is ruled out because the noun *belief* does not have Case features. As a result, *there* cannot be licensed with respect to Case theory by incorporating into the higher head, as it is in (5a–b). (See section 3.2. Recall that I assume with Lasnik (1995a) that *there* has Case.)

12. More evidence for Greed is given in section 4.4. For evidence for Greed, also see Chomsky 1993, 1994, and Saito and Hoshi 1994. For discussion of traditional ECM constructions such as *John believes Peter to know French*, which at first sight appear to raise a problem for Greed, see section 4.4, where I show that ECM constructions are in fact compatible with Greed. Note also that I adopt Move here rather than Chomsky's (1995) Attract, since Greed more naturally fits in with Move.

13. Martin (1992a) and Groat (1993) propose that adjunction to *there* is driven by the need to check the agreement features of the associate, which at first sight seems

to be in accordance with Greed. Chomsky (1994) apparently adopts this analysis. However, Lasnik (1995a) shows convincingly that upon closer scrutiny the agreement analysis turns out to be compatible with Enlightened Self-Interest but not with Greed. (See in this respect the discussion of (49a–b) below, which indicate that ϕ features of NPs need not be checked and therefore cannot serve as a driving force for movement consistent with Greed.) As a result, given the above discussion, the agreement analysis cannot be maintained.

14. I assume that adjunction to arguments is allowed if the element undergoing adjunction is an expletive, which seems natural if, as suggested by Chomsky (1986a), ungrammatical instances of adjunction to arguments disrupt θ-role assignment. It seems safe to assume that semantically empty elements do not affect θ-role assignment.

15. Note that under Chomsky's (1993) conception of the EPP, which reduces to the requirement that the N feature of I be checked in the overt syntax, there is no need for SpecIP to be filled at LF as far as the EPP is concerned. I should also point out that in (5a–b), *there*, an element that is "ambiguous" between XP and X^0, would undergo lowering after adjoining to the higher verb for Case checking. The lowering would be an instance of excorporation, which is consistent with the theory of excorporation argued for in chapter 5.

16. I am grateful to Howard Lasnik for bringing the data to my attention.

17. See Baltin 1987 and May 1985, among others, for alternative analyses, and Hornstein 1994, Lasnik 1993, and Takahashi 1993 for arguments against these analyses. Note that Lasnik (1993, 1995b) shows that antecedent-contained deletion constructions involving appositive relatives are actually more amenable to the minimalist analysis discussed in the text than antecedent-contained deletion constructions involving restrictive relatives. However, since most of the analyses of antecedent-contained deletion constructions in the literature are based on restrictive relatives, I will illustrate my point with respect to restrictive relatives.

18. My informants found (24a,c) significantly better than constructions such as *There is four men in the house*; these judgments indicate that we are indeed dealing here with first conjunct agreement and not some kind of default third person singular specification. The results of Sobin's (1994) experimental study of agreement phenomena point to the same conclusion. Sobin's subjects found *There is a pen and a stamp on the desk* to be significantly better than *There is four keys on the desk*.

   It is worth mentioning here that although my informants found *There is four men in the house* to be unacceptable, they still found it to be somewhat better than *Four men is in the house*. Sobin reports a similar finding. As will become clear below, on my analysis as well as Lasnik's this difference in the degree of unacceptability can be accounted for if agreement mismatches in Spec-head agreement configurations lead to stronger ungrammaticality than violations of Lasnik's requirement that an affix and its host not disagree in ϕ features. On the other hand, it is difficult to see how the difference in the degree of ungrammaticality can be accounted for in a principled way in Chomsky's (1993) system. Note that I am disregarding here existential constructions involving contracted *be*. For a number of speakers such constructions exhibit agreement patterns not found with full forms of *be* (compare ??*There's four keys on the desk* with **Is there four keys on the desk* and **There is four keys on the desk*), presumably because contraction minimizes the salience of agreement conflicts.

19. Note that the whole conjoined phrase is a BP, headed by *and*, and not an NP, and thus is not an appropriate host for expletive *there* since this host must be an NP. However, some speakers marginally accept agreement with the whole conjoined phrase. One possibility is that for these speakers BP can marginally serve as a host for *there*. Alternatively, the plural agreement for these speakers may be a result of extralinguistic self-correction, having nothing to do with their "mental grammar."

20. Howard Lasnik (personal communication) notes that if the configuration in which A is an affix on B, which contains a trace of A, is disallowed, **It$_i$ was believed t$_i$ to be someone in the garden* would be ruled out even if *it* can in principle attach to [−tense] clauses.

21. In principle, it should be possible to check whether or not (30) involves first conjunct agreement by making the first conjunct plural. However, it is very difficult to construct relevant examples.

22. There is an alternative way of accounting for (30) under the expletive replacement analysis that does not involve first conjunct agreement. Let us make the rather natural assumptions that clauses only optionally bear ϕ features and that, in contrast to expletive *there*, which can be taken from the lexicon with any set of ϕ features, expletive *it* is obligatorily specified as third person singular. If we choose the option without ϕ features for the clauses in (30), *it* and the conjoined clauses will be trivially nondistinct in their ϕ feature specification. On this analysis we still need to account for the fact that the agreement option is preferred in (29b); we can do this by adopting the proposal in Bošković 1995a (see also Emonds 1976 and Kitagawa 1986) that there are both nominal and nonnominal clauses. As shown in Bošković 1995a, nominal clauses have some NP properties such as having Case features, to which we should add ϕ features in light of the above discussion. It seems safe to assume that nonnominal clauses have neither Case nor ϕ features. In (29b) we need to choose the nominal option for the conjoined clauses; otherwise, the Case feature of the matrix I will remain unchecked. Since nominal clauses must have ϕ features, the obligatoriness of agreement in (29b) follows. (Note that in my 1995a analysis, nonnominal clauses, which have neither Case nor agreement features, must be used in Caseless environments such as (30).) However, McCloskey's (1991) observation that only contradictory coordinated clauses trigger plural agreement remains to be accounted for, regardless of whether the expletive replacement analysis is adopted.

23. Both Chomsky's (1995) and Lasnik's (1995b) analyses are based on Enlightened Self-Interest, rather than Greed. (Lasnik actually also adopts a version of Greed, as discussed below.)

24. Lasnik (1995b) actually considers another, less principled alternative. As will become obvious in the text, to account for (34a–c) in Lasnik's system, it suffices if

object shift can be overt in English. However, the data to be discussed, in particular (36a–d), force Lasnik to adopt the stronger position that object shift *always* takes place overtly in English. It should also be pointed out that Lasnik considers ellipsis to involve PF deletion rather than LF copying.

25. I assume here that direct object NPs are generated lower in the tree than adverbials, contra Larson (1988). (This is also Lasnik's position.) For evidence against Larson's position, see Bošković, in press a, Branigan 1992, and Stjepanović 1996.

26. Note that Chomsky assumes that *there* has no Case features. He therefore cannot account for (41) by appealing to Case theory. On Lasnik's and my analyses, in which *there* bears a Case feature, (41) is ruled out because $there_2$ cannot be Case-checked. In addition, if, as suggested by Lasnik (1995a), the complex $there_2$ + *someone*, formed by adjunction of the lower *there* to the indefinite NP, is not considered to be a partitive NP, the requirement that *there* be affixed to a partitive NP is also violated in (41). ((42) can be ruled out for the same reason.)

27. It is easy to verify that the contrasts in (44) can be accounted for under both Lasnik's (1995b) analysis and the affix-hopping analysis. Note that I am abstracting away here from a problem that arises in Chomsky's (1995) system even with respect to simple existential ECM constructions such as (i).

(i) The DA proved [there to be someone in the garden]

In Chomsky's system FF features of the associate must adjoin to Agr_O in the LF representation of (i). In addition, the N feature of the associate must raise to *there*. After FF movement of the associate to *there* takes place, it is not clear how the associate can be Case-checked in Chomsky's system. Raising the complex *there* + FF(*someone*) to Agr_O does not help since only the features of *there* would be available for checking with Agr_O in the relevant configuration. (If the associate were visible for checking in this configuration, Chomsky's account of double *there* constructions would be lost; after the associate adjoins to the lower *there* to check its D feature in *There seems there to be someone in the room*, the complex *there* + FF(*someone*) could adjoin to the higher *there*, thereby licensing it.) Since Chomsky's system bans movement of traces or, more generally, elements that do not head chains, the associate could not be Case-checked through LF movement to Agr_O of the trace of the associate left by "expletive replacement." We could perhaps account for (i) by assuming that FF(*someone*) adjoins to *there*, checking its D feature (the N feature of the associate would do the actual checking), and then excorporates to move to Agr_O. However, if we allow this kind of excorporation in Chomsky's system, we lose Chomsky's account of double *there* constructions, since one NP would be able to license indefinitely many expletives.

28. Chomsky (1995) actually gives two arguments that the associate of *there* is interpreted in its raised position. However, Lasnik (1995c) shows convincingly that the arguments do not go through.

29. Chomsky actually leaves room for the former possibility. However, he does it in a very stipulatory way, based on a distinction between deletion and erasure.

30. The underlying, empirically necessary assumption here is that Greed operates on chains and not on chain links, whose formation is licensed by the Minimize Chain Links Principle. Note that I am adopting here a strictly derivational approach to the Minimize Chain Links Principle, on which an element X undergoing the operation Form Chain of the type Y must make the shortest move of the type Y measured in terms of *nodes traversed*. This approach differs from that proposed in other works such as Jonas and Bobaljik 1993, where the length of a chain link is allowed to be unlimited unless a filled Spec intervenes. Under this view, but not under the strictly derivational view adopted here, the Minimize Chain Links Principle has essentially the same effects as a strictly representational constraint such as Rizzi's (1990a) Relativized Minimality. (See Bošković 1995a, Saito 1994, and especially Takahashi 1994 for arguments that the derivational approach is superior to the representational approach on empirical grounds. Among other things, Takahashi shows that the derivational approach allows a principled account for the full range of Subjacency effects, including Huang's (1982) Condition on Extraction Domain effects. Note also that it is not at all clear how the full range of Subjacency effects (essentially anything but the *Wh*-Island Constraint) can be accounted for if, instead of Move, Chomsky's (1995) Attract is adopted; thus, these effects seem to provide an argument for Move. For relevant discussion, see also note 59.)

It is worth mentioning here that Manzini's (1994) Locality, another derivational constraint that requires every chain link to be as short as possible, also has the effect of forcing *John* to move through the embedded SpecIP in (50).

31. Essentially following Ura (1993b), and contra Johnson (1991), Koizumi (1993), Lasnik (1995a), and Runner (1995), I will argue that overt object shift in English takes place in ECM constructions, but not in simple transitive constructions. I will also provide a theoretical explanation for the difference between ECM and simple transitive constructions.

32. Chomsky (1994) assumes that Greed cannot be violated to ensure convergence, which amounts to assuming that violating Greed leads to nonconvergence, an assumption that I adopt here.

33. Note that I am not claiming here that the N feature of Agr_O is strong in English. Under the analysis developed here, object shift has to take place overtly in English ECM constructions to ensure convergence even if the relevant feature is weak, as is standardly assumed. In fact, I will show that there is empirical evidence for the standard assumption—more precisely, I will show that there is empirical evidence that accusative NPs in simple transitive constructions remain in their base-generated position at SS and undergo movement motivated by Case checking only in LF. Given this, the N feature of Agr_O must be weak in English, as is standardly assumed.

34. Ura's (1993b) analysis of *wh*-movement out of *wager*-class infinitivals, adopted in section 3.3, may be inconsistent with this assumption. An alternative analysis of the relevant facts that is consistent with the assumption will be proposed in section 4.4.2.

35. In section 4.4.1.7 I will show that constructions such as *John has believed Mary to be sick* do not differ from (55) with respect to the possibility of overt object shift and V-movement outside Agr$_O$P, though the precise landing site of V-movement may be different (see in this respect chapter 5).

It is well known that adverbs cannot intervene between the raised verb and the shifted exceptionally Case-marked NP. Koizumi (1993) argues that adverbs cannot adjoin to the semantically vacuous Agr$_O$P, thus accounting for the adjacency effect.

Note that in Yoruba, adverbs cannot intervene between the verb and the direct object, although V undergoes overt movement (see Dekydtspotter 1992 for relevant data). Transitive constructions in Yoruba thus may involve the same structure in the relevant respect as English ECM constructions.

36. See Haegeman 1985 and Washio 1989 for evidence that *get* passives involve the same kind of structure as *be* passives.

37. Given the above analysis, we would expect traditional raising constructions involving PRO and *all to* sequences to be better than the corresponding nonraising constructions. As in (57), PRO in (i) must move to check its Case feature overtly; otherwise, the derivation will crash, either because Greed is violated or because the EPP is violated. (Recall that the N feature of [−tense, −finite] I is strong, as indicated by **John believes to be the students crazy.*)

(i) ?*The diplomats tried all to seem to like Yeltsin

Some, but not all, of my informants do find (i) to be better than (56a), though the difference is not overwhelming even for the speakers who detect it. This is actually not surprising. Notice that (i) involves the same structure as (56a) plus one additional level of embedding, which makes it more difficult to parse than (56a). The ambiguity of traditional subject-to-subject raising predicates between control and raising predicates (see chapter 2, note 11, and chapter 3, note 23) is another interfering factor here. It is well known (see Lasnik and Fiengo 1974) that the subject must be able to exert at least partial intentional control over the predicate embedded under *try*, as illustrated by the anomalous status of *The diplomats tried to receive good news* (see also the interpretation of (56)–(57)). The intentional control requirement may completely rule out the raising option for *seem* in (i), leaving only the control option, which expresses agentivity of the subject of *seem* but reduces to (56) with respect to the possibility of PRO moving overtly to SpecIP, a prerequisite for deriving the *all to* sequence. In fact, it is rather difficult to construct fully acceptable sentences involving unambiguous subject-to-subject raising structures embedded under a control verb, as illustrated by the strong preference for agentive/control *seem* in relevant constructions.

38. The ungrammaticality of (58b) could be interpreted as evidence against overt object shift in simple transitive constructions; that is, it could be taken as evidence that direct object NPs do not undergo overt A-movement in English, which is consistent with the analysis developed here (see section 4.4.1.4). However, the evidence is not conclusive since the ungrammaticality of the passive **The students were arrested all* and the ergative **The students arrived all* may indicate that for

some reason floating quantifiers cannot be stranded in θ-positions in English; that is, they cannot be associated with traces in θ-positions. Note, however, that floating quantifiers are not universally banned from being stranded in θ-positions. For example, Sportiche (1988) claims that they can be stranded in θ-positions in French. Icelandic seems to pattern with French in this respect, and Japanese with English (for relevant data, see Jonas and Bobaljik 1993 and Koizumi 1993, respectively).

39. (60) actually involves the same structure as (61) in the relevant respect if, as argued by Lasnik (in preparation), *there* must be inserted into SpecVP.

40. The structure in (i) is ruled out for the same reason.

(i) *I$_j$'ve believed$_i$ [$_{VP}$ for a long time now [$_{VP}$ t$_j$ t$_i$ [$_{IP}$ there to be no solution to this problem]]]

In addition, if, as argued by Lasnik (in preparation), *there* is inserted into SpecVP, (i) also violates Greed (see also note 48).

41. The question now is where *there* is located in *There seems to be a man in the garden*. Given that, as is standardly assumed, Tense (the bearer of the nominative Case feature) must move overtly to Agr$_S$ in English, *there* can be Case-checked by moving to SpecAgr$_S$P in the construction in question. Since SpecAgr$_S$P and the position adjoined to the Agr$_S$+Tense complex belong to the same minimal domain, Case checking via movement to SpecAgr$_S$P and adjunction to the Agr$_S$+ Tense complex end up being equally economical. Note, however, that there are no obvious empirical obstacles to allowing *there* to be located under Agr$_S$ in the construction under consideration. This is so provided that the EPP feature is not required to be checked in a Spec-head relation, in which case the head movement option would be excluded altogether.

Note also that exceptionally Case-marked referential pronouns, which I have argued to be analyzable as X^{0}s, (see section 3.2), appear to be able to precede higher-clause adverbials in constructions such as (i), which indicates that they are undergoing movement to SpecAgr$_O$P rather than incorporation in the construction in question.

(i) I've believed him for a long time now to be a liar

The grammaticality of (i) together with the data discussed in section 3.2 lead me to conclude that, in contrast to *there*, which is a pure nonbranching X^0/XP element and is therefore required to incorporate in ECM constructions by the economy principles, referential pronouns come in two forms: branching (XP) and non-branching (X^0/XP). Interestingly, the examples in which I argued in section 3.2 that referential pronouns must undergo incorporation are acceptable only when the pronoun is unstressed, a sort of a clitic (e.g., *Mary never alleged him to be crazy*, where the option of undergoing object shift is excluded); this condition does not seem to hold in (i). (Compare (i) with (59a).) This indicates that only pure clitic referential pronouns are nonbranching and therefore analyzable as X^{0}s. This is essentially the conclusion reached by Chomsky (1994), who argues that clitic pronouns are nonbranching X^0/XP elements that undergo movement to an X^0 position (via XP positions). However, under Chomsky's analysis, if *him* in *Mary has kissed him* and *lui* in its French counterpart *Marie l'a embrassé lui* remain in situ at SS, they have to be analyzed as involving a branching structure. (This is so even if *him* is unstressed in the construction in question. In Chomsky's system this follows from adopting Kayne's (1994) Linear Correspondence Axiom into his (Chomsky's) bare phrase structure.) *Him* thus seems to be ambiguous between a pure X^0/XP clitic pronoun and an unambiguous XP pronoun. (Lack of stress appears to be necessary but not sufficient to indicate that we are dealing with X^0/XP *him*.)

42. Notice also that since, according to Keyser and Roeper, the abstract clitic position is to the right of the verb, this analysis accounts for the fact that *there* incorporated into a verb follows the verb.

43. Kayne's (1985) *They're trying to make advantage out to have been taken of them* and *They're trying to make out advantage to have been taken of them*, involving idiom chunks, may be amenable to the same analysis. See Keyser and Roeper 1992 for discussion concerning which elements occur in the abstract clitic position. (They claim that even some complex idiom chunks can occur in this position.)

44. (64a–b) could actually also be analyzed as involving gapping of the higher verb with coordination of some higher constituent.

(i) a. John [[believes$_i$ [$_{IP}$ Peter to be crazy]] and [e$_i$ [$_{IP}$ Mary to be smart]]]
   b. John [[believed$_i$ [$_{IP}$ Peter to have played football]] and [e$_i$ [$_{IP}$ Mary to have played basketball]]]

However, the ungrammaticality of classical gapping constructions such as (iia–b) makes the gapping analysis of (64a–b) highly unlikely to be correct, since it shows that gapping is simply not possible in the relevant context.

(ii) a. *John [[believes$_i$ [$_{IP}$ Peter to be crazy]] and Jane [e$_i$ [$_{IP}$ Mary to be smart]]]
   b. *John [[believed$_i$ [$_{IP}$ Peter to have played football]] and Jane [e$_i$ [$_{IP}$ Mary to have played basketball]]]

It does not seem possible to rule out (iia–b) in a principled way without ruling out (ia–b).

Notice that complement + adverbial constructions such as *Peter talked to his boss on Tuesday and to his supervisor on Wednesday* and *I bought roses for Sally and lilies for Jane* may be amenable to a gapping analysis, given the grammaticality of Sag's (1976) *Peter talked to his boss on Tuesday and Betsy to her supervisor on Wednesday* and Postal's (1974) *I bought roses for Sally and Jack lilies for Jane*. (Neijt (1979) and Sag (1976) observe, and my informants agree, that gapping is generally quite good with complement+adverbial remnants.)

45. Postal (1974) claims that some conjunctions (e.g., *both ... and*) cannot be used to conjoin ECM infinitivals.

(i) (*) John believed both Peter to be crazy and Mary to be smart

However, my informants find such constructions acceptable. Not having access to speakers who find (i) degraded, I will merely speculate here on the nature of its unacceptability for the speakers who reject such constructions. Under the overt object shift analysis, the ungrammaticality of (i) for these speakers can be accounted for if they cannot use *both ... and* for Agr_OP-level coordination. (If this speculation is correct and if the analysis of double object constructions suggested in note 49 is on the right track, the speakers who reject (i) should also reject *John gave both Mary a car and Peter a house*, which under the analysis suggested in note 49 also involves Agr_OP-coordination.) Alternatively, *both* could be taken to block head movement of *believe* outside Agr_OP at least for some speakers. (Kayne (1994) also appeals to the blocking effect of *both*. However, he uses it to block XP-movement.)

46. Postal (1974) argues that the ungrammaticality of (67a) provides evidence for raising to object in ECM constructions. However, his exact argumentation does not carry over to the current system, which involves movement to $SpecAgr_OP$ instead of raising to object.

Note that the discussion in this section is restricted to specificational pseudoclefts. I ignore predicational pseudoclefts here (see Akmajian 1970 and Higgins 1979).

47. In this work I show that some superficial counterexamples to the claim that pseudocleft *what* does not have to be Case-checked are all independently ruled out.

48. Notice also the ungrammaticality of (i).

(i) *What John believes is [$_{IP}$ there to be someone in the garden]

As mentioned in note 39, Lasnik (in preparation) argues that *there* is inserted into SpecVP, as a result of which, under my analysis, *there* must undergo overt Case checking even in simple existential constructions, such as the infinitival clause in (i). Given Lasnik's proposal, (i) is ruled out by Greed, on a par with (67a). The ungrammaticality of (i) may in fact provide evidence for Lasnik's proposal.

It is worth noting here that there is an overt object shift derivation for (67a) and (i) that also must be ruled out. Suppose that the post-*be* constituent in (67a) is an Agr_OP, with *Peter* located overtly in $SpecAgr_OP$ and *believe* moving from Agr_O into the *wh*-clause after Case-checking *Peter*. This captures the above generalization that accusative NPs in the post-*be* constituent are Case-checked by the *wh*-clause verb. Since *John* is θ-marked by *believe*, under the predicate-internal subject hypothesis *John* would also have to be generated within the post-*be* constituent.

(ii) *What John$_j$ believes$_i$ is [$_{Agr_OP}$ Peter$_k$ t$_i$ [$_{VP}$ t$_j$ t$_i$ [$_{IP}$ t$_k$ to like Mary]]]

A-movement of *Peter* in (ii) clearly does not violate Greed. Recall, however, that Chomsky (1995) argues that all overt movement must take place to a c-commanding position. This is clearly not the case with the movement of *believe* and *John* in (ii). The structure can then be straightforwardly ruled out. In fact, it is ruled out for the same reason as *What John gave$_i$ was [$_{VP}$ Mary t$_i$ a book] (however, see note 49 for discussion of double object constructions) and *What John$_i$ seems is [$_{IP}$ t$_i$ to be crazy].

49. Note that object shift may also take place overtly in at least some ditransitive constructions. For example, consider the first object NP in double object constructions, which I assume is Case-checked under Spec-head agreement with the Agr_O+give complex.

(i) John gave Mary a book

There are two lines of research concerning such constructions. In one line of research, both objects are assumed to be generated within a projection of *give* (see Barss and Lasnik 1986, Chomsky 1981, Larson 1988, and Oehrle 1976, among others). Under this approach, given that the N feature of Agr_O is weak in English, we would not expect object shift to take place in double object constructions before LF. (I am focusing here on the first object NP.)

There is another line of research that predicts, under some rather natural assumptions, that object shift would take place overtly in double object constructions. This line of research, pursued by Collins and Thráinsson (1993), Den Dikken (1995), Johnson (1991), Kayne (1984), Kitagawa (1994), and Tremblay (1990), among others, holds that the object NPs in (i) are generated as part of a small clause that excludes the verb *give*. (Similar analyses have been proposed for other ditransitive constructions. See, for example, Den Dikken 1995, Kayne 1984, and Mulder 1991.) Depending on what structure is assumed for small clauses, under this analysis the first object NP is generated either in the Spec of the second object NP or adjoined to the second object NP. Alternatively, Collins and Thráinsson (1993), Den Dikken (1995), and Kitagawa (1994) argue that the small clause in question contains a null *have* and that the first object is generated within its maximal projection. However, a number of authors have argued that small clauses are actually headed by a functional element. Chomsky (1993), Den Dikken and Næss (1993), Hornstein and Lightfoot (1987), Kitagawa (1986), and Kreps (1994), among others, argue that small clauses are projections of I; if this is correct, the complement of *give* in (i) would have to be an IP. Given the plausible assumption that the N feature of the I is strong, forcing overt movement to SpecIP, and given the analysis presented above, we would expect the NP undergoing movement to the small clause subject position to move overtly to $SpecAgr_OP$ to be Case-checked. Remaining in SpecIP, which I assume is a Caseless position, would lead to a violation of Greed.

(ii) John$_i$ gave$_j$ [$_{Agr_OP}$ Mary$_k$ t$_j$ [$_{VP}$ t$_i$ t$_j$ [$_{IP}$ t$_k$ [$_{NP/VP}$ t$_k$ a book]]]]]

There is some evidence suggesting that the first object NP indeed undergoes overt A-movement, which, given the above discussion, would have to land in $SpecAgr_OP$. Thus, *John gave the students all a book* shows that the first object in double object constructions can be associated with a floating quantifier, thus providing evidence that it undergoes overt A-movement under Sportiche's (1988) analysis of quantifier float. (See Déprez 1989 for evidence that quantifier float is a property of A-movement, but not Ā-movement.) ?*What did John give students of a book* shows that the first object NP resists being extracted from, a limitation that can also be accounted for if the NP in question is located in $SpecAgr_OP$ at SS. The construction can then be considered a Subject Condition violation. (The minimalist accounts of the Subject Condition cited with respect to (75) would assign the construction the status of a Subject Condition violation if the first object NP moves overtly to either $SpecAgr_OP$ or the small clause SpecIP, but not if it remains in situ at SS.) It is thus possible that object shift takes place overtly in double object constructions for essentially the same reason it does in ECM constructions.

50. In Bošković, in press a, I offer two possible theoretical explanations for this, one based on Case theory and one on economy of derivation. Unless additional assumptions are adopted, the Case explanation is inconsistent with certain proposals concerning Case theory made in section 4.4.2. The economy explanation is, however, compatible with the system developed here. The gist of the economy account is that it is more economical for an accusative NP to pass through SpecAgr$_O$P on its way to a higher Ā-position than to undergo direct movement to the Ā-position, followed by LF movement of the *wh*-trace to SpecAgr$_O$P, or Move F to the verb. (Fewer nodes are crossed on the former derivation.)

In Bošković 1995a I develop a system in which accusative *wh*-NPs are forced to pass through their Case-checking SpecAgr$_O$P on their way to SpecCP by the Minimize Chain Links Principle. The essentials of this analysis can also be incorporated into the current system given some straightforward modifications.

51. Following standard assumptions, I assume that with *wh*-NPs, the variable (i.e., the *wh*-trace) is the trace located in the Case-checking position. Note that for ease of exposition I ignore intermediate traces of Ā-movement throughout this section.

I should point out here that I assume in Bošković, in press a, that the verb in (81) remains in situ. However, nothing seems to go wrong if we assume that the verb moves to the first head position above Agr$_O$P, in order to enable the direct object to reach SpecAgr$_O$P and the subject to move from SpecVP to SpecIP without violating the Minimize Chain Links Principle.

52. *When* modifies the matrix clause on the relevant reading in (83). A possible answer to the question is *John proved Mary to be guilty during her trial and he proved Fred to be guilty during a recess.* Notice that (83) contrasts with (i) on the relevant reading.

(i) ?*Who$_i$ did John [$_{VP}$[$_{VP}$ prove [$_{IP}$ t$_i$ was guilty]] when]

This is expected since, unlike in (83), in (i) the embedded-clause subject undergoes Case checking in the embedded SpecIP and therefore starts with *wh*-movement from that position, which is lower than the position in which the matrix adverbial is generated. In other words, the variable of *who* is c-commanded by *when* in (i). This leads to a Superiority condition violation.

53. There is an alternative analysis of (93) on which *students* does not have to move outside VP. Shlonsky (1991) argues that in some languages the NP Q order in constructions such as (93) can be derived by movement of the NP within the direct object (QP under Shlonsky's analysis). Shlonsky shows that this option is available in Hebrew, but not in French. If Serbo-Croatian patterns with Hebrew rather than French in the relevant respect, (93) could not be taken as providing evidence that the direct object *students* is undergoing A-movement outside of the VP. It is, however, possible to show that NP-movement internal to Q NP complexes is not an available option in Serbo-Croatian. If it were, it would be difficult to explain why constructions involving quantifier float within coordinations are unacceptable in Serbo-Croatian. Note that in the relevant respect Serbo-Croatian (ia) patterns with French (ic) rather than Hebrew (ib), which according to Shlonsky allows NP-movement within Q NP complexes. ((ib) is taken from Shlonsky 1991.)

(i) a. *[Svi momci] i   [devojke sve] gledaju film
       all boys   and girls   all watch movie
   b. [Kol ha-banim] ve [ha-banot kul-an] ra'u seret
      all the-boys and the-girls all   saw movie
   c. *[Tous les garçons] et [les filles toutes] regardent un film
       all the boys   and the girls all   watch   a movie

(ii), containing the second position clitic *su*, provides more evidence that in Serbo-Croatian the NP Q order cannot be derived by NP-movement internal to the Q NP complex.

(ii) Studente (*sve) su istukli
     students   all are beaten
     'They beat the students all'

Serbo-Croatian second position clitics must be located either after the first constituent or after the first word of their sentence (see Browne 1974 and chapter 5). Given this, (ii) indicates that NP Q sequences in Serbo-Croatian do not form constituents, which is unexpected if such sequences can be derived by NP-movement within QPs/DPs.

54. The question that arises now is whether the movements shown in (94) are optional or obligatory. It is difficult to determine this conclusively for object shift. I will simply assume here that object shift is optional in Serbo-Croatian, that is, that the feature driving the movement can be either strong or weak. As for participle movement, I show in chapter 5 that participles must undergo overt movement in Serbo-Croatian. There I also identify the landing site of Serbo-Croatian participle movement.

55. The impossibility of overt object shift in auxiliary + participle constructions in Icelandic (i.e., the ungrammaticality of Icelandic constructions corresponding to (88)), then may indicate that Icelandic differs from Serbo-Croatian and English with respect to the availability of a landing site for participles outside Agr_OP. The whole phenomenon of object shift in Icelandic should actually be reexamined. Given that what is generally referred to as "object shift" in Icelandic can place an NP into a position higher than sentential adverbs, which, as argued in Watanabe 1993 and Bošković 1995b and discussed extensively in chapter 5, cannot be located lower than the TP-adjoined position, it seems unlikely that the landing site of the operation in question is $SpecAgr_OP$, as is generally assumed. An NP undergoing the operation in question would have to be much higher in the tree, and this would "push" a participle preceding it even higher. ((i) is taken from Bures 1993. For much relevant discussion, see also Vikner 1995.)

(i) Í gær   las Pétur bókina$_i$ eflaust   ekki t$_i$
    yesterday read Peter the-book doubtlessly not
    'Yesterday, Peter doubtlessly didn't read the book'

As discussed by Holmberg and Platzack (1995), the element undergoing the operation in question cannot bind an anaphor from its SS position (it can bind a pronoun, though); this casts further doubt on the standard analysis, which places *Ólaf og Martein* in (iib) in $SpecAgr_OP$, an A-position.

(ii) Hann taldi   Ólaf   og   Martein$_i$, þeim$_i$/*sér$_i$/*hvorum öðrum$_i$ til
    he   considered Olafur and Marteinn them/REFL/each other   to
    undrunar [t$_i$ vera jafn   góða]
    wonder   be   equally good
    'He considered Olafur and Marteinn, to their surprise, to be equally good'

Holmberg and Platzack observe that, in contrast to the shifted object in (ii), the passivized subject in (iii) can bind an anaphor within the adverbial in question.

(iii) Ólafur og   Martein$_i$ voru, *þeim$_i$/sér$_i$/?hvorum öðrum$_i$
     Olafur and Marteinn were   them/REFL/each other
     til undrunar, taldir   [t$_i$ vera jafn   goða]
     to wonder   considered be   equally good
     'Olafur and Marteinn were, to their surprise, considered to be equally good'

A thorough examination of Icelandic "object shift" should be undertaken in light of the data in (i)–(iii), which seriously undermine the SpecAgr$_O$P analysis.

56. I ignore other intermediate copies in (96). (Copies are given in italics.) Note that, given the operational view of Case checking argued for in the next section, *who* could also pass through the embedded SpecAgr$_O$P without causing the derivation to crash (see note 66).

57. The tacit assumption here is that A-movement can feed Ā-movement, that is, that both A- and Ā-positions are potential landing sites for an element located in an A-position that is eventually to end up in an Ā-position. However, once the element in question moves to an Ā-position, it must proceed with Ā-movement to avoid violating the Improper Movement Constraint, which follows from the economy principles (see Saito 1992 and Takahashi 1994). For much relevant discussion, see also Bošković 1995a, where I give several other examples in which the Minimize Chain Links Principle forces elements in A-positions undergoing Ā-movement to land in intermediate A-positions. However, there I take a different view of the relation between Greed and the Minimize Chain Links Principle.

58. I assume here that phrases do not block movement of their own features, an assumption that seems to be necessary in the Move F framework. I also assume that features of a chain form a unit. If one member of a chain is affected by feature checking, they all are. Note that since the element in the VP-adjoined position is an exact copy of *who*, it bears a Case feature. (Here I am essentially following Chomsky (1993). For an alternative view, see Bošković, in press a.)

59. For relevant discussion, see Takahashi 1994. Only the relevant intermediate copy is shown in (97a). The slight marginality of the construction is due to a Subjacency violation. Note that (97a) raises a serious problem for Chomsky's (1995) system, based on Attract α, which essentially prohibits intermediate adjunctions.

60. It is unclear how to apply standard locality conditions on movement to pure feature movement. Note that I assume that traces of heads do not block movement to head positions, as discussed extensively in Bošković 1995b and chapter 5. However, in the derivation under consideration, feature movement of *the students* into the matrix clause would have to skip some lexically filled head posi-

tions. For much relevant discussion concerning the effect that locality constraints on movement have on feature movement, see Bošković, in press c.

61. The data in (i) parallel the data in (101) and can be accounted for in the same way.

(i) a. ??What$_i$ did John wager that Peter conjectured t$_i$
    b. *What$_i$ did Peter conjecture t$_i$

62. Of course, this point can be made only with respect to the speakers who find (101b) degraded. Some speakers accept (101b), a judgment that indicates that for them *conjecture* can function as a Case assigner.

Note that my informants find that (ia) does not improve significantly if embedded under a Case-assigning verb that takes a [+wh] complement. This indicates that *who* cannot be Case-checked through feature movement from SpecCP. (However, a slight contrast may still be detected between (ia) and (ib).)

(i) a. *Who did John conjecture to know French
    b. ?*I know [$_{CP}$ who John conjectured to know French]

If there is no contrast between (ia) and (ib), we can assume that either undergoing Spec-head agreement or the operator status of *who* freezes it for the possibility of feature movement. (Something like this must be assumed in the Move F theory independently of the particular analysis developed here.)

63. (i), where the complement of *know* is a [+tense] clause, does not seem to be any better than (102a). (Note that the accusative Case of *know* may actually be available for the *wh*-trace in (i).)

(i) *Who$_i$ did you [$_{AgroP}$[$_{VP}$ t$_i$ [$_{VP}$ wager that it$_j$ seems [$_{IP}$ t$_i$/t$_j$ to [$_{VP}$ t$_i$ know that Mary speaks French]]]]]

(i) can be taken to indicate that the tensed clause headed by *that* is too far away from expletive *it* to function as its associate. We can ensure this either by having LF lowering of the expletive to the clause violate locality restrictions on movement or by positing restrictions on the insertion of expletive *it*. I will tentatively adopt the latter approach here. As noted above, Lasnik (in preparation) suggests that expletive *there* cannot be freely inserted anywhere into the tree. In particular, he suggests that *there* must be inserted into SpecVP. Suppose that there is a similar restriction on the insertion of expletive *it*. To be more precise, suppose that *it* must be inserted into the Spec position of the predicate whose complement functions as its associate. Given this, *it* would have to be inserted into the Spec of *know* in (i), which is not possible. (For relevant discussion, see Bennis 1986 and Zwart 1993a, 1994a, where it is also argued that *it* is not inserted directly into SpecIP.)

64. I put aside here constructions involving auxiliary *be* and obligatory participle agreement. For some relevant discussion, see Branigan 1992, where it is suggested that obligatory participle agreement in such constructions is a result of the presence of the auxiliary *be* and therefore is not relevant to present concerns.

65. The metaphor is due to Howard Lasnik. A similar proposal is made independently by Ura (1994).

66. There may actually be some exceptions. For example, *John* may pass through SpecAgr$_O$P on its way to SpecIP in *John knows French*. It seems plausible that the derivation would not crash as long as *John* does not undergo Case checking in SpecAgr$_O$P. In LF *French* can check its own and the verb's Case features by adjoining to Agr$_O$.

67. Given the above discussion, a derivation is available in which *John* is not Case-checked in the embedded SpecIP. Instead, it can be Case-checked after undergoing LF feature movement to the matrix I. On this derivation (124) violates Greed in addition to the EPP and the Inverse Case Filter. Since I adopt the standard assumption that judgments always reflect the best possible derivations, which has good empirical motivation but is yet to receive an explanation, I will ignore this derivation, which is a superset of the derivation discussed in the text in terms of the constraints it violates.

68. Here I avoid using double object verbs with a clausal second object, which could serve as a host for *it* in the passive construction, since this could lead to additional violations (see note 63).

69. Mamoru Saito (personal communication) suggests a way of eliminating the redundancy between the Inverse Case Filter and the Case Filter discussed with respect to (129). He suggests that the accusative Case on the verb and the noun in (129) could be considered two instances of a single Case feature, rather than two Case features; if this is correct, only one feature would remain unchecked in the derivation in which the direct object NP in (129) does not move in LF. The idea is appealing, though difficult to implement formally.

Chapter 5

1. Some parts of this chapter are taken from Bošković 1995b. Sections 5.3 and 5.4 are completely new.

2. P-to-C movement is assumed to be optional. Thus, the participle is not assumed to be located under C when it follows the auxiliary.

(i) Petra *je* istukao
    Peter is beaten
    '(He) beat Peter'

Both (1) and (i) are simple declarative sentences in the past tense, which is formed by using the present tense form of *biti* 'to be' and the participle of the main verb. (The auxiliary in (1) and (i) is a second position clitic. Throughout this chapter second position clitics will be given in italics. See below for discussion of second position cliticization.)

3. A note is in order concerning the grammaticality judgments given below. It is well known that word order violations in scrambling languages such as Serbo-Croatian generally do not result in strong ungrammaticality, as in languages with relatively fixed word order such as English. Below, I abstract away from this and assign a full * even to the Serbo-Croatian examples that are less than strongly ungrammatical. Needless to say, all the judgments are comparative.

4. One should be careful in (4b,d) not to pause before the adverb since it is well known that such pauses make available readings that are otherwise not present. (Compare *John kissed Mary probably* with *John kissed Mary, probably*, with a pause before the adverb.) Note also that the judgment in (4b) holds only for the sentential reading of *nesumnjivo. Nesumnjivo* does not have to have a sentential reading, however. It can also modify the object NP, especially when the object NP is focused. On this reading the sentence means something like *It is undoubtedly Peter that Jovan beat.* For some discussion of the nonsentential reading of adverbs such as *nesumnjivo,* see Belletti 1990, where it is suggested that on this reading the adverbs in question are adjoined to the phrase they modify (the object NP in (4b)). Since this reading is irrelevant to the phenomena under consideration, I will disregard it below.

5. Note that (8a,c), simple declarative clauses, cannot be ruled out on a par with (i), whose marginal status is generally attributed to the incompatibility of sentential adverbs with questioning.

(i) ?*Will John probably run out of gas

(i) does not improve if movement to C is eliminated, which indicates that the degraded status of the construction cannot be attributed to a blocking effect of sentential adverbs on movement of verbal elements to C.

(ii) ?*I wonder whether John will probably run out of gas

In fact, the following V2 example from Swedish shows that sentential adverbs do not in principle block movement of verbal elements to C:

(iii) Sin make$_i$ har$_j$ hon troligen   t$_j$ inte sett   t$_i$
      her husband has she probably   not seen
      'she probably has not seen her husband'

6. See, however, Anderson 1993 and Radanović-Kocić 1988. For Franks and Progovac (1994), Progovac (1996), Wilder and Ćavar (1994a), and Tomić (1996) all Serbo-Croatian clitics are located under C^0; for Percus (1993) and Roberts (1994) they are located in a head position immediately below C and above I; and for Rivero (1994b) they are located in the Spec of an XP immediately below C and above I. Halpern (1995), on the other hand, suggests that Serbo-Croatian clitics are adjoined to the complement of C.

7. Note also that P-movement in (16) cannot cross sentential adverbs. Thus, (ia–b) are ungrammatical and in (ic) and (id) the adverb can have only the manner reading, which indicates that, like P-preposing in front of auxiliary clitics, P-preposing in front of nonauxiliary clitics lands below TP.

(i) a. *Istukao$_i$ bejaše nesumnjivo t$_i$ Petra
       beaten was   undoubtedly   Peter
       'He had undoubtedly beaten Peter'
    b. *Kad istukao$_i$ bude nesumnjivo t$_i$ Petra, pozovi me
       when beaten be   undoubtedly   Peter call   me
       'When he undoubtedly beats Peter, call me'
    c. Istukao$_i$ bejaše mudro t$_i$ Petra
       beaten was   wisely Peter
       'He had beaten Peter in a wise manner'

    d. Kad istukao$_i$ bude mudro t$_i$ Petra, pozovi me
        when beaten be   wisely Peter call   me
        'When he beats Peter in a wise manner, call me'

8. Hagit Borer (personal communication) has also suggested an adjunction analysis. Note that Wilder and Ćavar explicitly argue against Rivero's and Roberts's long head movement analysis of Serbo-Croatian P-preposing.

9. Note that all instances of excorporation given in the text involve excorporation of the host head. I leave it open here whether moved heads can undergo excorporation.

    Note also that excorporation may not be forced in the configuration in (21) if Z is an affix that is lexically specified as requiring Y to be its host. Economy of derivation compares only derivations that converge, that is, contain only legitimate PF and LF objects (see Chomsky 1993). It seems plausible that stranded affixes and improperly affixed elements (elements affixed to the "wrong" types of heads) are illegitimate PF objects. In other words, derivations containing such elements crash. Given this, if excorporation of Y in the configuration in (21) would leave Z either a stranded affix or an improperly affixed element, it would not be allowed to take place. Y would thus be allowed to pied-pipe Z only if the pied-piping is necessary for PF convergence.

10. (25a) also contains pro, which can be located either in SpecAgr$_S$P or in SpecVP. Note that (i) indicates that subjects do not have to move to SpecIP at SS in Serbo-Croatian (see section 5.2.2 for evidence for the structure in (i)).

(i) [$_{AuxP}$ Poljubio$_i$ *je* [$_{VP}$ Jovan t$_i$ Mariju]]
        kissed   is   Jovan   Maria
    'Jovan kissed Maria'

Note that I am using AuxP strictly for ease of exposition. The maximal projection of *je* should probably also be considered to be a VP. Here I omit functional projections intervening between AuxP and VP since they are irrelevant to current concerns (see section 4.4.1.7 for relevant discussion).

11. Some elements that can be analyzed as X^0s can actually marginally intervene between the participles.

(i) ??Vas dvoje *ste* bili   nju čekali
      you two   are been her waited
      'You two had been waiting for her'

Given that, as argued below, the participles in (i) and (27) are located under the same X^0 node and given the standard assumption that X^0s but not XPs can adjoin to X^0s, the contrast between (i) and (27b–c) can readily be accounted for.

12. Rivero (1991) regards (28b) as ungrammatical. However, she also notes that such constructions are grammatical in Bulgarian, a closely related language. In my judgment, just like Bulgarian, Serbo-Croatian allows preposing of the second participle. Note that the ungrammaticality of (i) provides evidence that (28b) does not involve remnant preposing of the VP headed by the second participle, containing a trace of the rightward-moved object. If remnant preposing of the VP in

question were possible, we would also expect preposing of the whole VP to be possible, which is not the case. (As will become clear below, the ungrammaticality of (i) is in fact predicted under the analysis presented here.)

(i) *čekali Marijinu prijateljicu *ste* bili
    waited Maria's friend   are been

13. Having one element check the same kind of feature on two different elements is not a general pattern but has already been proposed in the literature. Thus, Baker (1988) shows that some verbs in Kinyarwanda, as well as other languages, are capable of checking two structural accusative Cases. I in Japanese seems to be capable of checking more than one nominative Case (see Ura 1993a). In most languages negative heads can check the [+neg] feature on more than one negative polarity item (see Lee 1994). Subject NPs in Serbo-Croatian can apparently check agreement features more than once (see chapter 4). Given this, the possibility of one element checking the same kind of feature on two different elements should not be ruled out in principle.

14. The landing site of *čekali* and t_i also belong to the minimal domain of the chain ($čekali_j$, t_j). However, this should be irrelevant, since the chain in question does not exist at the moment of targeting the *ste*-adjoined position by *čekali*, that is, when the position is considered as a target. The chain is created by adjoining *čekali* to *ste*. (If a chain α created by movement of X could create equidistance relations for the very movement of X that creates the chain α, we would essentially lose all locality restrictions on X^0-movement.)

15. Notice, however, that in Bošković 1995b,c I achieved the desired result by simply assuming that traces of heads do not block head movement. A similar proposal is made in Chomsky 1995.

16. Some speakers marginally allow a pause after the first participle in (33), which suspends the second position effect (see Bošković 1995b). For these speakers (33a) is marginally acceptable. (33b) is still unacceptable, however.

17. As pointed out by Daiko Takahashi (personal communication), the A-over-A Principle would have to be refined, so that it does not rule out excorporation of the host head in a head + head complex. The ban on adjunction to the lower segment of a branching segmented category could plausibly be a result of failure of the head undergoing adjunction to c-command its trace. Note that Chomsky (1995) also argues that X^0-adjunction always takes place to the "maximal" X^0, never to one of its "constituents."

18. There is actually another derivation for (33a–b) that must be considered. Suppose that the second participle right-adjoins to the first participle and then the participles adjoin to the left of the auxiliary. This derivation gives (33b) without violating the A-over-A Principle. I assume, however, that P-to-P movement, crucial for this derivation, is ruled out by Greed, since it has no morphological motivation; that is, it does not involve feature checking.

19. Kayne (1994) notes that in some cases it is also possible to delete a clitic in one conjunct under identity with a clitic in another conjunct in French. However,

clitic deletion in French can only occur in the second conjunct. In this respect, notice that (36b) is better than (36a).

20. I will not discuss VP-preposing in past tense constructions involving clitic auxiliaries. Such constructions are unacceptable for most speakers. I will also ignore VP-preposing in past perfect tense constructions, which in my judgment is degraded regardless of whether or not the auxiliary participle is affected by the preposing.

21. Following Huang's proposal concerning remnant topicalization in German, I assume that if it holds at all, the Proper Binding Condition is satisfied with Serbo-Croatian remnant AuxP-preposing under LF reconstruction.

22. As shown by (45), when the auxiliary is not a clitic, P-movement is allowed in the presence of a lexical complementizer. (45) thus provides conclusive evidence that (43b) is ungrammatical because the auxiliary is a clitic rather than because P-movement to C has taken place.

23. All the structural accounts proposed in the literature crucially depend on adopting additional assumptions that also turn out to be rather problematic. For example, Rivero's and Wilder and Ćavar's analyses are crucially based on assuming that P-preposing is a last resort operation that takes place to provide a host for clitic clusters when they are found in sentence-initial position, a position that I showed to be untenable in section 5.2.

24. Embick and Izvorski (1995) show that P-movement in front of nonclitic auxiliaries is also possible in the corresponding Bulgarian constructions.

25. Note that, as illustrated in (18), no XPs can intervene between the preposed participle and the auxiliary in pluperfect and future II constructions, as expected under the P-to-Aux adjunction analysis.

26. Belletti actually considers the adjunction analysis for Italian and rejects it owing to the inability of auxiliaries to pied-pipe participles when moving to I. However, as argued above, the possibility of pied-piping is ruled out in the relevant constructions by the economy principles.

27. The feature [+aux], which I assumed drives P-movement, may thus be wrongly named. "[+participle]" could be a more appropriate term.

28. P-movement similar to that of Standard Dutch is also found in other Continental West Germanic languages. I choose to examine Standard Dutch here because it presents a very intricate paradigm concerning P-movement, which can be rather straightforwardly accounted for by essentially extending my analysis of P-movement in Serbo-Croatian. To the extent that it is successful, the analysis of the Dutch data considered below will thus provide further confirmation of my analysis of Serbo-Croatian. I should point out that the phenomenon of P-movement, and more generally V-clustering, in Dutch itself presents an outstanding empirical problem, which has attracted a great deal of attention. For discussion and further references, see Broekhuis et al. 1995, Den Besten and Edmondson 1983, Den Dikken and Hoekstra 1995, Evers 1975, Haegeman 1992, 1994, Haegeman and Van Riemsdijk 1986, Hoeksema 1988, Hoekstra 1994, Kaan

1992, Rutten 1991, and Zwart 1993a, 1994b, 1995, among many others. All the Dutch data discussed below either come from Zwart 1994b or were provided by C. Jan-Wouter Zwart (personal communication).

Following Zwart (1994b), for ease of exposition I will indicate the SS order of verbal elements through numbering next to the examples, the numbers corresponding to the order in which the verbal elements are generated. Note that I will discuss here only modal+auxiliary+participle sequences of verbal elements. I will ignore passive constructions formed by using the participle of *worden* 'become', which introduce some additional complexities (see Zwart 1994b).

29. Zwart (1993a, 1994b) analyzes *uit* as the predicate of the small clause *het boek uit* 'the book out', which functions as the complement of *gelezen*. He argues that *uit* must be licensed overtly in a Spec position. I assume that the relevant Spec is SpecVP. I assume, then, that ignoring V2 clauses, *uit* must be in a Spec-head configuration with a lexical verb at SS. Other facts concerning the distribution of *uit* follow from the analysis presented below without additional assumptions. Note that Zwart (1994b) suggests that *uit* moves to the Spec of a functional projection. This is so because in his analysis SpecVP is often occupied by a participle, which is not the case under the analysis presented here. Note also that if, as Zwart argues, the lowest position in which *het boek* can be located in (i) is SpecAgr$_O$P, which is higher than VP, the ungrammaticality of (ia) can readily be accounted for if the Spec *uit* occupies at SS is SpecVP.

(i) a. *dat Jan uit het boek moet hebben gelezen 1-2-3
        that Jan out the book must have   read
        'that Jan must have finished reading the book'
    b. cf. dat Jan het boek uit moet hebben gelezen
        (cf. also (50) and (51))

30. My analysis is similar to that of Zwart (1993a) in that I analyze P-movement in terms of head movement of the participle to the left of its base-generated position. In later work, however, Zwart (1994b, 1995) analyzes P-movement as involving movement into SpecVP. Since, when P has a clausal complement, P-movement leaves behind the clausal complement (in Zwart's system, the clausal complement remains in its base-generated position), I assume that P-movement involves head movement.

(i) a. dat Jan verteld zal hebben [dat hij Marie gekust heeft]
        that Jan told   will have   that he Marie kissed has
        'that Jan will tell that he has kissed Marie'
    b. *dat Jan verteld [dat hij Marie gekust heeft] zal hebben
    c. *dat Jan [dat hij Marie gekust heeft] verteld zal hebben

31. This is not necessarily the case in other Germanic languages featuring P-movement.

32. Zwart (1994b) notes that (54) is slightly degraded in Standard Dutch. What is important here is that (54) is clearly better than (56), discussed below.

33. Recall that, as discussed with respect to the Serbo-Croatian (33) (see note 18), there is actually another way of deriving the illegitimate order in (56). *Gelezen*

could first adjoin to the right of the auxiliary, and the complex head formed by the adjunction could then adjoin to the left of the modal. I ruled out a similar derivation in Serbo-Croatian by arguing that the first adjunction, P-to-P adjunction in the case of Serbo-Croatian, violates Greed, because it has no morphological motivation. The ungrammaticality of the *hebben-gelezen* order in (56) suggests that the *gelezen*-to-*hebben* adjunction is also ruled out for lack of morphological motivation. In other words, *gelezen* has a feature to check through adjunction to *moet*, but it has no feature to check through adjunction to *hebben*.

34. The relative freedom of word order in Serbo-Croatian and Dutch may be relevant here. Serbo-Croatian is a language with extremely free word order, freer in a number of respects even than the word order of "traditional" scrambling languages such as Japanese and Korean. Turning off (62) may be one way of achieving free word order in Serbo-Croatian. The discussion becomes moot here, since the nature of the phenomenon in question is unclear.

35. Note that the locus of adjunction does not have to be a finite element, although it happens to be a finite element in the examples discussed above. Thus, the locus of adjunction is not a finite element in (i).

(i) dat Jan Piet dwingt het boek gelezen$_i$ te hebben t$_i$
    that Jan Piet forces the book read to have
    'that Jan forces Piet to read the book'

36. The first XP above the conditional *by* can be either a VP or an IP (if *by* is generated under I). Note that Borsley and Rivero (1994) generate the conditional and the perfective auxiliary under the same node without providing real evidence for this move. However, they provide evidence that the perfective auxiliary is an independent lexical item. Thus, they show that it is generated under an independent head position in (65). I will assume that the perfective auxiliary is always generated under an independent head position, which is the null hypothesis. Following a proposal by a *Natural Language & Linguistic Theory* reviewer considered by Borsley and Rivero, I assume that *by* takes the AuxP headed by the perfective auxiliary as its complement.

37. Mamoru Saito (personal communication) suggests an interesting modification of the analysis pursued here. He suggests that instead of adjoining to the highest verbal head in the sequence, all verbal heads in a sequence of Vs adjoin to a functional head immediately above the highest verbal head. An appealing consequence of this analysis is that the locus of adjunction can be kept constant; it should therefore be easier to state the adjunction in terms of feature checking. As far as I can tell, the data examined above are consistent with this analysis. I see no obvious way of empirically teasing apart the adjunction-to-the-highest-V-head and the adjunction-to-a-functional-head analyses.

References

Akmajian, A. 1970. Aspects of the grammar of focus in English. Doctoral dissertation, MIT, Cambridge, Mass.

Anderson, S. 1993. Wackernagel's revenge: Clitics, morphology, and the syntax of second position. *Language* 69, 68–98.

Aoun, J., N. Hornstein, D. Lightfoot, and A. Weinberg. 1987. Two types of locality. *Linguistic Inquiry* 18, 537–578.

Authier, J.-M. 1991. V-governed expletives, Case theory, and the Projection Principle. *Linguistic Inquiry* 22, 721–742.

Authier, J.-M. 1992. Iterated CPs and embedded topicalization. *Linguistic Inquiry* 23, 329–336.

Bach, E. 1977. Review article: *On raising: One rule of English grammar and its implications. Language* 53, 621–654.

Baker, M. 1988. *Incorporation: A theory of grammatical function changing.* Chicago: University of Chicago Press.

Baker, M., K. Johnson, and I. Roberts. 1989. Passive arguments raised. *Linguistic Inquiry* 20, 219–251.

Baltin, M. 1982. A landing site theory of movement rules. *Linguistic Inquiry* 13, 1–38.

Baltin, M. 1987. Do antecedent-contained deletions exist? *Linguistic Inquiry* 18, 579–595.

Banfield, A. 1973. Grammar of quotation, free indirect style, and implications for a theory of narrative. *Foundations of Language* 10, 1–39.

Barbosa, P. 1994. Towards a new look at the null subject parameter. Paper presented at the Workshop on the Minimalist Program, University of Maryland, College Park.

Barss, A., and H. Lasnik. 1986. A note on anaphora and double objects. *Linguistic Inquiry* 17, 347–354.

Belletti, A. 1988. The Case of unaccusatives. *Linguistic Inquiry* 19, 1–35.

Belletti, A. 1990. *Generalized verb movement.* Turin: Rosenberg and Sellier.

Bennis, H. 1986. *Gaps and dummies*. Dordrecht: Foris.

Besten, H. den, and J. Edmondson. 1983. The verbal complex in continental West Germanic. In *On the formal syntax of the Westgermania*, edited by A. Werner, 155–216. Amsterdam: John Benjamins.

Besten, H. den, and G. Webelhuth. 1987. Remnant topicalization and the constituent structure of VP in the Germanic SOV languages. Paper presented at the 10th GLOW Colloquium, Venice.

Bobaljik, J. D. 1994. What Does Adjacency Do? In *MIT Working Papers in Linguistics 22: The morphology-syntax connection*, edited by H. Harley and C. Phillips, 1–32. MITWPL, Department of Linguistics and Philosophy, MIT, Cambridge, Mass.

Borer, H. 1995. The ups and downs of Hebrew verb movement. *Natural Language & Linguistic Theory* 13, 527–606.

Borsley, R., and M.-L. Rivero. 1994. Clitic auxiliaries & incorporation in Polish. *Natural Language & Linguistic Theory* 12, 373–422.

Bošković, Ž. 1992. Clausal selection, subjacency, and minimality. Ms., University of Connecticut, Storrs.

Bošković, Ž. 1994a. Categorial status of null operator relatives and finite declarative complements. *Language Research* 30, 387–417.

Bošković, Ž. 1994b. D-Structure, θ-Criterion, and movement into θ-positions. *Linguistic Analysis* 24, 247–286.

Bošković, Ž. 1994c. Participle movement in Serbo-Croatian and related issues. Paper presented at the Third Annual Workshop on Formal Approaches to Slavic Linguistics, University of Maryland, College Park.

Bošković, Ž. 1994d. *Wager*-class verbs and existential constructions: A case for Greed, lowering, and partitive Case assignment. Ms., University of Connecticut, Storrs.

Bošković, Ž. 1995a. Case properties of clauses and the Greed Principle. *Studia Linguistica* 49, 32–53.

Bošković, Ž. 1995b. Participle movement and second position cliticization in Serbo-Croatian. *Lingua* 96, 245–266.

Bošković, Ž. 1995c. Principles of economy in nonfinite complementation. Doctoral dissertation, University of Connecticut, Storrs.

Bošković, Ž. 1996a. On right-node base-generation. Ms., University of Connecticut, Storrs.

Bošković, Ž. 1996b. Selection and the categorial status of infinitival complements. *Natural Language & Linguistic Theory* 14, 269–304.

Bošković, Ž. 1997. Coordination, object shift, and V-movement. *Linguistic Inquiry* 28, 357–365.

Bošković, Ž. In press a. On certain violations of the Superiority Condition, Agr_O, and economy of derivation. *Journal of Linguistics*.

Bošković, Ž. In press b. Pseudoclefts. *Studia Linguistica*.

Bošković, Ž. In press c. Superiority effects with multiple *wh*-movement in Serbo-Croatian. *Lingua*.

Boster, C. 1991. On numerical quantifiers and quantified noun phrases in American Sign Language. Ms., University of Connecticut, Storrs.

Bouchard, D. 1984. *On the content of empty categories*. Dordrecht: Foris.

Bowers, J. 1987. Extended X-bar theory, the ECP and the Left Branch Condition. In *Proceedings of the West Coast Conference on Formal Linguistics*, vol. 6, edited by M. Crowhurst, 47–62. Standford, Calif.: CSLI publications. [Distributed by Cambridge University Press.]

Branigan, P. 1991. Variables, Case, and economy. In *MIT working papers in linguistics 15: More papers on* wh-*movement*, edited by L. Cheng and H. Demirdache, 1–29. MITWPL, Department of Linguistics and Philosophy, MIT, Cambridge, Mass.

Branigan, P. 1992. Subjects and complementizers. Doctoral dissertation, MIT, Cambridge, Mass.

Bresnan, J. 1969. Remarks on adsententials. Ms., MIT, Cambridge, Mass.

Bresnan, J. 1971. Contraction and the transformational cycle. Ms., MIT, Cambridge, Mass.

Bresnan, J. 1972. Theory of complementation in English syntax. Doctoral dissertation, MIT, Cambridge, Mass.

Bresnan, J. 1991. Locative case vs. locative gender. In *Proceedings of the Seventeenth Annual Meeting of the Berkeley Linguistics Society*, edited by L. A. Sutton, C. Jonhson, and R. Shields, 53–68. Berkeley Linguistics Society, University of California, Berkeley.

Brody, M. 1993. θ-theory and arguments. *Linguistic Inquiry* 24, 1–23.

Broekhuis, H., H. den Besten, K. Hoekstra, and J. Rutten. 1995. Infinitival complementation in Dutch: On remnant extraposition. *The Linguistic Review* 12, 93–123.

Browne, W. 1974. On the problem of enclitic placement in Serbo-Croatian. In *Slavic transformational syntax*, edited by R. D. Brecht and C. V. Chvany, 36–52. Department of Slavic Languages and Literatures, University of Michigan, Ann Arbor.

Bures, A. 1993. There is an argument for a cycle at LF here. In *CLS 28*, Vol. 2, *The Parasession*, edited by J. M. Denton, G. P. Chan, and C. P. Canakis, 14–35. Chicago Linguistic Society, University of Chicago, Chicago, Ill.

Cheng, L., and H. Demirdache. 1990. Superiority violations. In *MIT working papers in linguistics 13: Papers on* wh-*movement*, edited by L. Cheng and H. Demirdache, 27–46. MITWPL, Department of Linguistics and Philosophy, MIT, Cambridge, Mass.

Chomsky, N. 1981. *Lectures on government and binding*. Dordrecht: Foris.

Chomsky, N. 1986a. *Barriers*. Cambridge, Mass.: MIT Press.

Chomsky, N. 1986b. *Knowledge of language: Its nature, origin, and use.* New York: Praeger.

Chomsky, N. 1991. Some notes on economy of derivation and representation. In *Principles and parameters in comparative grammar,* edited by R. Freidin, 417–454. Cambridge, Mass.: MIT Press.

Chomsky, N. 1993. A minimalist program for linguistic theory. In *The view from Building 20: Essays in linguistics in honor of Sylvain Bromberger,* edited by K. Hale and S. J. Keyser, 1–52. Cambridge, Mass.: MIT Press.

Chomsky, N. 1994. Bare phrase structure. MIT Occasional Papers in Linguistics 5. MITWPL, Department of Linguistics and Philosophy, MIT, Cambridge, Mass.

Chomsky, N. 1995. Categories and transformations. In *The Minimalist Program,* 219–394. Cambridge, Mass.: MIT Press.

Chomsky, N., and H. Lasnik. 1993. The theory of principles and parameters. In *Syntax: An international handbook of contemporary research,* edited by J. Jacobs, A. von Stechow, W. Sternefeld, and T. Vennemann, 506–569. Berlin: Walter de Gruyter.

Collins, C. 1987. Part I: Conjunction adverbs. Ms., MIT, Cambridge, Mass.

Collins, C. 1994. Toward a theory of optimal derivations. Ms., Cornell University, Ithaca, N.Y.

Collins, C., and H. Thráinsson. 1993. Object shift in double object constructions and the theory of Case. In *MIT working papers in linguistics 19: Papers on Case and agreement II,* edited by C. Phillips, 131–174. MITWPL, Department of Linguistics and Philosophy, MIT, Cambridge, Mass.

Déchaine, R.-M. 1993. Predicates across categories: Towards a category-neutral syntax. Doctoral dissertation, University of Massachusetts, Amherst.

Dekydtspotter, L. 1992. The syntax of predicate clefts. In *NELS 22,* edited by K. Broderick, 119–133. GLSA, University of Massachusetts, Amherst.

Delahunty, G. 1983. But sentential subjects do exist. *Linguistic Analysis* 12, 379–398.

Déprez, V. 1989. On the typology of syntactic positions and the nature of chains: Move α to the specifier of functional projections. Doctoral dissertation, MIT, Cambridge, Mass.

Diesing, M. 1992. *Indefinites.* Cambridge, Mass.: MIT Press.

Dikken, M. den. 1995. *Particles.* Oxford: Oxford University Press.

Dikken, M. den, and E. Hoekstra. 1995. Parasitic participles. Ms., Holland Institute of Linguistics/Vrije Universiteit, Amsterdam, and Meertens Instituut, Amsterdam.

Dikken, M. den, and A. Næss. 1993. Case dependencies: The case of predicative inversion. *The Linguistic Review* 10, 303–336.

Doherty, C. In press. Clauses without complementizers: Finite IP complementation in English. *The Linguistic Review.*

Embick, D., and R. Izvorski. 1995. On long head movement in Bulgarian. In *Proceedings of the 11th Eastern States Conference on Linguistics*, edited by J. M. Fuller, H. Han, and D. Parkinson, 104–115. DMLL Publications, Cornell University, Ithaca, N.Y.

Emonds, J. 1976. *A transformational approach to English syntax: Root, structure preserving and local transformations*. New York: Academic Press.

Enç, M. 1991. On the absence of the present tense morpheme in English. Ms., University of Wisconsin, Madison.

Epstein, S. 1990. Differentiation and reduction in syntactic theory: A case study. *Natural Language & Linguistic Theory* 8, 313–323.

Epstein, S. 1995. Un-principled syntax and the derivation of syntactic relations. Ms., Harvard University, Cambridge, Mass.

Evers, A. 1975. The transformational cycle in Dutch and German. Doctoral dissertation, University of Utrecht.

Franks, S., and N. Hornstein. 1992. Secondary predication in Russian and proper government of PRO. In *Control and grammar*, edited by R. Larson, S. Iatridou, U. Lahiri, and J. Higginbotham, 1–50. Dordrecht: Kluwer.

Franks, S., and L. Progovac. 1994. On the placement of Serbo-Croatian clitics. Paper presented at the 9th Biennial Conference on Balkan and South Slavic Linguistics, Literature, and Folklore, Indiana University, Bloomington.

Frazier, L. 1978. On comprehending sentences: Syntactic parsing. Doctoral dissertation, University of Connecticut, Storrs.

Freeze, R. 1992. Is there more to V2 than meets the I? In *NELS 22*, edited by K. Broderick, 151–162. GLSA, University of Massachusetts, Amherst.

Fukui, N. 1993. Parameters and optionality. *Linguistic Inquiry* 24, 399–420.

Fukui, N., and M. Speas. 1986. Specifiers and projection. In *MIT working papers in linguistics 8: Papers in theoretical linguistics*, 128–172. MITWPL, Department of Linguistics and Philosophy, MIT, Cambridge, Mass.

Grimshaw, J. 1979. Complement selection and the lexicon. *Linguistic Inquiry* 10, 279–326.

Grimshaw, J. 1990. *Argument structure*. Cambridge, Mass.: MIT Press.

Grimshaw, J. 1994. Minimal projection, heads, and optimality. Ms., Rutgers University, New Brunswick, N.J.

Groat, E. 1993. English expletives: A minimalist approach. In *Harvard working papers in linguistics 3*, edited by H. Thráinsson, S. D. Epstein, and S. Kuno, 81–88. Department of Linguistics, Harvard University, Cambridge, Mass.

Guasti, M. T. 1991. Incorporation, excorporation, and lexical properties of causative heads. *The Linguistic Review* 8, 209–232.

Haegeman, L. 1985. The *get*-passive and Burzio's generalization. *Lingua* 66, 53–77.

Haegeman, L. 1992. *Theory and description in generative grammar: A case study in West Flemish*. Cambridge: Cambridge University Press.

Haegeman, L. 1994. Verb raising as verb projection raising: Some empirical problems. *Linguistic Inquiry* 25, 509–521.

Haegeman, L., and H. van Riemsdijk. 1986. Verb projection raising, scope, and the typology of rules affecting verbs. *Linguistic Inquiry* 17, 417–466.

Hale, K., and S. J. Keyser. 1993. On argument structure and the lexical expression of syntactic relations. In *The view from Building 20: Essays in linguistics in honor of Sylvain Bromberger*, edited by K. Hale and S. J. Keyser, 53–110. Cambridge, Mass.: MIT Press.

Halle, M., and A. Marantz. 1993. Distributed Morphology and the pieces of inflection. In *The view from Building 20: Essays in linguistics in honor of Sylvain Bromberger*, edited by K. Hale and S. J. Keyser, 111–176. Cambridge, Mass.: MIT Press.

Halpern, A. L. 1995. *On the placement and morphology of clitics*. Stanford, Calif.: CSLI Publications.

Hankamer, J., and I. Sag. 1976. Deep and surface anaphora. *Linguistic Inquiry* 7, 391–428.

Hegarty, M. 1990. On adjunct extraction from complements. In *MIT working papers in linguistics 13: Papers on wh-movement*, edited by L. Cheng and H. Demirdache, 101–124. MITWPL, Department of Linguistics and Philosophy, MIT, Cambridge, Mass.

Hegarty, M. 1991. Adjunct extraction without traces. In *Proceedings of the Tenth West Coast Conference on Formal Linguistics*, edited by D. Bates, 209–222. Stanford, Calif.: CSLI Publications. [Distributed by Cambridge University Press].

Hegarty, M. 1992. Adjunct extraction and chain configurations. Doctoral dissertation, MIT, Cambridge, Mass.

Higginbotham, J. 1983. Logical form, binding, and nominals. *Linguistic Inquiry* 14, 395–420.

Higgins, F. R. 1979. *The pseudo-cleft construction in English*. New York: Garland.

Hoeksema, J. 1988. A constraint on governors in the West Germanic verb cluster. In *Morphology and modularity: In honor of Henk Shultink*, edited by M. Everaert, A. Evers, and M. Trommelen, 147–161. Dordrecht: Foris.

Hoekstra, E. 1994. Analysing linear asymmetries in the verb clusters of Dutch and Frisian and their dialects. Ms., Meertens Instituut, Amsterdam.

Holmberg, A., and C. Platzack. 1995. *The role of inflection in Scandinavian syntax*. Oxford: Oxford University Press.

Hornstein, N. 1994. An argument for minimalism: The case of antecedent-contained deletion. *Linguistic Inquiry* 25, 455–480.

Hornstein, N., and D. Lightfoot. 1987. Predication and PRO. *Language* 63, 23–52.

Huang, C.-T. J. 1982. Logical relations in Chinese and the theory of grammar. Doctoral dissertation, MIT, Cambridge, Mass.

Huang, C.-T. J. 1993. Reconstruction and the structure of VP: Some theoretical consequences. *Linguistic Inquiry* 24, 103–138.

Huot, H. 1981. *Constructions infinitives du français: Le subordonnant de.* Genève: Librairie Droz.

Iwakura, K. 1978. On root transformations and the structure-preserving hypothesis. *Linguistic Analysis* 4, 321–364.

Jackendoff, R. 1972. *Semantic interpretation in generative grammar.* Cambridge, Mass.: MIT Press.

Jaeggli, O. 1980. Remarks on *to* contraction. *Linguistic Inquiry* 11, 239–245.

Johnson, K. 1991. Object positions. *Natural Language & Linguistic Theory* 9, 577–636.

Jonas, D., and J. D. Bobaljik. 1993. Specs for subjects: The role of TP in Icelandic. In *MIT working papers in linguistics 18: Papers on Case and agreement I,* edited by J. D. Bobaljik and C. Phillips, 59–98. MITWPL, Department of Linguistics and Philosophy, MIT, Cambridge, Mass.

Kaan, E. 1992. A minimalist approach to extraposition of CP and verb (projection) raising. *Language and Cognition* 2, 169–179.

Kaisse, E. 1983. The syntax of auxiliary reduction in English. *Language* 59, 93–122.

Kayne, R. 1984. *Connectedness and binary branching.* Dordrecht: Foris.

Kayne, R. 1985. Principles of particle constructions. In *Grammatical representation,* edited by J. Guéron, H.-G. Obenauer, and J.-Y. Pollock, 101–142. Dordrecht: Foris.

Kayne, R. 1989. Facets of Romance past participle agreement. In *Dialect variation and the theory of grammar,* edited by P. Beninca, 85–103. Dordrecht: Foris.

Kayne, R. 1991. Romance clitics, verb movement, and PRO. *Linguistic Inquiry* 22, 647–686.

Kayne, R. 1994. *The antisymmetry of syntax.* Cambridge, Mass.: MIT Press.

Keyser, S. J., and T. Roeper. 1992. Re: The abstract clitic hypothesis. *Linguistic Inquiry* 23, 89–125.

Kiparsky, P., and C. Kiparsky. 1970. Fact. In *Progress in linguistics,* edited by M. Bierwisch and K. E. Heidolph, 141–173. The Hague: Mouton.

Kitagawa, Y. 1986. Subjects in Japanese and English. Doctoral dissertation, University of Massachusetts, Amherst.

Kitagawa, Y. 1994. Shells, yolks, and scrambled e.g.s. In *NELS 24,* Vol. 1, edited by M. Gonzàlez, 221–239. GLSA, University of Massachusetts, Amherst.

Kitahara, H. 1993a. Contraction: PF evidence for the theory of feature checking. In *Harvard working papers in linguistics 3,* edited by H. Thráinsson, S. D. Epstein, and S. Kuno, 120–128. Department of Linguistics, Harvard University, Cambridge, Mass.

Kitahara, H. 1993b. Deducing the superiority effects from principles of economy. Ms., Harvard University, Cambridge, Mass.

Kitahara, H. 1994a. A minimalist analysis of cross-linguistically variant CED phenomena. In *NELS 24*, Vol. 1, edited by M. Gonzàlez, 241–253. GLSA, University of Massachusetts, Amherst.

Kitahara, H. 1994b. Target α: A unified theory of movement and structure-building. Doctoral dissertation, Harvard University, Cambridge, Mass.

Koizumi, M. 1993. Object agreement phrases and the split VP hypothesis. In *MIT working papers in linguistics 18: Papers on Case and agreement I*, edited by J. D. Bobaljik and C. Phillips, 99–148. MITWPL, Department of Linguistics and Philosophy, MIT, Cambridge, Mass.

Koizumi, M. 1995. Phrase structure in minimalist syntax. Doctoral dissertation, MIT, Cambridge, Mass.

Kolb, H., and C. Thiersch. 1991. Levels and empty categories in a principles and parameters approach to parsing. In *Representation and derivation in the theory of grammar*, edited by H. Heider and K. Netter, 252–322. Dordrecht: Kluwer.

Koster, J. 1984. On binding and control. *Linguistic Inquiry* 15, 417–459.

Kreps, C. 1994. Another look at small clauses. In *UCL working papers in linguistics 6*, edited by J. Harris, 149–178. Department of Phonetics and Linguistics, University College London.

Kuno, S. 1973. Constraints on internal clauses and sentential subjects. *Linguistic Inquiry* 4, 363–385.

Laka, I. 1990. Negation in syntax: On the nature of functional categories. Doctoral dissertation, MIT, Cambridge, Mass.

Larson, R. 1988. On the double object construction. *Linguistic Inquiry* 19, 335–391.

Larson, R. 1991. *Promise* and the theory of control. *Linguistic Inquiry* 22, 103–139.

Lasnik, H. 1985. Illicit NP movement: Locality conditions on chains? *Linguistic Inquiry* 16, 481–490.

Lasnik, H. 1992. Case and expletives: Notes toward a parametric account. *Linguistic Inquiry* 23, 381–406.

Lasnik, H. 1993. Lectures on minimalist syntax. University of Connecticut Occasional Papers in Linguistics 1. [Distributed by MITWPL, Department of Linguistics and Philosophy, MIT, Cambridge, Mass.]

Lasnik, H. 1994. Weakness and Greed: A consideration of some minimalist concepts. Paper presented at the Workshop on the Minimalist Program, University of Maryland, College Park.

Lasnik, H. 1995a. Case and expletives revisited: On Greed and other human failings. *Linguistic Inquiry* 26, 615–633.

Lasnik, H. 1995b. Last Resort. In *Minimalism and linguistic theory*, edited by S. Haraguchi and M. Funaki, 1–32. Tokyo: Hituzi Syobo.

Lasnik, H. 1995c. Last Resort and Attract F. In *Papers from the Sixth Annual Meeting of the Formal Linguistics Society of Midamerica*, edited by L. Gabriele, D. Hardison, and R. Westmoreland, 62–81. Indiana University Linguistics Club, Indiana University, Bloomington.

Lasnik, H. 1995d. Verbal morphology: *Syntactic structures* meets the Minimalist Program. In *Evolution and revolution in linguistic theory*, edited by H. Campos and P. Kempchinsky, 251–275. Washington, D.C.: Georgetown University Press.

Lasnik, H. In preparation. Pseudogapping. Ms., University of Connecticut, Storrs.

Lasnik, H., and R. Fiengo. 1974. Complement object deletion. *Linguistic Inquiry* 5, 535–571.

Lasnik, H., and M. Saito. 1984. On the nature of proper government. *Linguistic Inquiry* 14, 235–289.

Lasnik, H., and M. Saito. 1991. On the subjects of infinitives. In *CLS 27*. Part 1, *The General Session*, edited by L. M. Dobrin, L. Nichols, and R. M. Rodriguez, 324–343. Chicago Linguistic Society, University of Chicago, Chicago, Ill.

Lasnik, H., and M. Saito. 1992. *Move α: Conditions on its application and output*. Cambridge, Mass.: MIT Press.

Law, P. 1990. *Na*-clause complement and extraction in Modern Greek. In *MIT working papers in linguistics 13: Papers on* wh-*movement*, edited by L. Cheng and H. Demirdache, 179–192. MITWPL, Department of Linguistics and Philosophy, MIT, Cambridge, Mass.

Law, P. 1991. Effects of head movement on theories of subjacency and proper government. Doctoral dissertation, MIT, Cambridge, Mass.

Lee, R. 1994. Economy of representation. Doctoral dissertation, University of Connecticut, Storrs.

Li, Y. 1990. Conditions on X^0-movement. Doctoral dissertation, MIT, Cambridge, Mass.

Lillo-Martin, D. 1990. Parameters for questions: Evidence from *wh*-movement in ASL. In *Sign language research: Theoretical issues*, edited by C. Lucas, 211–222. Washington, D.C.: Gallaudet University Press.

Lobeck, A. 1990. Functional heads as proper governors. In *Proceedings of NELS 20*, vol. 2, edited by J. Carter, R.-M. Déchaine, B. Philip, and T. Sherer, 348–362. GLSA, University of Massachusetts, Amherst.

Long, M. E. 1974. Semantic verb classes and their role in French predicates. Doctoral dissertation, University of Indiana, Bloomington.

Longobardi, G. 1994. Reference and proper names. *Linguistic Inquiry* 25, 609–666.

Mahajan, A. 1990. The A/A-bar distinction and movement theory. Doctoral dissertation, MIT, Cambridge, Mass.

Manzini, M. R. 1994. Locality, minimalism, and parasitic gaps. *Linguistic Inquiry* 25, 481–508.

Martin, R. 1992a. Case theory, A-chains, and expletive replacement. Ms., University of Connecticut, Storrs.

Martin, R. 1992b. On the distribution and Case features of PRO. Ms., University of Connecticut, Storrs.

Martin, R. 1994. Null Case and the distribution of PRO. Ms., University of Connecticut, Storrs.

May, R. 1985. *Logical Form*. Cambridge, Mass.: MIT Press.

McCloskey, J. 1991. *There, it*, and agreement. *Linguistic Inquiry* 22, 563–567.

Motapanyane, V. 1994. An A-position for Romanian subjects. *Linguistic Inquiry* 25, 729–734.

Mulder, R. 1991. An empty head for object control. In *NELS 21*, edited by T. Sherer, 293–307. GLSA, University of Massachusetts, Amherst.

Munn, A. 1987. Coordinate structure and X-bar theory. In *McGill working papers in linguistics 4–1*, edited by Z. Laubitz and E. Guilfoyle, 121–140. Department of Linguistics, McGill University, Montreal.

Munn, A. 1991. Binding in gerunds and the Leftness Condition. In *MIT working papers in linguistics 14: Papers from the Third Student Conference in Linguistics*, edited by J. D. Bobaljik and A. Bures, 163–178. MITWPL, Department of Linguistics and Philosophy, MIT, Cambridge, Mass.

Munn, A. 1993. Topics in the syntax and semantics of coordinate structures. Doctoral dissertation, University of Maryland, College Park.

Murasugi, K., and M. Saito. 1994. Adjunction and cyclicity. In *Proceedings of the Thirteenth West Coast Conference on Formal Linguistics*, edited by R. Aranovich, W. Byrne, S. Preuss, and M. Senturia, 302–317. Stanford, Calif.: CSLI publications. [Distributed by Cambridge University Press.]

Muysken, P. 1982. Parametrizing the notion head. *Journal of Linguistic Research* 2, 57–75.

Neijt, A. 1979. *Gapping: A contribution to sentence grammar*. Dordrecht: Foris.

Nemoto, N. 1991. Scrambling and conditions on A-movement. In *Proceedings of the Tenth West Coast Conference on Formal Linguistics*, edited by D. Bates, 349–358. Stanford, Calif.: CSLI Publications. [Distributed by Cambridge University Press.]

Oehrle, R. 1976. The grammatical status of the English dative alternation. Doctoral dissertation, MIT, Cambridge, Mass.

Ormazabal, J. 1995. The syntax of complementation: On the connection between syntactic structure and selection. Doctoral dissertation, University of Connecticut, Storrs.

Ormazabal, J., J. Uriagereka, and M. Uribe-Etxebarria. 1994. Word order and *wh*-movement: Towards a parametric account. Paper presented at the 17th GLOW colloquium, Vienna.

Percus, O. 1993. The captious clitic: Problems in Serbo-Croatian clitic placement. Ms., MIT, Cambridge, Mass.

Pesetsky, D. 1982a. Complementizer-trace phenomena and the Nominative Island Condition. *The Linguistic Review* 1, 297–344.

Pesetsky, D. 1982b. Paths and categories. Doctoral dissertation, MIT, Cambridge, Mass.

Pesetsky, D. 1989. The Earliness Principle. Ms., MIT, Cambridge, Mass.

Pesetsky, D. 1992. Zero syntax, vol. 2. Ms., MIT, Cambridge, Mass.

Petronio, K. 1992. *Wh*-questions in ASL. Ms., University of Washington, Seattle.

Plann, S. 1986. On Case-marking clauses in Spanish: Evidence against the Case Resistance Principle. *Linguistic Inquiry* 17, 336–345.

Pollock, J.-Y. 1989. Verb movement, universal grammar, and the structure of IP. *Linguistic Inquiry* 20, 365–424.

Postal, P. 1974. *On raising: One rule of English grammar and its implications.* Cambridge, Mass.: MIT Press.

Postal, P. 1993. Some defective paradigms. *Linguistic Inquiry* 24, 357–364.

Progovac, L. 1996. Clitics in Serbian/Croatian: Comp as the second position. *Approaching second: Second position clitics and related phenomena*, edited by A. Halpern and A. Zwicky, 411–428. Stanford, Calif.: CSLI Publications. [Distributed by Cambridge University Press.]

Radanović-Kocić, V. 1988. The grammar of Serbo-Croatian clitics: A synchronic and diachronic perspective. Doctoral dissertation, University of Illinois, Urbana-Champaign.

Radford, A. 1994. The nature of children's initial clauses. Ms., Essex University, England.

Riemsdijk, H. van. 1978. *A case study in syntactic markedness.* Dordrecht: Foris.

Rivero, M.-L. 1989. Barriers in Rumanian. In *New analyses in Romance linguistics*, edited by D. Wanner and D. A. Kibbee, 289–312. Amsterdam: John Benjamins.

Rivero, M.-L. 1991. Long head movement and negation: Serbo-Croatian vs. Slovak and Czech. *The Linguistic Review* 8, 319–351.

Rivero, M.-L. 1993. Bulgarian and Serbo-Croatian yes-no questions: V^0 raising to *-li* versus *-li* hopping. *Linguistic Inquiry* 24, 567–575.

Rivero, M.-L. 1994a. Clause structure and V-movement in the languages of the Balkans. *Natural Language & Linguistic Theory* 12, 63–120.

Rivero, M.-L. 1994b. On two locations for complement clitic pronouns: Serbo-Croatian, Bulgarian, and Old Spanish. Paper presented at the Third Diachronic Generative Syntax Conference, Vrije Universiteit, Amsterdam.

Rizzi, L. 1980. Nominative marking in Italian infinitives and the Nominative Island Constraint. In *Binding and filtering*, edited by F. Heny, 129–157. Cambridge, Mass.: MIT Press.

Rizzi, L. 1990a. *Relativized Minimality*. Cambridge, Mass.: MIT Press.

Rizzi, L. 1990b. Speculations on verb second. In *Grammar in progress*, edited by J. Mascaró and M. Nespor, 375–386. Dordrecht: Foris.

Roberts, I. 1991. Excorporation and minimality. *Linguistic Inquiry* 22, 209–218.

Roberts, I. 1992. *Verbs and diachronic syntax*. Dordrecht: Kluwer.

Roberts, I. 1994. Second position effects and agreement in Comp. Paper presented at the Third Annual Workshop on Formal Approaches to Slavic Linguistics, University of Maryland, College Park.

Rochemont, M. 1989. Topic islands and the subjacency parameter. *Canadian Journal of Linguistics* 34, 145–170.

Rochette, A. 1988. Semantic and syntactic aspects of Romance sentential complementation. Doctoral dissertation, MIT, Cambridge, Mass.

Ross, J. R. 1967. Constraints on variables in syntax. Doctoral dissertation, MIT, Cambridge, Mass. [Published as *Infinite syntax*. Norwood, N.J.: Ablex, 1986.]

Runner, J. 1995. Noun phrase licensing and interpretation. Doctoral dissertation, University of Massachusetts, Amherst.

Rutten, J. 1991. Infinitival complements and auxiliaries. Doctoral dissertation, University of Utrecht.

Ruwet, N. 1982. *La grammaire des insultes et autres études*. Paris: Seuil.

Safir, K. 1985. *Syntactic chains*. Cambridge: Cambridge University Press.

Safir, K. 1993. Perception, selection, and structural economy. *Natural Language Semantics* 2, 47–70.

Sag, I. 1976. Deletion and Logical Form. Doctoral dissertation, MIT, Cambridge, Mass.

Saito, M. 1985. Some asymmetries in Japanese and their theoretical implications. Doctoral dissertation, MIT, Cambridge, Mass.

Saito, M. 1989. Scrambling as semantically vacuous A'-movement. In *Alternative conceptions of phrase structure*, edited by M. Baltin and A. Kroch, 182–200. Chicago: University of Chicago Press.

Saito, M. 1992. The additional *wh*-effects and the adjunction site theory. Ms., University of Connecticut, Storrs.

Saito, M. 1994. Improper adjunction. In *MIT working papers in linguistics 24: Formal approaches to Japanese linguistics 1*, edited by H. Ura and M. Koizumi, 263–294. MITWPL, Department of Linguistics and Philosophy, MIT, Cambridge, Mass.

Saito, M., and H. Hoshi. 1994. Japanese light verb construction and the Minimalist Program. Ms., University of Connecticut, Storrs.

Saito, M., and K. Murasugi. 1990. N'-deletion in Japanese. In *University of Connecticut working papers in linguistics 3*, edited by J. Ormazabal and C. Tenny, 86–107. Department of Linguistics, University of Connecticut, Storrs.

Saito, M., and K. Murasugi. 1993. Subject predication within IP and DP. Ms., University of Connecticut, Storrs, and Kinjo Gakuin University, Japan.

Schachter, P. 1984. Auxiliary reduction: An argument for GPSG. *Linguistic Inquiry* 15, 514–523.

Selkirk, E. 1972. The phrase phonology of English and French. Doctoral dissertation, MIT, Cambridge, Mass.

Shlonsky, U. 1987. Null and displaced subjects. Doctoral dissertation, MIT, Cambridge, Mass.

Shlonsky, U. 1991. Quantifier phrases and quantifier float. In *NELS 21*, edited by T. Sherer, 337–350. GLSA, University of Massachusetts, Amherst.

Snyder, W., and S. Rothstein. 1992. A note on contraction, Case, and complementizers. *The Linguistic Review* 9, 251–266.

Sobin, N. 1994. Non-local agreement. Ms., University of Arkansas, Little Rock.

Speas, M. 1994. Null arguments in a theory of economy of projection. In *University of Massachusetts occasional papers 17: Functional projections*, edited by E. Benedicto and J. Runner, 179–208. GLSA, University of Massachusetts, Amherst.

Sportiche, D. 1983. Structural invariance and symmetry in syntax. Doctoral dissertation, MIT, Cambridge, Mass.

Sportiche, D. 1988. A theory of floating quantifiers and its corollaries for constituent structure. *Linguistic Inquiry* 19, 425–449.

Stjepanović, S. 1996. Is inherent Case structural? Paper presented at the Fifth Annual Workshop on Formal Approaches to Slavic Linguistics, Wabash College, Crawfordsville, Ind.

Stowell, T. 1981. Origins of phrase structure. Doctoral dissertation, MIT, Cambridge, Mass.

Stowell, T. 1982. The tense of infinitives. *Linguistic Inquiry* 13, 561–570.

Stowell, T. 1983. Subjects across categories. *The Linguistic Review* 2, 285–312.

Takahashi, D. 1993. On antecedent-contained deletion. Ms., University of Connecticut, Storrs.

Takahashi, D. 1994. Minimality of movement. Doctoral dissertation, University of Connecticut, Storrs.

Tanaka, H. 1995. Reconstruction and chain uniformity. Paper presented at Student Conference in Linguistics 7, University of Connecticut, Storrs.

Terzi, A. 1992. PRO in finite clauses: A study of the inflectional heads of the Balkan languages. Doctoral dissertation, CUNY, New York.

Tiedeman, R. 1987. *Wh*-questions, parametric variation, and the ECP. In *University of Connecticut working papers in linguistics 1*, edited by Y. Ishii, R. Thornton, S.-H. Ahn, and E. Bar-Shalom, 116–142. Department of Linguistics, University of Connecticut, Storrs.

Tomić, O. M. 1996. The Balkan Slavic clausal clitics. *Natural Language & Linguistic Theory* 14, 811–872.

Travis, L. 1991. Parameters of word structure and verb-second phenomena. In *Principles and parameters in comparative grammar*, edited by R. Freidin, 339–364. Cambridge, Mass.: MIT Press.

Tremblay, M. 1990. An argument sharing approach to ditransitive constructions. In *Proceedings of the Ninth West Coast Conference on Formal Linguistics*, edited by A. L. Halpern, 549–563. Stanford, Calif.: CSLI Publications. [Distributed by Cambridge University Press.]

Ura, H. 1993a. L-relatedness and its parametric variation. In *MIT working papers in linguistics 19: Papers on Case and agreement II*, edited by C. Phillips, 377–399. MITWPL, Department of Linguistics and Philosophy, MIT, Cambridge, Mass.

Ura, H. 1993b. On feature-checking for *wh*-traces. In *MIT working papers in linguistics 18: Papers on Case and agreement I*, edited by J. D. Bobaljik and C. Phillips, 243–280. MITWPL, Department of Linguistics and Philosophy, MIT, Cambridge, Mass.

Ura, H. 1994. Varieties of raising and their implications for the theory of Case and agreement. MIT Occasional Papers in Linguistics 7. MITWPL, Department of Linguistics and Philosophy, MIT, Cambridge, Mass.

Uriagereka, J. 1996. Multiple Spell-Out. Ms., University of Maryland, College Park.

Vikner, S. 1995. *Verb movement and expletive subjects in the Germanic languages*. Oxford: Oxford University Press.

Washio, R. 1989. The Japanese passive. *The Linguistic Review* 6, 227–263.

Watanabe, A. 1992. *Wh*-in-situ, Subjacency, and chain formation. *Journal of East Asian Linguistics* 1, 255–291.

Watanabe, A. 1993. Agr-based Case theory and its interaction with the A-bar system. Doctoral dissertation, MIT, Cambridge, Mass.

Webelhuth, G. 1992. *Principles and parameters of syntactic saturation*. Oxford: Oxford University Press.

Wexler, K., and P. Culicover. 1980. *Formal principles of language acquisition*. Cambridge, Mass.: MIT Press.

Wilder, C., and D. Ćavar. 1994a. Long head movement? Verb movement and cliticization in Croatian. *Lingua* 93, 1–58.

Wilder, C., and D. Ćavar. 1994b. Word order variation, verb movement, and economy principles. *Studia Linguistica* 48, 46–86.

Williams, E. 1978. Across-the-board extraction. *Linguistic Inquiry* 9, 31–43.

Wood, W. 1979. Auxiliary reduction in English: A unified account. In *Papers from the Fifteenth Regional Meeting, Chicago Linguistic Society*, edited by P. R. Clyne, W. F. Hanks, and C. L. Hofbauer, 366–378. Chicago Linguistic Society, University of Chicago, Chicago, Ill.

Zwart, C. J.-W. 1991. Clitics in Dutch: Evidence for the position of INFL. *Groninger Arbeiten zur germanistischen Linguistik* 33, 71–92.

Zwart, C. J.-W. 1993a. Dutch syntax: A minimalist approach. Doctoral dissertation, University of Groningen.

Zwart, C. J.-W. 1993b. Verb movement and complementizer agreement. In *MIT working papers in linguistics 18: Papers on Case and agreement I*, edited by J. D. Bobaljik and C. Phillips, 297–340. MITWPL, Department of Linguistics and Philosophy, MIT, Cambridge, Mass.

Zwart, C. J.-W. 1994a. Shortest move vs. fewest steps. *Groninger Arbeiten zur germanistischen Linguistik* 37, 277–290.

Zwart, C. J.-W. 1994b. Verb clusters in Continental West Germanic dialects. Paper presented at the 18th Meeting of the Atlantic Provinces Linguistic Association, University of New Brunswick, Saint John.

Zwart, C. J.-W. 1995. A note on verb clusters in the Stellingwerfs dialect. Ms., University of Groningen.

Index